CHASING

THE

MIC

"A story of Self-Censorship
& American Counter-Culture
in a time when **NOTHING** is funny."

By: PATRiCK DiMARCHi

CHASING THE MIC

"A Story of Self-Censorship
& American Counterculture
in a time when NOTHING is funny."

Published Spring 2023
Written by: Patrick DiMarchi

Edited by: Alivia Sley
& Patrick DiMarchi

COVER ART MADE POSSIBLE BY
EDUARDO J MEZA
(MEZ.ART)

ISBN: 978-1-7341139-4–5 (paperback)

Published by Kindle Direct Publishing
A Palabras by Patrick Production

The Opening Act:

Hello there. To those of you picking this up after reading my previous works, I appreciate you sticking around. To those reading my work for the first time, thanks for giving it a chance. Hopefully it'll convince you to give my previous book a shot as well. If so, *"The Stateside Wanderer: Two Weeks of Hangouts and Hideaways Along the Pan-American Highway"* can help you fill in any blanks this story may leave. In some ways *Chasing the Mic* is kind of a continuation on the story from my first book, but in many ways it's a look into a completely different side of life that I was lucky to experience after college. Under the best of circumstances this will find you at a time where you already know of me. Even if only superficially. Otherwise, why bother reading this? The thoughts and happenings of some interesting stranger isn't usually enough to keep one in their seat under the constant pressures of a weird life in an ever-changing world. Now assuming, even if only with blind hope, that I *make-it* someday, it shouldn't be a surprise that you've picked this book up, I'm famous damnit. Why wouldn't you wanna read a collection of my experiences? Since it seems like you do, lets move onto a few things about my work.

With regards to my writing style, criticisms that I usually receive include how I can go from present tense to past tense memories in a matter of only one sentence and back again. Sometimes this book is going to be happening in the now, other times it's going to be talking about the past, and sometimes you're going to feel like you're right there with me. Even during a few times where I wish you didn't. So if you don't like that type of jumping around you should exclude yourself from the reading of this book. Also, some of these paragraphs will be a page long. My bad. Don't blame my editor. She told me to do otherwise. I've also included a bit of history about the things which I think matter around the topics at hand, hope it doesn't bore you. I also believe this life is more in the mind than anywhere else, so a lot of this book is the internal ramblings of a guy on the go. I would even call it more thoughts than happenings. That being said, each of these chapters should address only a few things at a time. Even so, if you think I'm long winded in person, you should see what happens when they don't give me page limits. I try not to ramble on about any one thing too much, but this book did take place in a certain time in my life as well as a very particular time in society, so I do get situationally topical. I've had the great fortunate to drive across the United States seven times as of this publishing, and I certainly used these pages to give you an idea of my thoughts on some of the cities and subcultures that make up this country. Before writing this or getting into comedy I had spent most of the decade prior living a much more international existence, so that might also layer how I view or speak about some of these things.

Speaking of jumping around, much like my last book, this one was written and edited a little bit of everywhere. During its creation I typed away throughout parts of Los Angeles, Washington D.C., Puerto Rico, North Carolina, Virginia, Northern Europe, The Pacific Northwest, and countless other locations. I did some of this on trains, a lot on planes, some in my car, a lot in my car actually. Some of it sober, some of it not. Some of this was written while seriously wild stuff went on around me (that's for another book). Other times in the quietest place I could find. The writing of this started right around the beginning of the pandemic, but the story which led to it was experienced nearly 6 years prior. Because this was based on a road trip I owe a special thanks to countless people who made this trip possible. From the friends no longer here who put a $50 in my hand all the way to the strangers whose names I don't remember, but whose couches kept me rested for the next leg of my trip. I also couldn't print this without thanking anyone who lived with me during this time in my life. It was a lot of fun getting to do this work while being surrounded by some of the most interesting people this world has to offer.

Anyone out there who has ever produced anything creative should relate to this next part. I would argue there is nothing more useful and yet equally hard to come by in the creative world than a combination of encouragement and honesty. Which is why my editor Alivia deserves a special thanks here. Too many people worry about hurting your feelings in the creative process, even when you're asking for truth. Alivia has done more for my readers than I have, and anyone who enjoys this book owes a lot of it to her. I couldn't be happier to have met her as accidentally as I did and how this little bookworm has helped me grow as a writer goes beyond what any graduate program or job could have ever done. Our meet ups and late nights texts often starting with, *"What the hell are you trying to say here?"* will forever be some of my favorite memories in the writing of this book. It's a lonely process doing this and I am forever grateful for her help. As always this book had many silent editors along the way; friends, family and strangers alike, I thank you all. Hope you enjoyed this as much as I did.

READ IT. REVIEW IT. SHARE IT.

This book is itself a combination of several arts; writing, performing, and graphics. In regards to the graphics I owe a huge thank you to a long time friend and fellow artistic soul. As a friend I know him as Chino, as an artist I know him as Mez. I can't thank this guy enough for sitting with me through several cover renditions and ultimately being the man who helped create the first impression of this book that anyone will ever get. Whether it was at his house or sitting in the tattoo shop, this guy was a pro the whole time and his input was invaluable to me. Thanks is never enough, but a solid *muchas gracias* to you buddy.

Lastly, to the comedians and show runners trusting enough to put a stranger from out of town on their mics, I can't thank you enough for your hospitality and situational encouragement. Prior to getting into comedy all I knew was the negative reputation for this industry being without anyone willing to help you and I can only speak to the opposite of this as a reality in my time spent experimenting on the stage. For the purpose of this book most of the names who helped me have been changed, and sadly some were even forgotten, but it was the time spent in rooms with complete strangers chasing the same dream that made this journey so special. While I hope it does so much more, at the very least I hope this book shows some of those who don't understand just what kinda struggle can go into this type of career. Though after all I can only hope to offer my perspective of the scene as it was during my time. Now to those who've never seen me perform and have no experience on which to base their opinion on my comedy, here's my personal take; I don't claim to be anything more than a guy willing to get on stage and give it a shot. Sometimes people laugh, sometimes they don't. I'm willing to call most of the times they don't my fault. Now that this book is done hopefully I'll have much more time to go up on stage and hone this craft into something I can be more proud of. For now, please enjoy this story of a journey as I remember it. And as always,

Travel Well, Travel Often.
Patrick DiMarchi

READ IT. REVIEW IT. SHARE IT.

Trigger Warning & Disclaimer

If you need any type of warning about what you're about to read you should probably put this down and go call a therapist. It's just words. If my grandma could handle it, so can you.

*This book is dedicated
to my grandmother Dorthy.
A person for whom my love was infinite
and unattached all at once.*

(Dorthy, 1924-2017)

My grandmother loved nature and would hate for me to waste an entire page of paper dedicated just to her, so this page is also being used to let you know that a percentage of profits from this book will be donated towards the replanting of trees via the One Tree Planted Organization. They basically plant one tree per one dollar, which I think is a damn good deal. If you're interested in donating beyond the purchase of this book, please visit www.onetreeplanted.org as a means of doing so. For the record I'm doing this because I actually want people to read physical books and the only way I can push this without feeling guilty is by knowing that over time I am going to be replacing more trees than I destroy. As of this publishing we've planted 220 trees throughout Appalachia and Central America and I promise to continue to stay ahead of the game as far as the tree count goes using whatever percent of profits that takes.

READ IT. REVIEW IT. SHARE IT.

TOUR SCHEDULE

OPEN-MIC NIGHT

THE FIRST 5 MINUTES

LONE STAR GRINGO

BREAK A LEG

ENCORE

MIC DROP

INSIDE THE GREEN ROOM

OPEN-MIC NIGHT

Days: 5 months
Miles Traveled: Approximately 1,200
Times on stage: Around 150

New York City, N.Y.
January 2016

"How'd you get into stand-up?"

A s far as I can tell there are only two languages we can call truly universal, tears and laughter; the rest are just words trying to get us from one to the other. That doesn't mean we all come into the light crying, but it's not long before we see attention and laughter as currencies to be used to move us along through this life. No doubt I used them a time or two in my younger years, but by the time I first stepped on stage and started telling jokes, I had already been placing my feet in front of a mic for over 20 years. All of this despite not growing up thinking that I wanted to be a comedian. Truth be told, I don't even remember feigning the thought until somewhere in my mid-twenties, though the idea of being some type of performer had always resonated with me. Perhaps that's why I stayed with bartending so long ago after graduating from college. As far as comedy goes, I had zero exposure to stand-up beyond the applause filled tapes I would listen to as I painted the insides of newly constructed homes during a summer job I took one year in high school. Even then it wasn't until a buddy took me to a late night comedy show in Los Angeles that I fully appreciated the intimate nature of the experience when sitting next to a crowd of no more than thirty people. Nor did I know that 30 people was more than most comedians would ever get in front of on a given night. One of the more common misnomers is that we all get our 15 minutes of fame. Truth is, most of us don't. Not beyond the mini-stages of our own existence and the lifetime members who stay by our side wondering if we'll ever make it. The reality is that in the beginning anyone in my game is only looking for 5 minutes, before then 15 feels like a pipe dream. What follows is about what I did with those 5 minutes.

From inside of a crowded subway car riddled with new graffiti and old advertisements, I watched one stop after another speed by as the express train moved me closer to where I was scheduled to meet Jax in Midtown Manhattan. Departing the station my feet were met with a wet layer of snow starting half-way up the concrete steps leading me out of the subway and into the cold January air off of the West 4th street metro stop across from the IFC theatre. I hadn't seen Jax since that winter I spent living on the west coast a few blocks from Santa Monica Beach. Back then he spent most of his time doing everything he could to keep himself in the spotlight, but even though his lifestyle of performance seemed nomadic he had managed to concrete more of a stabilized existence than myself. I had never understood why I was even able to meet him in college when we did. I had always looked at kids going for a degree in theatre as out of their fucking minds and I'm sure it came out in our conversations. Sometimes subtly and sometimes not so subtly. Standing there scanning the faces around me I heard a voice cutting through the snow, *"PAT! What's good?"* With a bright smile peaking out of a fleeced parka, Jax removed his gloves and pulled me in for a handshake and a full embrace. Noticing my lack of appropriate clothing and the light weight of my summer hoodie he patted me on my back and inquired as to my choice of uniform. *"Nobody told you it was snowing?"* Letting out a sigh I rolled my eyes in an annoyed response, *"Bro. It's been a long 24 hours,"* shivering a bit more now I rubbed my hands together vigorously, *"Mind if we take this inside?"*

"Sure thing bro. My bad. You want some pizza or something before we go in? This Artichoke joint is really dope, kinda different, but it's good. Or we can go to this spot here on the corner..."

"I'm good with whatever is closest. My fucking feet are freezing."

"Aight cool, we'll hit up Artichoke."

"Awesome, so what's good? Catch me up. You're working at a club now?"

"Yeah. I bartend there a few nights a week. Tonight's different tho. No drinks. Just jokes."

"Nice. Sure we have time for pizza before your show?" Looking at his watch and rubbing off the layer of moisture gradually caking its' baby blue face he brushed off my concerns, *"Absolutely. I'm not even going on til midway through. I just like to get there early so I don't walk in late and make any noise. Plus it's always nice to see who you gotta follow ya know?"*

Looking around I noticed how each building towered above me until somewhere close to the 30th floor where the remainder slowly faded over the next two floors and into the snowy night skies. *"I really can't believe I'm here right now. I was literally barefoot in a jungle like three days ago."*

"That's some white people shit."

"Bro. You're a quarter Spanish. Your name is Jax. You're white as me to anyone in this city."

"Whatever man. I still wanna hear your jungle story even if you're gonna be mean."

"I'll catch you up on it later when I can show you the pictures to go with it."

"Sounds good man. You got a place to crash yet?"

"Not yet. I figured I would get a hotel based on where you said was good."

"Fuck that. You can stay with me. My girlfriend's in New Hampshire right now anyway, we can crash at her place uptown if we need."

"Works for me. What area you living in?"

"I got a spot in Brooklyn. It's kinda far, but I love my rooftop. Plus the other bar I work at is off the same train."

"Nice."

"Yeah. It's sweet. So how long you around?"

"Technically I gotta be back to work on Tuesday evening, so as long as I get on the bus before noon I should be good. With no traffic and no delays."

"Nice. That'll give us plenty of time to fuck around. We'll get you some boots from my spot tomorrow. I'll keep us inside best I can tonight. That work?"

"Yeah totally. I appreciate that."

Grabbing a slice of pizza and a root beer the two of us walked to the club entrance and scarfed down our slices before a doorman larger than your average NFL lineman greeted Jax with a keen familiarity and ushered us past a short line of fans waiting to be filtered through. Eyeing up the Goliath of a man I looked over at Jax, "Security that tight here?"

"What? Oh no. He's harmless. Just there for show. Bitch can't do anything about hecklers. I don't see why we pay him." A comment to which the big man glared the way a man large enough to destroy you with his hands does while he's holding back the urge to do so. Following him down the steps into an English basement Jax put his fingers up to his lips and shushed me as we entered a dark room with a large curtain holding in the sound of the room before us. As we moved beyond the veil we sat down at two seats near the back of a room holding about 80 people and Jax leaned with the volume of a whisper to tell me he would see me after the show. "I'll come find you when it's over. The bartenders name is Ericka, tell her you're with me."

Watching the line up was like listening to several very different radio stations back to back. With some topics pulled at from all sides without over stretching. Others beaten so hard you wouldn't know it was ever a horse. Between each person my mind went back and forth between reflecting on other times I had been a part of such a crowd and the words I was hearing come out of their mouths. The longer I stayed there the more it brought me back to the history of comedy I had seen throughout my life. Before that night, I had only seen stand-up performed twice outside of the formatted for T.V. versions projected into my living room. Once at an arena in the days of Dane Cook, and another at an emerging event in Los Angeles called the *Kill Tony Show* at *The Comedy Store.* Both times I was taken to the performances by the original desires of others, but quickly hooked by the entertainment at hand. Though admittedly the two shows were vastly different. Dane in all of his glory stood in the middle of a sports arena surrounded by crowds of 20,000 people looking down at the trademarked *SuFi* finger outline which had become tightly associated with his *Vicious Circle* act. That night I watched him exude more energy in an hour and some odd minutes on stage than most people would put out in an entire week. While nothing about his energy was relatable, his material about working at *Burger King* really hit home. At the time I had never entertained the thought which came to me as I was sitting there at Jax's comedy show that night. The thought which told me, *I could do at least as good as the worst guy here*. In thinking further I knew I would at least have better presence than those who held on nervously to the mic-stand and paced around with their heads down fumbling for their next thoughts. That idea dwelled inside of me all night, but it took a back seat each time I saw someone go up and kill it. Quickly realizing that those who could do it could *really* do it.

We all grow up watching someone on a stage; our parents, our family, our politicians, our stars. Every form of celebrity finds itself on a pedestal above the rest as means of standing out. It's perhaps why we enjoy the tall, they're just a little easier to see and we never know where to look until we're told. There was something much different about seeing the act of someone who you knew rather well, and yet in watching them divulge their inner thoughts you began to think you knew them far less than you really did. As the weekend went on I loved walking around with Jax and seeing how he would adjust his jokes as he went, trying to find the best word or turn of the wrist to change how the audience perceived the message it was receiving. He was more physical on stage than I remembered him being in real life and it was like his face had ten different layers of emotion that he never showed to

4

the world at large. Absorbing all that I could that night I floated back and forth between talking peoples ears off and standing there in abstract silence as I soaked up the array of characters around me. After the third show of the night I found myself standing outside talking with one of the comedians somewhere just before 1 A.M., accepting a cigarette from the first one to offer as a means of extending the conversation as long as I could. Despite the purpose it had served I hated the smell in my hands and had anyone from my past seen me at that moment they woulda been more than surprised. To say I was against smoking was an understatement, I had become known in my family for refusing to go to my brothers wedding unless he finally quit the habit, a form of blackmail which ultimately didn't prevail, but probably helped him cut down on his intake when he was around me for the months leading up to his matrimony. Who knew he would stick to his guns like Chappell did receiving his *Mark Twain Award*? Nonetheless that didn't keep me from sharing a drag here and there as we walked around from club to club, something I justified by telling myself that the warm air entering my lungs was temporarily more helpful than harmful. That and it always led to more conversations or more things to smoke. You could always tell a weed smoker by how they handed you a cigarette. From there it was just a matter of remembering which one to drag and which one to hit. At one point Jax ended up on a call to someone who ran a spot around the corner and I soon found myself feeling the slight buzz of tobacco as the cigarette stayed in my hands for more than a few would be rotations. *"Throw that out, we gotta get inside."*

Standing off to the side of the room I felt the room around me silence as I watched this kid grace the stage with a noticeable confidence gleaming from his skinny frame. His expressions were deep and his movement was quick, but most importantly, his jokes were on point, each time lighting up the crowd with a laugh from one side to the other. In-fact, in my entire time there that weekend I dare say he was the most seasoned, although nothing about him looked seasoned. When he got off the stage I made it a point to go up and start talking to him, curious about the personality behind the persona. As we started talking I noticed a bit of hurry in his motions, like someone looking for the door, not out of disinterest, but out of necessity. After giving him the usual compliment and talking about his process he suddenly interrupted me and apologized for the fact that he had to go. Looking at the time and noticing it was nearly 2 A.M. I asked him where it was he had to go off to so quickly, assuming it was some girls spot, a reason for which I could have easily forgiven him and would have moved out of his way. However, it wasn't that, it was something even more surprising. *"I got school in the morning. My mom is gonna be pissed if she sees I'm not there when she gets up for work."* A comment which suddenly brought together all of the other clues about him, the clothes that didn't fit, the boyish charm in his presentation, and the backpack slung across his shoulders. *"Wait, how old are you man?"* Remembering that black didn't crack I had expected he was younger than his face would lead me to believe, but his answer of *"sixteen"* which was given with a casual nature that I've still yet to comprehend as it literally shook me and everything I thought I knew about how long it could take to get an act together. As we shook hands I watched him dart out and up the stairs. I think I stood there for a good minute as I contemplated this kids existence. There he was coming into 21 and up clubs and crushing it on stage at that age. I imagine it must have been like seeing Lebron James play back in high school. The 90's kid in me wants to say Michael Jordan here, but the fact is LJ was more impressive in high school even though I think that MJ was more impressive in the NBA. Though that's an argument for another time and for more qualified individuals to debate.

There was something about my first time in the back of a club that felt natural to me. I was always a bit of an instigator when I was younger and this felt like the first time I was around others who were raised like me and the most likely to be raising hell. *(You would know that already if you've read my first book).* Perhaps that's why I liked the personality of comics so much. Something about how the wiring worked. Have you ever watched monkeys and noticed how much the joke around? If not I suggest finding your local zoo or referring to David Attenborough's works on *Planet Earth* and giving them a look. I'll sum up the part that matters for this situation though, they laugh at each other all the time. Granted they don't get much done beyond establishing dominance, but to the extent you consider yourself and the rest of us similar to chimps with regards to interactional tendencies, it all just seems so natural. This is seen most prominently in comedic roasts where one comedian sits there and roasts another willing participant, with roast having the meaning of making very personal jokes about the victim of the night. Which on many levels seems like the most personal type of comedy, because it wasn't just you who had to have the material, but you had to have pretty damn personal knowledge about the person you were roasting and at that same time some sort of permission to go so deep with the receiver of the heat sitting there in front of you. Like the ultimate moment for inside jokes, except totally exposed in front of anyone willing to watch the original or the rerun. A process which sits right by me because from the history I've lived poking fun at one another is how you let someone know how close you are to them. There's something about telling someone something about themselves that they're not picking up on. Which is the opposite of the amount of self-awareness needed to be a comedian trying to do a certain level of self-deprecation.

That weekend Jax took me in a ton of places worth mentioning, but the only place I was really interested in were the comedy clubs. Probably didn't hurt that the warmth of those dark basements were far more preferable than the windy streets of Manhattan in the middle of January, especially for a guy who had just gotten off a plane coming from the tropics. At his convincing, which took no great level of diplomatic delivery, I ended up staying through Monday and buying a ticket to leave on the first bus out of the city the next morning. On that extra night Jax tried to get me to go up and it's likely that I would have, but I was somewhat happily humbled by the fact that I was visiting on the weekend and this weekend had been extended for the winners. *"Don't take it so seriously. Just tell them that raccoon story you told me earlier. But try to talk slower. You talk so damn fast."* Of course we didn't know that when we entered the club and looked around for the sign-up sheet. Noticing there wasn't one Jax went around looking for the organizer of the show that night and pulled me by the shirt to get in front of him when the time came. Asking where the sign up sheet was and how I could get on stage I was met with a hesitant glance and a situationally serious voice which asked, *"How long you been doing comedy?"*

"This is my first time."

"Yeah. No."

Jumping in with the hope to sway him Jax grabbed the guys arm, *"Come on. It's a Monday night! Let the guy go up!"*

"Look Jax we got show runners here tonight. No can do."

Walking away without another word the man quickly broke my spirit and all of the excitement I had for the moment. Let down as I was, he probably saved me by telling me *no* on a night of importance. Not only did he save me from going up completely unprepared to a crowd several comedians into their night of laughter, but he also ignited a side in me that didn't like being told *no*. A side that thought, *"Fuck you then, wait til you see me next time. I'm gonna make you wonder why you didn't let me up in the first place"*. More than being told what I should do, I always hated being told what couldn't do. It just irked me. Especially if the reason for which I was being told I could not do the said action in question felt like an arbitrary reason construed for the moments use to keep me in my place. Often times an excuse made up on the spot for the mere fact that they hadn't had someone do such a thing in that particular manner before which deemed such damning. I'm a walking conflict between thinking we have too many rules and being fully aware that humans are wild animals with little bounds to decency once all lines are lifted. Nonetheless the guy had a point as far as his business was concerned and I wouldn't learn until much later that there were just some nights where only the best were allowed to go up and those nights often served as a sort of audition for something bigger, so I guess I shouldn't be surprised that no one wanted to waste five minutes on a first timer. Not being one to be easily discouraged Jax blew the whole thing off and brought it up to me later after we watched a few of the cities best go up. *"You outta come back up during the week sometime. Honestly you coulda gone on at almost any other spot this weekend. We just happened to come on the one wrong Monday night of the year."*

"That would be awesome. Not sure I'm gonna have much time off anytime soon, but if I can make it work I will."

"You could find some mics down in D.C., I don't really make it down there often, but every city's got a scene."

That night after the final shows Jax and I headed to his girlfriends place and I crashed on her couch as he tried to slip into her room quietly as not to wake her. From what Jax told me I would end up saving a good 45 minutes in the morning by staying there instead of at his place. Apparently the trains are a bit spotty in the morning. Before going into the room he threw me a blanket and we said our goodbyes, *"You know how to get to the bus tomorrow?"*

Through the fading light of a blinking eye I responded, *"Yeah man I'll be good. Thanks for everything."*

"Anytime. And feel free to take those boots with you."

With that gesture I felt like my toes needed to thank him just as much as I did. *"Good looks. I'll see you soon."* From there I shut my eyes and quickly fell to sleep for what felt more like a nap than a long night before I was woken up by an alarm as a precursor to the morning commotion.

Only hours before I was running down these streets with Jax trying to make it to the next show. Now I was wandering those same streets attempting to find the Chinatown bus stop at the edge of the city; gaining a peak of blue amongst the grey in the early morning sky. Joining the line of weekend travelers headed back to a set of assorted East Coast cities I waited in an oversized red coat and a set of thick socks between me and my beaten up sandals. As much as I had wanted to take him up on his offer I was already carrying all of the shit I had taken with me to Costa Rica and I needed to travel as lightly as possible. Plus I knew if I did I would somehow put undue importance on the task of returning his shoes and likely prioritize it far above some of the other things I actually needed to do. I didn't need that kind of anxiety to start my year. Finally scanning my ticket and getting on the bus I found a seat near the front and placed myself next to the window, resting my head on a twisted pile of shirts I used to make the best replica of a pillow I could. As the bus meandered around city blocks taking us to the Lincoln Tunnel I stared across the Hudson River and looked on into Bergenline County N.J. where I saw the edges of Union City and West New York hugging the palisades; a scattered set of blocks slowly brightening to illuminate the beginning of the day to the dwellers within. Through a series of turns we made our way to 42nd street where we approached the Lincoln Tunnel, creating an uncertainty in me as I looked at the clearance to the tunnel getting closer and closer to the top of the bus ultimately allowing for a few inches between us and the rows of lights lining the tiled interior of a 1.56 mile long journey underneath the Hudson River. From inside the bus I looked on as we exited the tunnel and turned the proper corners to see kids playing with each other while a set of early 20's mothers paid more attention to their dogs interactions than that of their children. Which seems fair as the one group is far more prone to barking. The more I see them the more I feel like we should all watch children to understand human nature at it's core; they're always joking with each other when the parents aren't watching. Hell, they might be the most honest thing next to chimps. Only difference is kids can actually call you out on your bullshit. It's why everyone should be around a 9-year old once in a while, as that seems to be the age where they're smart enough to tell you you're wrong, but not socially aware enough to know they're supposed to be polite about it. This is not a secret of course. It was long discovered by the teams of a show from my childhood called *Kids Say The Darnedest Things* that children were the way to go for outright honesty. Those kids had it good. They were still young enough to get away with saying whatever it was they wanted on public television. Even though they would soon cross the threshold into members of polite society and not be forgiven for saying something stupid again until they were near the ages of claimed senility. For the rest of the ride back to D.C. I sat staring out of the window at the passing metropolises of the East coast corridor finally decompressing from the last few weeks. Prior to that weekend I assumed I would go about my business after leaving Costa Rica and find myself a new job in the states that was more attuned to true nature, but after spending 72 hours hopping around the city it was hard to see my life or where it was going the same again.

Two days later I found myself unable to sleep, still riding a high and unable to stop replaying the scenes from the clubs in my mind. Every time I was at work I would notice the laughter around me and wonder what had sparked it. Each evening I found myself pacing back and forth diverting between the how's and who's of making another weekend trip to NYC work as soon as it could be done. For whatever reason I kept this internal excitement within me at first, not mentioning to anyone other than the walls of my room. I wanted to, but the idea just seemed so crazy and far fetched at first. Although in some ways the idea felt completely natural each time I tried to dissect it. As my personal history will show, I've had a lot of brushes with members of the comedy world over the years far beyond viewing them from a stage. Perhaps the dumb luck of circumstance, but I found it harder and harder to believe it wasn't something more the more I gave it consideration. Maybe the world had been speaking to me for longer than I had been listening.

Figuring that I could try it for my first time in my own city I started searching for open mics nearby. The city had an IMPROV, but I went with the logical guess that they weren't letting an amateur on stage anytime soon. Which was only partially true. They accepted amateurs, but only those who had a 5 to 15 minute tape to send along as an informal audition. I soon discovered the crazy reality that there was never more than one show per night, which I found to be a far cry from my three days in New York City which managed to somehow expose me to at least eight different spots that one weekend. I scrolled down towards the bottom and found a contact page with a name next to a set of instructions about who to get in touch with. Little did I know that D.C. may have been a city of the arts, but it lacked in certain artistic environments, with only one clique of comedians controlling the local scene. The largest barrier was that the majority of the shows were run by one person who was unenthusiastic about letting outsiders enter his circle. An odd amount of bureaucracy as I reflect on it now, but very D.C. in a lot of ways. Along with that I was also informed that for my first time I needed to do a bringer show in which I provided a group of no less than five people to join at the club and stick around for the entirety of the show. Having no idea what that was I nodded along as he explained it to me and then went onto his next point. On top of that he also gave me this far off date of six weeks from the day we were talking. *WTF?* With that bit of discouraging news I gave my thoughts a break and continued about my life figuring I would eventually get myself back up to the NYC and go on stage when time and opportunity allowed. Easier to travel four hours sleeping on a bus than to jump the hurdles of a limited funnel to stage time currently blockading my freshman debut.

It wasn't until two weeks later that life forced me into a moment of clarity with a violent wake up call about the topic of *someday*. An awakening which happened one night as I had to take a friends car to the airport after he had left it at my house for the duration of his vacation under the promise that he would bring me back something cool from Europe. Per his request I was set to arrive at the airport in his car and let him take the wheel from there. His flight was scheduled to come in around 8:30, which is why I found myself at a stop light a few miles from the airport around 8:20. Which means it must have been close to 8:21 when the lights of a red Toyota Camry suddenly filled my review mirror as the car took no mercy upon me or the red light causing me to sit in the middle of the road in the first place. Only grasping the pending reality a mere moment before the impact I was unable to do anything to brace myself and soon found both me and the car shaking in the middle of the intersection as the Camry plowed into the back of my car and on through the intersection. Looking up from the steering wheel I watched as the car which had just hit me quickly

11

recovered from one swerve to the next and attempted to flee the scene. Lucky enough to still have control of the car and the functionality of all of its mechanical capabilities I pursued and soon steered my way into the middle of a parking lot where I began discussing the incident with a man who appeared to be a mix of tired and intoxicated. Unsure which of the two were overwhelming him more. Knowing the realities of what was likely in my own trunk I exchanged information with the driver and was forced to let him on his way as we were both in somewhat of a predicament. It wouldn't be til days later that I would find myself laying in bed wandering what would have happened if that had been a truck, or just the same vehicle going faster. I was lucky that the impact was only somewhere in the 30MPH range and that there had been no real damage done other than to my friends bumper. Nonetheless it caused me to ask myself a few things. Most importantly of which was, *"What if you had died that night? What would you regret NOT having done?"* I had never been in an accident like that before. I had been in plenty of situations which could have killed me, but something about this one shook me. All I would have been on the news is *"some man"*; just a dude sitting at a stoplight waiting for life to let him continue on his way.

With taking a stab at stand-up as the only thing being dragged from one to-do list to another I decided to reach back out and see when the next show was and how long it would be before I could go up. Once sent the schedule of possible shows I took a few days to delay my response and went to scope them out to see which one was the best possible location. Among the two finalists in my decision were a spot named *The Big Hunt* and another called *The Wonderland Ballroom*, both in different parts of the city and both bringing different types of crowds. *The Big Hunt* was off of Connecticut avenue just south of Dupont Circle in a vibrant area filled with bars and bar hoppers alike. *Wonderland* was more of a neighborhood spot in an area that looked less than ideal for parking your car, but was also right across from a school. Aside from their surroundings the two environments were very different internally. *The Big Hunt* placed its stage in the basement below a bustling bar and had the proper set up for comedy; a stage in the middle, chairs spread out evenly from the middle to either side, and a small bar off to the back left next to a few tables where the comics could sit before going up. Meanwhile *Wonderland* had more of a narrow hallway wide enough for a table on either side and an isle to walk down leading you towards the stage. It was like you were up there performing a wedding. The lighting was also worse and the environment itself only allowed for a few people to pay great attention at any one time. However, *The Big Hunt* created a feeling that the stakes were much higher, even on the slower nights the basement filled up quickly and the crowd would be right at your feet the moment you went up. Knowing that this may be the only time I tried such things I decided to go for the fully immersive experience and sent back a message stating that I was good to do either of the Monday or Wednesday shows at *The Big Hunt*, to which the head of the group agreed provided that I could bring five people. With reluctance I assured him I could and went about brainstorming who would be best to invite for my debut and possibly my only time.

As time went on I thought my biggest issue was going to be coming up with jokes, but finding a group of five friends to come along held much more weight in my soul as the day come near. For starters who the fuck wants five friends there for their debut? The proposition alone sounded unreasonable enough to almost consider calling the whole thing off. It was then I wished that I had been able to keep in touch with a few groups from college who saw me as a possible performer before I ever tried. I can remember this girl who used to tell me that while some people had a sparkle in their eye, I had what she called a naughty sparkle, like I was either thinking something naughty, or knew something naughty was going on somewhere. In a lot of ways she was right, being the local bartender I knew of plenty of naughty and I suppose when the light hits just right I do have a bit of a glimmer in my eye, but if anyone else ever noticed anything they didn't say. It was some of those observing me early on in life which had led to me considering this path long before I was even presented with it as an option. Now as I was saying, no matter the occasion there are fewer and fewer people available at a moments notice the older you get, and even less that can just pick up and go to a comedy show last minute with a few people to tag along. Which is why I was lucky one of my first texts hit the mark. *"Hey Q, you have a girlfriend these days?"*

"I got someone I'm talking to..." - Q

"You and her ever been to a comedy show?"

"Yeah man. We saw Bob Saget a few weeks back." - Q

"Awesome. So I need you to clear your schedule next Wednesday and bring her to see me go on stage."

13

"You serious? Where? I didn't know you did stand up." - Q

"That's the enthusiasm I need. Uh next Wednesday, at the Big Hunt, it's off of Conn. Ave. And yeah I know, it's my first time, so don't expect too much outta me."

"No way. We've been there. Yeah, I'll tell Chelsea and get her roommates to come with!" - Q

"Nice. Appreciate it. I actually gotta bring like 5 people, so if you know anyone else who wants to go, appreciate you telling them to come along. Otherwise I'll hit up a few other people and try to fill the crowd a bit."

"Nah don't even stress that. I'll get a few coworkers that'll be down to show up. Just worry about getting your act together." - Q

"It's the only thing on my mind. Look forward to seeing you. Hit me up on Wednesday and we'll figure out what time to meet before."

"Bet. Be easy. See you then!" - Q

I'm sure it seems unlikely that I had some backlog of jokes, but I had kept journals in one form or another for somewhere over ten years of my life by the time I got to this moment. Not to mention the years I spent working behind the bar hearing the hilarious stories of others. At the very least I could find five minutes worth of stories to spew out while tryin to find a funny twist. Admittedly no easy task, the most tedious part was taking the time to go through my notebooks and pull out the funny stuff. It took a level of labeling that I was far from used to and a level of mental organizing that I didn't know I had. Still, even once you have the material labeled setting up your first five minutes is hard. For me it was way harder than the actual decision of going on stage.

When I finally had my five minutes together the next step was to get it burned in my mind. The thing particularly different about this preparation was the need to remember what I was going to be saying and in what order. Despite having given all of the previous mentioned types of speeches and presentations I had never been in a situation where the precision of wording and timing were so equally necessary. In attempting to prepare I recorded my act and became religiously attached to my headphones and listened to my voice repeating my act over and over for days leading up to my performance. Something which I would imagine to be as cringeworthy for you to imagine as it was for me to experience. I can't say for sure how many minutes I spent listening to my own voice that week, but it was easily the part of the process which most contributed to my feeling of comfort. The only thing I couldn't be sure about was the actual level of humor. I had said a few of these things in front of friends throughout the last week, but none of this would be crowd tested until that night came.

Saying I had come up with five minutes of jokes implies that I had the ability to go up and speak for that long without stopping or repeating myself, all while generating enough laughs along the way to keep people in their seats. I was not going up there and splitting sides for five minutes. Even still, the one thing I wasn't going to do was show up unprepared. I didn't care as much if they laughed or not as whether or not the crowd saw me as someone who might know what he's doing, especially since I had gone through the second part of my life fairly certain that I was projecting anything but that about myself. Deep down that's all I really wanted, it didn't matter so much that I did great as long as I looked prepared.

With that mindset I stood in front of the mirror silently performing, trying to perfect every bit of my act possible, each time with the awareness that I was relying on the punchlines to hit as I planned for them to, each time uncertain that they would be as funny to the audience as they were to me in my half-baked moments. Truth be told I wasn't sure any of it was funny. I've always been seen as far more serious than comical and even though I mentioned a history of going on stage a time or two, I was never much of a fan of the spotlight. For a number of reasons, one of the largest being how the light gleams off of my forehead. I do however enjoy the stage and as previous stories of mine would tell you, I've always been uncomfortable when it came to mischief, but I was always the one to be put in front talking once the authorities had gotten involved. It's weird wanting to do something that people rank as their highest fear. Though even that label isn't without some lies. It's actually the fear of rejection that those with stage fright fear. This is probably why early speakers saw the power of words. The acknowledgement of that power has been known since the beginning of time and recognized worldwide as even the Nation of Islam was started under a man who was honored by his ability to produce words without any formal education; a feat as impressive now as it was then.

The prep that went into this event had me recollecting one of the weirder weeks of my life when I was preparing for my first time performing as a stripper. Nothing official, no platform or anything of that, but the whole thing was meant to entertain a group of women celebrating a bachelorette party for a coworker set to put the reigns on a man of the older persuasion later that summer. As a piece of advice here I will tell you that a lot of funny things can come from just saying yes; funny or interesting, sometimes both. Still being in college at the time and a full time bartender I had to take the only gaps in my schedule that I could find and meet with a buddies girlfriend and her roommates in their living where we were instructed and critiqued on our lap dancing abilities. I assure you it was way more awkward a picture than I can even paint it here. Of all the lessons learned that evening the one which stuck with me the longest and applies the most in this particular situation was that of alleviating my soul of shame. When you've been stripped down to nothing in front of a room full of strangers it becomes hard to feel any sort of embarrassment over anything else ever again. And I do mean stripped; I can still vividly recall the moment I felt a collection fingertips crest over the waistband of my boxers moving in a downward motion as I came to terms with what was about to happen. I imagine it would have been more embarrassing to hurriedly scramble my coverings back on that it was to just stand there and deal with the reality of that which they had wanted. As the above story should show, I am somewhat of an odd person or an unusual case when it comes to people who find themselves getting up on stage to perform for the masses. Which I find odd because I don't have any overwhelming desire to be heard. Something which I'm sure seems like a narcissistic denial since I am not only projecting my thoughts on the stage, but also in books. I just know I have the ability to do this and it would seem dumb not to try. This wasn't necessarily some childhood desire as much as it was a final realization that I was beyond qualified to give this lifestyle a try.

My first memory on a real stage took place somewhere in elementary school when a friend of mine asked me to perform in a talent show with him. My buddy Matt had written a few raps and needed another person to go along with him. I remember the prep of sitting in his room trying to go back and forth reciting the lines. I remember the photo of us, but I can only recall one moment from actually standing on the stage. We had two nicknames of no mention beyond my own embarrassment, and if I can keep a few things private then why not, you're getting plenty out of this book as it is. We had about two minutes among the stanzas and the rap went back and forth between the two of us as we gripped our microphones and rapped about who knows what. I guess if there is a privilege I have beyond any doubt it's my lack of fear about being on stage in front of others. I can only imagine standing in front of a classroom had done plenty to alleviate that modern fear. Still not sure if that ability was aided by all of that experience or whether the ability is the reason I was allowed those experiences. Nonetheless, it came to no surprise to anyone in that gym room that day or to any of those who knew me throughout school that I would eventually find my way back to the stage as I was about to. When we were in the classroom I was always the one used as a voice to present group projects and class opinions alike. I eventually moved on to write an entire book about people using my voice as a way to get around Central America. I really don't know what else I've got to say to sell myself on this fact, but it just never bothered me to talk in front of others. Now I don't mean to sound like it has always gone well, that is so not the case. It has gone bad on more occasions than I care to remember. I once performed a wedding after having received the personalized vows only moments before. Oh, and it was in Spanish. So I've had some hiccups. Now, that being said, I've never felt shy or apprehensive about the human aspect of this, the speech part of this was always easy. I think part of it has to due with the fact that I came from a group of friends that was ridiculously shameless, to an extent that I don't know if anyone ever really *one-upped* anyone.

That night of my performance I arrived to The Big Hunt about an hour before the doors opened and peaked inside to get a look at the early arrivals. The first thing I needed to do was make sure I was on the list and noted as having arrived. When I found the list I wrote my name down and then took a picture of it a few moments later once the other spots around me had filled in. I worked it out to realize that I had about 45-50 minutes before going up if each person before me did at least five minutes. Before walking away from the table I was stopped by the guy I can only assume was the one in charge. *"You're the new guy right?"*

"Yeah that's me. I think we spoke over email?"

"Okay look, just a few things so you know. Sets are 5 minutes. We'll give you the light at 4 and a half. Don't go over your set. And make sure to put the mic back when you leave the stage."

"Got it."

Lucky to round the hour I had plenty of time for the crowd to pile in. As the show went on I'd never taken such diligent care in listening to the order of people called and memorizing the names before mine. My nervousness wasn't a nervousness in the normal sense. It was a tension. Standing there I waited with a glass of water in my hand, taking slow sips as the condensation thickened around my palms. Living in my own head I barely noticed his hand as Q came up from behind and smacked me on the shoulder with a greeting and a question all at once, *"You nervous?"*

Floating in uncertainty I took a shot of tequila with Q and then watched the guy before me go up. In the first minute or so of his act I sort of zoned out and heard a light buzz in the room drowning out my thoughts and his act. Somewhere in the final stretch he went into this bit about gummy bears and I listened for the final two minutes as he got the crowd to a steady laugh. When he started walking off of the stage my palms got sweaty and I took a deep breathe as I listened for the host to introduce me to the stage. By the time the moment came I was excited to get on there and see if I was right about my thoughts on what was funny versus what wasn't. Though it didn't hit me right that moment there was something empowering about being about to go on stage and test my material only moments after thinking of it as I did with my opening line.

The next five minutes were some of the best of my entire life. I walked onto the stage and ducked at first sight of the pipes dangling above my head as a compliment to the low ceiling. Though I looked natural to those around me, in my mind I was robotic. I said my words, I gazed at the crowd, and I even got some laughs, but the entire time I barely noticed a single face. I would argue my eyes wouldn't let me take in any one look for the fear that it would be one of boredom and throw me off my beat. Four minutes in I saw the flash of the light in the back of the room alerting me I had a minute left and so I picked up the pace of my words and rushed through my final joke. Ending on a lighter laugh than I would have preferred I thanked the crowd for listening and handed off the mic to the host who came up and tried to shake my hand as we passed. Stepping off stage I floated back towards my friends and a set of smiling faces who gave me a quick congrats before we went about listening to the rest of the show. I knew from that moment I was addicted and I would be chasing the mic for the rest of my life.

The rest of the night is a relative blur to me. I watched the last of the comedians and made sure to thank the show runner before I left.

My friends invited me for a drink afterwards but I used the excuse of work the next day as a reason to deflect. Truth was, I spent the rest of the night walking around the city reflecting on the night and this new feeling it had invigorated inside of me. Once I got that feeling inside of me I had to figure out a way to jumpstart things so that I could keep doing it. I needed material. I needed regular stage time. I needed fans. I had lived in Los Angeles years before spending seemingly wasteful time going to and from the casting offices, each time wondering if anyone would ever watch that stupid video I had just stood in line all day to drop off, but this was different, this didn't require sending my tape all over town, this just took me finding a stage with a mic. Seeing how easy it was I almost felt stupid for how long I had been in the scene without realizing how close I was to some of the better spots in the nation for such an endeavor. I had to jump start it like the Japanese playing catch up in the late 1860's, I was behind, but I could catch up if I did it right. In order to get myself in the mode I had to be honest with myself and began asking myself some of the very questions they had asked themselves back then, for instance, *What could I do to speed this up? What could I do to improve this?* In answering these questions I knew I needed time to write, time to perform, and time to reflect. In order to take this type of art seriously and give myself a chance, I had to treat it like a *real* job. For the first time in my entire life I felt like I knew where I belonged, and at this time in the world the place which had the most clubs to play such a character was NYC. Knowing that I started taking trips up on every day off I could find and signing up at open mics throughout the city, often being the first person to arrive, but still putting my name no sooner than fourth on the list each time. At first I used Jax's place as a spot to crash with a couch usually available. The nights it wasn't Jax usually wasn't home anyway. He took advantage of his girlfriends downtown apartment more so than he led on. His roommates didn't seem to mind, so having a place to stay I soon adopted NYC as my second city. A few times I didn't even mention it to Jax, I would just text his roommate and make sure the door was unlocked. He may have had his act together on stage, but his day to day personality was increasingly flakey and unreliable, usually unresponsive to messages for days at a time. This wasn't something entirely unique to him. That was another thing about NYC, everyone was somewhat noncommittal. Plans could be broken in an instant and no one was ever mad.

The more time I spent in the city the more I thought on the fact that I had often heard those abroad say NYC was the only place in America they had ever visited. Which I dare say gave them a warped sense of reality about my country, but I was still glad to hear they were interested in stopping by to take a look at what craziness Times Square could offer. The whole city was like an open-air office for the world with the best design of intersecting patterns genuinely constructed by the passage of peoples on their way in and out of the favorite city of the 21st century. When I look at what it was and what it became NYC might represent the best example of the ability of the American collective to get a ton of shit done in only a little bit of time; relative to time that is. Modern NYC was a city built by a combination of the three hands of American society which existed cohesively at the time of its inception; the government, the people, and the underworld. The history of the city is such an overlapping set of cluster-fucks in which the influences of all three battled back and forth as a plethora of realities surfaced within the 302.6 square mile island. This city was one of the largest culprits of corporate greed, though any hub eventually would be. More of a problem with people than with places. To understand how that all happened you gotta understand how Manhattan began. I know it's hard to imagine that there was a time when the island was best explored on foot and hiked as any elevated piece of land would be by newcomers. I think newcomers is the most appropriate word for those coming across the Atlantic from the late 1490's on, regardless of will or reason. Before we worry about getting political, that's something I always thought sounded crazy, the idea of coming across the Atlantic Ocean before what we know as modern technology. I just couldn't. Even under the best of conditions in any century.

My favorite part of this city was how I could walk around for hours without ever seeing the same thing or any moment on repeat, and never from the same angle. No other city in America had that. Other places were big, but no place was as condensed. All you had to do was stand outside of Times Square for a few minutes to really take it in. Although some moments didn't happen on repeat it's crazy to see how quickly trash can stack up on a busy street corner in rhythm with the timing of meals. Sometimes pausing a moment life felt like you're standing center of a time lapsed photo on full speed. Being raised in Virginia I have a particularly ingrained interest in the history of this country as it is and despite me wanting to tell you to visit Jamestown it's hard to say there's much to be missed involving American history if you just visit New York City and read every plaque you see. It is there that you can see the modern representations of each group that had its hand in the building of this country. Then in reading its history you'll see that some parts of the city were built by the mob, some by the government, and some by grey participants of both. At the end of the day it was power and culture which built all of these things. All the powers of the world grappled for control, but the one which held its grip the longest was that of the media. If we are to go back to NYC a minute I would say it was ultimately and most effectively conquered in construction by Robert Moses, and it was done so via the understanding of legislature of the funnels of power. If you're interested in that sort of thing I highly suggest you read the book the *Power Broker* by Robert Caro. It's phenomenal. You'll totally understand NYC after that, and you'll also hate toll roads, and tolls in general. I should mention that it's about a thousand pages, but I assure you, totally worth it. Caro, if you're out there, we love ya, keep up the good work, you're a damn genius.

Sometimes the best part about attending stand-up is watching the process of thought happening in live action on stage. Once you start doing comedy you begin to hear a few of the same sentences and questions over and over. One of them being someone asking you *what other comedians you are like?* As I was starting to think about figuring out my story I saw my country as a place trying to figure out its own. As previously stated, I wouldn't say I have an accent of any sort, but if you put me in NYC it's easy to hear I'm not from around the corner despite the fact that NYC has more accents than anywhere in the country, but even within itself it possesses many accents distinguishing members of one part of the city from another. America itself has around 30 distinct accents. In NYC one would see a separation amongst Americans unlike that witnessed in other cities. People in New York were New Yorkers, THEN Americans. A lot like Texans. Even people from New York have their own level to this. Go ask a man in the Bronx where he is from. It'll be the Bronx THEN New York! Something which I think has to do with living in the most touristy city in the world with an average of 66 million people visiting from around the world each year. When you're just going about your day there's gotta be a part of you that's like *"Hey! I'm a local, get the fuck out of my way."* Which is interesting because New Yorkers aren't exactly standing on land *gifted* to them by anyone. If

21

memory serves me the natives didn't even understand the concept of currency or owning land when the deal was made. I read once, *"All lands are stolen lands if you go back far enough."* I've alway wondered the same about thoughts. Except for the material things inserted into this new world are there any new thoughts amongst the people around me? Are they all not wondering some version of the same concerns repeated throughout history? Perhaps it should say all lands are constantly stolen, stolen by influence, stolen by funds, stolen by time. It's like a corner store that keeps changing its theme. Here and there little things are rearranged and coupled with previously unimagined or un-marketed combinations of side items. Sometimes they even brought entirely new items from all over the world. Though even with this natural tendency towards change the shifting narrative of America no longer being a place to be seems ridiculous.

I was still new to the idea of being back in the United States and was getting used to how people were talking about each other. Often times speaking of those from other parts of the country as being different, often even foreign like. Which in some ways was no surprise as I've found that how far away we are from our home most often impacts how we describe where we are from. The more I saw comics talking about themselves in NYC I started to think about myself and how I was viewed and how I had gotten to where I was. As a performer I was lucky to have somewhat of a neutral accent despite having grown up in the geographical South. A place where far before the ways of the woke I was used to hearing jokes about Southerners being stupid, with jokes specifically directed from Virginias to West Virginias, and this county claiming to be slightly less hick than the next. I myself had plenty of West Virginia jokes after having spent my life growing up only twenty miles or so from its borders. Yet hearing New Yorkers talk of Southerners I found myself conflicted because I continued to see a theme of blanketed statements about a group of people with majority of them thinking of them as hicks filled with hate and ignorance. Meanwhile, the people in the South, not free of their own assumptions, seemed to look at people in the North as disconnected from the way of the world and attempting to corrupt their beautiful way of life. Both groups with a great deal correct about the other. It's no wonder there was a feeling of a divide developing amongst the people around me. I would argue it's rooted in the natural consequence of geographical separation that took place in such a large country. The same separation that quickly inspired the building of a railroad system across the country as a way to keep people on both coasts connected culturally. Though geography is only part of the problem. Everyone has brought their own thing here, but in some instances the ingredients weren't stirred in the melting pot for which we are known. Which has created a lack of shared identity amongst an increasingly large portion of our population. Granted America has always been this malleable place, so a permanent label becomes no easy thing to make.

The American identity is very layered for a country so young, with several beginnings to speak of, first being that of the natives and that of the new arrivals. As they do new arrivals eventually became established, and everyone after came either on the favor of somebody already here or via the faith provided by the original selling of the American dream. A dream which painted America as a clean slate among everything else. This became a cycle of repetition for years to come. With those solidified further growing in influence, and those coming here ever more shifting this picture at the fringes of its borders. With a combination of identities evolved by having groups of people with the mindset of *having been here forever* combined other groups of people living with the mindset that they came here and worked hard and used the system to get the life they needed and in some ways ripped it from the greedy hands of those born here by a combination of genetic grace and geographical luck.

If we're looking for something collective, an American attitude might be the only thing we can claim to share across the board. Some type of sense of belonging that stems from our frontiersmen background. Something I would argue possible by a promotion of individual interests which makes each person here feel like there's a chance at any life no matter how crazy it may seem. This is because nowhere else does there exist more ways for which one can express themselves on an individualistic level than in the United States of America. And with that individualism at stake we need to get rid of the idea that we are as divided as led to believe. There's an importance to maintaining the union as it stands out of the mere lesson of having seen Europe splinter into factions and kingdoms to only see a few decades of unity before entranced ideals put up walls of legislation setting back the progress of those eventually re-united through clear thinking and the reflections of war.

Americans are constantly putting ourselves out there. Perhaps because we know we can reach fame. Fame for fame's sake. Fame for being ridiculous. Even the cast of *Jackass* found their time in the sun, and in many ways broadened the field of possibilities for which one was able to establish fame thereafter. Traveling abroad I constantly heard sentences like, *"Americans are too friendly"* or *"They act like they know you right away."* Even people in Europe were far from used to our boisterous ways despite the amount of interactions and similarities we share. A fact which I find neat when you consider that Europeans are more interconnected geographically as a people than Americans have ever been.

I was the combo of one first generation American and one transplant via a convoluted path from West Africa; ethnicity being a completely different story. With that my grip on the identity of an American is one which stems from shallow roots of only a generation ago, but nonetheless they're tightly wrapped up in the soil of this land I call my home. Having traveled the world I can tell you that at the moment where we are as a nation internally and where we are from an external perspective are very different. Despite seeing the comical nature to nationalism, there is a part of me that understands that a people living within the same borders and under one system must have some sort of shared identity no matter how small it may be at times, and in times when that shared identity is shrinking, they should convene with one another, not further divide. I suppose it naturally happens after a few generations when people become separated. North, South, East and West were the only separations people got to really have. That and whether they were first generation American or otherwise. Those were some of the divides. Land or no land. Renters and owners. We going to Mars or staying here? Those divisions are more prevalent than any others as far as understanding one another. Then again, we can't be expected to understand everyone we come across nor to be understood by them. We all evolved too differently to do so effectively. Even I was in a weird position having been planted in a transitional period of our time and people. I was in that weird in-between generation where I totally understood technology, but I wasn't really into documenting my day via pocket spies like Tik-tok and Snapchat. For the brief time either one of them were on my phone it was only as a means of reaching those who rather use it as a medium for communication, it was never my go to choice.

When you're trying to figure out your identity as a performer, there are some ups and downs. Unfortunately the obvious lows of a comedian take place in front of crowds. Luckily for me, that's never been too big a deal. As far as individuals go, I'm admittedly rare in my lack of stage fright so I can't claim to completely understand the mindset of someone who doesn't feel as good about going on stage. I assume the thing people are most afraid of is some form of bombing. Something which can be thought of as not only failing, but being truly alone in a room full of people who don't relate to what you're saying and continuing to talk with them via a microphone and heightened volume despite all of the obvious reason to no longer continue to do so. The audibility of it is alarming more so than anything. The first time I bombed on stage wasn't as bad as people make it out to be with regards to inner hate afterwards. It was more confusing than awful, even disorienting in a way. You feel like you're being ignored. Like they're not getting the point, but it's as if they start paying even more attention the longer you go. They want to be entertained, they want to laugh. You're just not delivering. And then the lights start to get hot. You feel the electrons slamming into your forehead. Three minutes in you're just rambling by any normal persons observance. That's what it is when you're talking on stage with no real point to the mission of the speech beyond laughter in a state where laughter is not being achieved. There I was just rambling away for about 7 minutes. First they heard about my girlfriend, the one I no longer had, then the dog. Next was how hard it was being back in the states. Five minutes in and still nothing. I started to realize I was gonna need to bring out the big guns. Like a good pick up line. Some of them worked no matter where you were. Those are the ones you keep in your back pocket for when you get panicked. So I tried my last *good* joke. Another flop. I knew my act enough to know how much time had gone by. I was after all at the end of my first set of jokes. The ones which had taken me through my first open mic were now falling flat on the audience...Great.

Now time for the new stuff. With a blind gaze I scanned the tops of their heads and went on about this and that, never really making sense, never creating anything halfway resembling a funny thought. In a dark room you notice a cell phone light up. You definitely notice 3, and then 7. During a show it's nothing to see a cluster of phones lighting up here and there. When I saw the light flash, alerting me of my 30 seconds, I lulled into a final joke, nodded my head, and ended with 12 seconds left to spare. Yes, I'm sure it was 12. I started counting down from the moment the first light flickered. One of the best things you can have happen in a room like this is having that one person with a distinct laugh latching on to your first few moments. However, that same distinct enthusiasm can work against you when you've been hearing it for every comic before you and then all of a sudden you don't and so you start to wonder, okay maybe they went to the bathroom? Maybe they died? Why would God take the one person giving laughs right before I go on? Fuck. Either way it doesn't matter because in this moment there was no laugh hungry audience member ready to save me. Of course this whole thing took place in a stadium styled auditorium so as soon as I finished, I had to go and walk back up the steps passing the crowd I had just let down. So much fun. From there I sat and watched 3 other comics go up before I gave myself permission to slip out into the bright red hallway of the New York Comedy Stand. The bulbs lining the edges of the ceiling seemed to touch my skin just as much as the light on the laugh-less stages had. Though these lights did not hide the shadowed silhouette of the disappointed.

When I was finally outside I wandered around for a moment and considered getting a slice of the nearest pizza to help heal my woes, maybe even drown them down with a 2nd root beer afterwards. Then somewhere in my stroll I decided to stop and pull out my phone to check on the location of the next mic. Seeing one starting in only an hour I resolved to go up again before the night was over as a means of making the evening end on a good note. This time I would throw myself even more under the fire by inviting a few friends to come see me. With that decision, I sent out a massive group text letting all of my NYC based friends know where I would be and when. *The Creek and the Cave @ 10 p.m.!* As usual a handful of people never responded and a couple others half committed. Nonetheless I did the best I could and made myself get on stage one more time for the evening that way I wouldn't go to bed with that as the last set I ever did. Much like the adage of not going to bed mad at the ones you love, I would also advise similar actions when considering your artistic endeavors, and for that matter three-pointers, never leave the court without the sound of a swish to end your session.

I later watched the video of my failed performance and realized that I needed to pay attention to much more than my words when I was on the stage. I don't wanna make excuses, but I kept moving out of the light. I never stood in it on any punchline. And when I was out of the light I was practically invisible. It was bombing on stage that night which helped me solidify confidence in my decision to move to the city. That combined with the realization that nobody growing up in NYC has the thought that they wanna grow up and get out. It's more like they wanna elevate to another experience in the game they're in. And if I was going to do the same I had to throw myself in the game. Because if previous hesitations had taught me anything, it was that a lesson was often better than a delay.

After going up to the city a few times and crashing with Jax I soon saw that on the lease it was him and his two roommates, but in reality it was always a cluster of humans, artistic and otherwise, crashing on this couch or that spot on the floor. Being there I lived somewhat of a frat house existence for a while and as long as I kept the fridge stocked each time I showed up no one seemed to mind. I took advantage of this Costco thing and from there I was able to supply the house with food for less than an average months rent. This all made it easier when the time came for me to ask them about having a place to stay for a few months. A question to which they responded, *"Okay. So you're going to be sleeping on the couch like you have been, and I'm going to pay $200 less a month?" - Jax*

"Basically." - Patrick

"Don't know why you thought that'd be a problem..." - Jax

"Well I just wanted to tell ya." - Patrick

"Great. I gotta run to my girls. Catch you later?" - Jax

"Yeah. I gotta run down to D.C. but I'll be back sometime this weekend." - Patrick

Just like that, I was given a key to the house and I became a permanent fixture. Well, as permanent as anyone is in their city apartment. Most people use it as a storage unit they're allowed to sleep in. From there I used his apartment as a hub for the next few weeks, taking the bus up whenever I could. Soon I felt like a pro at managing the schedule and making it to the bus on time. It was funny to me that I had gone without riding a bus in the states since leaving the unmonitored backseats of the school bus somewhere around 15 when one of my best friends got his license. I spent the next few weeks going back and forth, eventually anchoring my life in NYC with an apartment in Brooklyn amongst a few scattered artists.

Being in NYC allowed me to see the nighttime economy each city eventually develops once it reaches a certain size. Before this I thought

I had been a part of the late night crowd, leaving work at 1 AM, but it was here that I learned how wrong I was when I would find people, not just find people, but literally bump into them on the streets of Manhattan at 4 AM. Along with the idea of the nightlife I also really liked the idea of not having a lease. It was the most free I had felt in a while. Not that my twenties weren't a definition of freedom, but I was still anchored down by a series of one year contracts that would have made even the most qualified rookie nervous. Having a month left on my lease I slowly moved my stuff into storage and downsized my already small existence into the least amount of bags possible. I was up there often enough to convince a local bar that I was living around the corner and began working here and there in my commutes back and forth, sometimes picking up a shift on 4 or 5 hours notice to keep them from realizing I was 248 miles away until the day I wasn't.

New York City, N.Y. pt 2

March 2016

"Am I supposed to be following you?"

H ad I been giving any choice beyond circumstance and timing I wouldn't have pulled the trigger on moving to NYC in the middle of winter. It's easily the worst fucking time to try and get acclimated to the city. Unless you wanna wear rainboots all day you WILL go home with wet socks. It's almost impossible to avoid the random dips of slush remaining from the lack of sunlight to melt away the cities hidden crevices of sidewalk. On a brighter note my roommates were great. I slept on a futon at the end of Jax's bed, which he was barely in because he constantly stayed at his girlfriends place. Though still I had no idea which nights that would be so I often woke up in the morning looking at his comfortable mattress wondering why I had never just crawled into bed and set an alarm to make sure I wasn't caught off guard. The other guys were great too. One in particular was always up doing things. The kind of guy you wanted to be around if you were hoping to get into the arts. He inspired you to get your work done just by the presence of his robotic self doing the same each morning. My first night there the guys were in a hurry to show me the rooftop. Apparently, our apartment had the best access to it with a hatch above our stairwell leading you to the top. If you had the time to sit on a rooftop and do nothing then you had made it in life by the standards of any good Brooklyn resident.

It was no more a surprise that I had made it to NYC, than it was a cliche. My family had found it once before when they came over from Ireland, and even my father wouldn't pass up a chance to drive up I-95 to see the city for a long weekend away. Since sometime in the 1700's the city served as a beacon to the world from the newly found nation. Buildings were erected, and on top of those buildings were placed towers, and so started the spread of radio waves which would never cease. A city filled with people is the natural hub for a projection because you have the largest canopy to start with which is why NYC is the home of the media empire as a whole. It was from NYC that the message of America was first broadcasted to the globe and from where it continues to be broadcasted.

Although cities like New Orleans and San Francisco were attracting international crowds since the 1700's, but that's for another part of the book. America was that place everyone went to and wrote home about, at least for the era of existence in which I inhabited. The city on the top of the hill, bright lights shining far and wide for others to see, like a beacon speaking to every one with the ability to rummage up a few dollars and go.

New York City was long known as a hub where all cultures of the US and the world came to meet. Go there today and you'll see jerseys representing teams from all over the world. I swear every team has a bar with a fanbase to take refuge with on the weekends. This city was always the stage. Which is why it makes sense that stand-up comedy started here. The people of the 1950's just needed something to laugh about after experiencing the global turmoil of the 40's. Late night shows and comedy were just meant to break the tension. As a kid these shows were also a way to become informed about things from the past that you weren't around for, using SNL weekend update as a great way to hear of the news, with a comedic twist tied to every story. In my middle school and early high school life I watched as *Comedy Central* and a few of the late night hosts began to use the waves to capture a new audience of politically intrigued viewers. This twisted view of comedy and politics all tied into one helping to cultivate my interest further in both fields, though they were both only pursued on an intellectual level in the beginning. In recent days I sometimes ask myself whether it was good or not that news started the change in the way that it did. As most things are just a response to something that came before, there was some sort of cynical void which existed and allowed for such an emergence of what I would call *comedically driven news*. Satire is what it really was, but it always tried to edge into the realm of real news by showing you glimpses of sides that were completely ignored, sometimes things which were far more logical than that which we were being shown on the so-called *mainstream* media, which is to say the media which was given the best access to events as a result of reputation, longevity, and connections. I do feel like it got more people caring about the news and noticing more pertinent issues.

Day to day existence in NYC was something indescribable to people who haven't spent time there. Especially for someone like myself at first. I grew up in a more rural part of the country, about two hours from the closest major city, but seemingly a world away as the differences at the time were far more than political. The ways of life between my two existences early on were staggeringly different. In the city my friends would go over only a few cul-de-sacs to have a sleep over at their neighbors. Meanwhile, I drove 52 miles round-trip on a regular basis at the age of 17 to visit my girlfriend. Who despite going to a different high school, was still within the district of mine, and only attended the other because her mother was a teacher there and it just made sense when considering the early hour at which her daughter would have had to have been picked up at in-order to make her spot on the bus route work. I know that was a lot, the point is, shit was not close to each other when I was growing up. Things were spread out beyond all belief, which created one of the largest differences. Nothing was convenient, nothing other than finding a place to pull off the road and rest a bit should the need strike you. That being said, living in the city I saw a level of convenience like I had never seen before and from the outside witnessed an obvious addiction to it. Here I saw how proximity had created the addiction to convenience which had begun to take over city dwellers by their mid-twenties. It was one thing when things were just accessible, it's another when they're at the beck and call of your desire fueled finger tips. This was one of my problems with things like UberEats and DoorDash, besides the fact that they would overrun my restaurant with orders for people that had no interest in actually dining there, but would still be happy to take away the attention from the people who had actually gone out of their way to come out and enjoy an evening in one of our booths. With those attending the restaurant often being ignored or receiving a lesser quality of service because the person who should have been taking care of them was arguing with some delivery driver about why this or that wasn't ready. I fuckin' hate those apps, they should only be used for things like subs and sandwiches, no one has ever enjoyed pasta to-go. Truth be told I think those food delivery apps had a lot to do with the slow legalization of drugs in my country, I mean if you're a cop how the hell can you tell the difference between a drug deal and a food delivery these days? It's all just a bunch of sketchy bitches with brown bags handing them off to strangers at street corners behind the protection of a row of hazard lights blinking in non-sequential glares up and down each clogged avenue. There must have been an early saying amongst the force, *"If you don't see the cash, it ain't the hash"*.

Bartending seemed like a good way to get the word out about my stand-up, but I found for the most part it interfered more with my shows than it helped them. It was just as easy to get people from the park to come as it was anyone else. Something I learned one day when I was hanging out around Colombia Circle and wound up in a conversation with a family of Argentineans who had an uncle that really wanted to come see me that night if they weren't catching the late flight to Boston. This whole thing isn't to say that everyone who meets you and hears about your endeavors becomes excited. Some people have it programmed as some sort of trigger to either tune out or no longer take you seriously. Whether at the bar or out in the open the conversation would always go down the same roads until they would ask me something like, *"Okay so what kinda comedy do you do?"*. In some ways that question was a lot easier to answer when it came after a really long conversation when I had been given a few chances to be accidentally funny enough for them to not need too many qualifiers about my ability to create humor. I knew how it was that they saw me because it was how they were introduced to me, as just another guy bringing them a drink with a dream hoping to escape the scene forever. If someone asked me about my travels I could narrow some things down by saying they're mostly of Latin America and usually on the lighter side of luxurious. However, if someone asked me what type of comedy I did, I had no idea what to say. Not just for the fact that I was still establishing it, but that anyone I thought to compare myself to was incomparably famous. I also hadn't been doing it long enough to feel like I had any type of voice established. If someone came and saw me how would they sum me up?

With a life as inconsistent as my twenties I was never able to relate to the feeling of running into people within your industry. I was so far outside of everything that it didn't even compute to me. Which is why it felt kinda cool and oddly professional when I started to recognize other open mic performers around the city; at times walking with them from one show to another or staying behind at their request to check out their set or help record for a showcase they were trying to get on. Something I noticed is that I was a part of the right group of people. I was for once in the right circle of people for the things I was hoping to do with my life. I mean, I wanted to learn languages with the early part of my life, but it's not like I needed to be around other linguists, I only needed to be around those who spoke the language I wanted to speak. Luckily in this instance there was somewhere I could go to be around people who wanted to do what I wanted to do. Though oddly, I saw that I wasn't really gaining many friends in the stand-up community.

Not for a lack of friendliness or anything, but for the same reason people have a hard time dating in the city, everyone is so fucking busy. While you may be able to do, see, and find anything you want in the city, that same surplus of options leads to a plethora of distractions unlike anywhere else.

Given my history of getting into fun situations, I was really excited for my time living in a place like New York. Living there is like putting yourself in the lottery for experiences in life. That is as they relate to experiences related to interactions within civilization. It's not like you're gonna experience an avalanche. Aside from that, anything and everything is bound to happen if you just walk around for enough time. Sooner than later you'll find yourself in one of those *Only in New York* moments. One of my favorite ones happened some semi-warm afternoon in March when I was in a bookstore downtown looking for a new joke book. Browsing the shelves I soon found myself bumping into a man taking up a bit more space than myself. Apologizing and moving along I looked back and realized his face to be a familiar one. Turning back a moment I asked him, *"Hey man. You seem like an analog kinda guy, what kinda notebooks do you use?"* To which he responded with a series of choices by order of awesomeness and told me he was trying to find one in particular which he saw a few weeks back. From there he went about introducing himself, *"My name is, Jeff. Jeff Garlin."* His hello was met with a handshake and shortly after followed by, *"Lemme go upstairs and ask them about those notebooks,"* which he said just as he turned around and proceeded to knock over a whole stack of books from a tiny table behind him, immediately drawing attention to a previously quiet corner. I told him not to worry about it and started to reorganize the table as he went upstairs. By the time I had it done I found myself in an odd limbo not knowing what to do. Saving me in nearly the knick of time I heard a voice from upstairs say, *"Patrick, you coming?"* With that I bolted up the stairs and through the front door where I saw Jeff standing with a friend of his who was now listening to the explanation of where we were going. *"Book lady said they got some good notebooks at this place around the corner."* Getting further away from the store I turned to him and asked, *"Hey. I just wanna make sure, am I supposed to be following you....?"*

"Yeah. It's just a few blocks away. Do you mind?"

"No. Not at all."

Along the way we were stopped twice for selfies by passerby's and each time his friend obliged as if he had been through the routine 100 times today. Full disclosure here, but I neglected to tell Jeff I had been in the store we were talking about earlier in the week and knew for sure they didn't have what he was looking for because he was catching me on the tail end of a long journey searching for the perfect joke book. I had been as thrown off as he was to see that the store was a stationary store without any actual notebooks along for the ride. None aside from the overly priced leather ones they had with weak weighted paper. Still I couldn't miss the opportunity to go with him on this journey in hopes that somehow we would find some super secret magical notebook that they only give the stars. Though our journey ended with no such luck, I was able to make an impression on his buddy by asking for an autograph in my notebook instead of a selfie like the rest of the world. A decision which I still debate to this day, though his chose of words above his name added enough comical value to my day to make it feel worth it at the moment.

There's something debilitating and torturous about living in a city like NYC when you're broke, because there you are surrounded by every option known to man, yet you shouldn't spend your money on any of them. Leaving the city isn't easy either; leaving costs, coming back costs. It all costs. The whole city is one rotating toll road with differing financial barriers to entrance. I always tried to remind myself that I had decided to put myself in a place where I could practice every day. I was in a weird situation because a place like NYC made it easy to sell yourself to a thousand people a day, especially once you got a job as a bartender, providing you limitless access to the already endless streams of people. That being said, it felt really strange how often you were selling yourself to a person and you would realize, *well I'm not really that person, that's just who I'm trying to be*. Though I can remember doing the same before I could really speak Spanish. I would say the few things I knew with ridiculous confidence, and that inevitably led to a quick series of linguistic tongue twisters as the listener would ultimately assume that they were speaking with someone fluent. Creating moments of awkward denial as I had to remind them that I was still *just learning*. Although no matter how kind someone is when you're trying to learn their language, that kindness and patience soon fades when your failed attempts have led to them being delivered the wrong dish when they're in a hurry to eat and get to the next thing on the never ending to-do list that is life. That's why early in NYC you start to adapt your NYC personality. Once you do it's easy to figure out your way, you've just gotta take charge and find your line amongst the crowd. It's not to say I actually accomplished that anywhere by this point in the story, but I definitely saw the importance of it represented in the success of those who had reached it. Whether you're hurrying down the stairs to catch the subway or attempting to make the most out of those last 4 seconds on the cross walk, NYC soon forces you to adapt to a new speed and a new flow unlike any other.

Through a combination of the city and the drive of comedy I had developed a new found urgency to my life. I had a reason to do things. Most importantly, I had made myself promise, not just to keep up with it but to be honest about my intentions. In my earlier days I was a writer, expressing myself behind the guise of a campus nickname and an early avatar writing for those interested enough to drop in on my blog once in a while. The difference here was I couldn't do this secretly. I could hide it from my friends, but I had to perform in front of somebody. The issue of committing to something so publicly is that the public sees it first. Saying that I was going to do something so bold and to do it on such a public forum was nerve wracking no matter how much confidence I claimed to have. As a young student I was constantly put in front of the class every time a group assignment required one of us to get up there and start speaking. Once they shove you up front what are you supposed to do? Just leave? Walk down the stairs of the diving board like a fat kid shaking at the knees? No. But I didn't wanna perform in front of a screen. I was an in-person person. Which is ironic since most of us see the majority of our performances in life on a screen. The screen is where some of my most influential times came from. I can only imagine the the same combo of ideas is what led to many other unique souls like myself. The abundance of ideas is proof more than anything that a nation which cultivates individuals eventually finds those individuals at odds. Individuality no doubt has its drawbacks. I'm sure we all know someone who is a little *too* themselves for our likings. Nonetheless, I would still call it an essential part to our society and one of the things which defines us most as a country; our defense of and ability to be individuals.

As you start to sell yourself you come across some strange people. Which is to say you come across average people and you realize how different the world really is. Especially how different your idea of funny is. You would often start a conversation only to be thrown into another of an unsuspecting person whose friend would say something along the lines of, *"Oh my God you should talk to her, she has tons of funny stories!"* Everyone wanted you to hear their funny stories or somehow put their likeness on stage. Which was more or less annoying because you could never really explain to someone how difficult that translation would ultimately be. How am I supposed to tell a joke in which I am the mother of a daughter? Funny might be funny, but when it came to delivery, relatability mattered.

After a few weekends of consecutive visitors I experienced the duality of frustration and appreciation for anyone who was willing to come to one of my shows more than once. See, I wanted people to be intrigued, I needed them to be, but here I was selling myself without enough material to back it up. I had no infrastructure. No YouTube, a joke of an Instagram, and only the shell of a website converted for my use from a WordPress assignment given to me back in college. *Thank God I remembered the password.* Yet, a part of me felt like if someone had come to see me off of me selling myself on them it was somehow required of me to do at least one to two minutes that I knew would work, preferably material that would kill. Then there were the people who actually knew me, I felt like they should only see the best. For whatever reason in March this was a problem like no other. It was then that I became a part of the New York stop off list for layovers and 3-day weekends of friends on their way to and fro. Usually those few curious souls wondering what their former hometown friend or college days buddy was doing. The ones who had time to come along to a mic just sat amongst the crowds and stared. Others were the kids who had the money to travel and who doesn't have a reason to go to NYC for a weekend if they have the means? It was a hub for everyone. I even got a visitor from Spain along with countless friends on overnight layovers who would come to a show then crash on my couch. Similar to when I had been living in Los Angeles in my early twenties and found people wanting to find excuses to visit me. I wish I had earned more money back then. I wish I had been in a position to tell people to come visit me and stay at my place and crash on the floor and just come and go as they please, but instead it was more important for me to be free and to have the schedule I wanted which is why I was in a shared house and not a single apartment.

When I would first meet up with any old friends the conversation would quickly go to a question about what I was doing in the city and where I was traveling to next. Traveling was still the thing they remembered me for, so it seems almost fitting that I had to do something so out of left field to redirect their attention towards my newly intended future. What country I was going to next became the question which controlled my life before that point. Now I was here being asked where my next show was. Always amazing to me how quickly one narrative unhinges and a new one can begin. For all that it mattered I had to make this work. Even with this changing narrative I knew my friends might not save me again with last minute opportunities. I knew that by the time I might decide I need them again they could be near retiring. The narrative I was creating had to become a reality.

I remember a quote from the movie *Almost Famous,* where a journalist tells this up and coming writer in regards to many other writers,*"You'll meet them on their long journey to the middle."* While I love some of the in your face attitude coming from the statement, I never needed that type of *fuck them* satisfaction, nor did I hope for it. I just wanted to make it as an artist, for my own satisfaction, with no ties to their feelings about it before or afterwards. In that attempted transition I went from being the guy constantly on the go to the guy who hadn't left the radius of a few blocks in nearly five months. To help keep people from holding onto that image I decided to do something different. Unlike during the first few years after my college graduation, this time I promised myself that I would not bullshit people about who I was and what I was up to. If I was hoping to create a certain reality I had to be the first to speak of it. I can recall telling people for years after I knew it wasn't true that I was going to be getting myself into grad school any day. All the while lying to myself just as much as I was lying to them. Then in doing so I found myself living up to some of the realities of my lies by delaying myself in any of the necessary actions to advance my life. Not this time, this time I was going to be sure to tell everyone who I was and what I was doing. If they didn't like it then they weren't someone in my audience, that was that. As this attitude started to take form inside of me I would find myself sitting on park benches or the concrete surroundings of statues and eventually in the middle of a conversation with some family from God knows where. Noticing my notebook and my free time they would often inquire as to what I was doing. When I told them stand-up comedy I was usually met with one of two reactions, *"Oh that's so cool"* Or *"Oh. Uh, nice."*

Followed by a long conversation or a quick departure.

Then there was that one time when I ran into that family from Argentina. They embraced me at first and then I realized that they thought I was telling them that I was some type of salesman. I don't know how that was lost in translation, but it came across on my end when I heard them refer to me as a *charlatan* but with a Spanish accent, leading me to inquire further as to what they meant. A *charlatan* as far as I had known it to be defined was an individual who made his way selling the lies and follies of his existence; not one to be looked at with eyes of admiration. I suppose I should have suspected this. My moms husband once told me if he didn't know me that he would think I was bullshitting him the majority of the time I was telling a story. I was used to people not being able to read me my whole life. It was weird how some people would be amazed that you were a comedian, but then let down that you didn't have a Netflix special. It was like they no longer cared once they heard you couldn't be found somewhere on the airwaves once they left. Not being on YouTube meant you didn't exist. Each time I start to tell people about doing stand-up comedy I begin to feel like a liar. For one, it's kinda crazy, I get that. Two, I don't come off as some loud funny personality. Quite the contrary. I'm usually on the softer spoken side of the conversation, and would much rather sit with you in a quiet corner than to be trying to steal the conversation at a loud dinner party. I've always been more of a conversationalist. I even tried to make my first book sound like someone was speaking to you the entire time. If you haven't read it yet I suggest you check it out.

Given his age I totally understood why the guy thought I might be pulling his leg. He was from a time when the truth about my claims would have been much harder to substantiate. Ironic as the majority of our problem today is not knowing what is true or not based off of too much information being available, in his time it was so hard to get the information that you had to take a lot at face value, and nothing is often more difficult than believing the claim of an individual as to who they think they are versus who they've really become. That all being said, they didn't know how to read me, and that combined with me telling them what I do, I could only take but one meaning from their interpretation of me. Ultimately I had to ask myself *What seriousness do they even owe me? Did I even have enough talent to do this? Do I have anything worth putting out into the world and is doing so in a humorous manner the way to do so?* How could I feel confident in this when I already didn't handle it well as an exchange would go something along the lines of, *"Oh you're a comedian....?....Tell me a joke."* At which point I would stand there kinda dumbfounded not knowing how to tell the person across from me that I was more of a story guy.

Even as a stories guy my brief time in NYC allowed for a view into sides of life that I never knew were possible. An early spring evening at a rooftop party put me in the company of a physicist and the close relative of a few last names you would swear they were lying about if it weren't for the extravagant nature of their life and rooftop apartments. That being said the levels of imposture syndrome varied depending on the group I was around, but it's fair to say it was possible no matter the company. At times it was even surprisingly worse than you thought it would be. I remember being on the rooftop that one night and thinking to myself, *"Patrick, you gotta earn your way back to this rooftop."* Because I felt like such a fraud as I stood there. The people, though disheveled and heavily intoxicated, were all of high esteem and each one as interesting as the next. I wondered for how long they had diluted their own doubts in hopes of concreting the realities of their desired existence which they now portrayed in relaxed opulence. There's a certain amount of self delusion that must take place in order for you to be a successful artist no matter what your endeavor. I mean, you've gotta tell yourself that you really have a chance at this thing. Not only that you're qualified to do it, but that you have enough to say, for a long enough time, and not only have an audience, but have the capability and the determination to continuously draw in that audience over time. It was the first time I found myself wondering, did the sheer act of being in the act of trying make me worthy?

As I began to think of my identity as a comedian and the idea of imposture syndrome I realized that I don't think I ever even vaguely understood Shakespeares whole *to be, or not to be* nonsense until I got into comedy. The whole idea of *being* took on a whole new meaning. Identifying as a stand-up comedian and attempting to project that identity upon the world caused me to see a shift in how people responded to what I was doing. Not to say that they always looked at me like I was serious, or logical. I get it, but then again, I don't. If you're a doctor, you do one surgery and you're a surgeon. Right? If I have a friend who did one brain surgery they would always be the brain surgeon in my head, even if they only did it once. A waste of a long journey to a medical degree perhaps, but still a choice they can make. However, if you do stand up 100 times and have never been paid, are you a comedian? When am I allowed to tell comedians I am comedian and does that differ from when I'm allowed to tell a random person that I'm a comedian? How much does the opinion of either matter when put up against the laughing validation of an unknowing crowd?

New York City, N.Y. pt 3
April 2016

"I guess you had to be there...?"

Along with the endless probes of what my act was like, one
of the questions I was asked a lot was, *"How do you stand all
of the PC bullshit they try to bring you down with?"* Which
was a response to a growing narrative that our country is *too sensitive*
or *too politically correct*. While I would argue that such statements are
rooted in a history of facts, I would also argue that the assumed
outrage which is creating the perception of an enraged society is
actually something more recently fabricated by professionals of the
word who have decided that this is the best way to get attention and
follows; sometimes to incite descent, others to generate income, and at
times a disheartening combination of the two. Something done in
history time and time again, using hysteria and the human tendency to
overreact to facilitate states of seeming unrest. In my opinion it's not
oversensitivity so much as it is highlighted outrage. That's my opinion
as a whole. Though that doesn't mean that my act was without some
heated response. And despite my mindset, political correctness wasn't
something left back in 1991.

Even though I was loving the comedy scene it's not like everything
about it was perfect. Traveling the world, I would sometimes wonder
how people lived without cameras back in the day. Conflicted by the
days when we thought it was somewhat precious that certain cultures
didn't want their photos taken due to a fear of losing a piece of their
soul. Now a camera is more likely and more often to be on you than the
eyes of someone who loves you. I always had an aversion to having my
performances filmed and this made my least favorite of clubs the ones
where upon arrival you would learn that you had given up the right to
privacy that night by agreeing to stand in front of a camera which
would simulcast to a small group of subscribers. I hated this. Most of
us hated this. I was never okay with the idea of having someone who
was not a part of the present energy being able to participate in the
critique of it. One of the things I hated the most about this, was that too
many of us were giving up not just our privacy, but our right to

41

experiment as artists in order to eat up a few more followers from the exposure. When I would mention it to people coming to perform they would agree, but the ones controlling the show would usually just say something to the likes of, *"You're getting exposure. Soak it up."* As I saw it the a lot of comedians feared that the crowd wasn't aware that sometimes the bad stuff is a sort of defense mechanism for the fact that they don't have it all together right now, and then somehow it can get worked out overtime once they've gotten pass the part that they initially didn't see. The bottom line is the stage is where it gets worked out. The editing happens on the stage. So to hope to work it out while live streamed was no welcomed message. I was more so on the side of the comedians and clubs who decided to take your phone all together once you got in the door. The few times I was lucky enough to either perform or observe at one of those events I was blown away by the level of focus from the audience, the same audience that any other night would have their attention divided between me and their phones.

Contrary to popular belief the biggest reason for not having cameras somewhere isn't actually fear of concern for cancel culture. It's a matter of the fact that one of the largest necessary elements to the art of comedy actually working is the element of surprise. So as a lower level comedian without a lot of material how could it be beneficial for me to put all of my stuff out there depleting the eventual surprise? I like to think this is only an issue in the beginning when you're just getting started. Maybe if you're Jerry Seinfeld and someone sees you once they're not gonna be let down to see the same joke again a few weeks later, but how many shows in a row could that same trick be played before the crowd would stop coming and stop advising others to do the same? Then again who was I to assume that everyone was seeing everything I did anyway?

Despite the cameras I got up and delivered a few parts of my act as well as a few newer jokes. One of which was actually the first joke I ever really wrote. Though to say I wrote it is somewhat false, I just experienced it as a funny moment and then translated it into my act. See, at the time I was dating this girl from South America. Awesome girl, adorable smile, beautiful soul, and the prettiest curls I've ever seen. As happens with a lot of couples at my age the topic of kids came up, which eventually led to the topic of dogs. She lived in a tiny apartment at the time so she was advised to get a smaller dog despite her love of Huskies. One day while walking with her and her new dog in a local park we started talking about the process of registering the dog after purchasing. Which is when she started shuffling through her purse and pulled out a stack of documents and receipts all showing me that her dog had been registered with the AKC and a few local organizations. To which I replied, *"Wow. I guess I gotta get my shit together."* She then looked at me and said, *"What do you mean?"* and I responded with what would become my eventual punchline, *"I don't know. I just had the disheartening realization that my girlfriends dog has more papers than she does."* She laughed. I laughed. And I'm pretty sure I even saw the dog give me a smirk. Though this eventually led to a much deeper conversation about the necessities of citizenship than it did more puppies.

After my set, I went to the bar and found my buddy Q with a group of people he had made friends with during my time away. Doing my best to be friendly and normal despite the adrenaline rush I was going through I extended my hand and tried to give everyone a firm *'Great to meet you'*. The first two in the group were super friendly and receptive, even going out of their way to tell me what a great job I did. It wasn't until the third one that I was met with some resistance by a girl with dark curly hair and a forehead reaching my chest. To her I said, *"Thanks for coming,"* hoping to use that as a statement applying to all those being introduced. Then she took it upon herself to do what every comedian loves, give me some shit about my act with the opening line, *"I didn't like that joke about your girlfriend. It was kinda mean."*

Knowing immediately the joke to which she referred I decided to take the conversation to Spanish. *"De Donde Eres?"*

Met with a, *"Huh?"* I repeated myself and waited as a confused look remained on her face. Considering that perhaps the volume of the crowd around me had hindered her hearing I asked again, *"De Donde Eres?"* Met again with a blank response I went back to English, *"So, are you even Hispanic?"*

"No..."

"Okay....So you're not offended. You were just offended FOR her...?"

Being met with an overall blank look I gave no more moments for a response and yet again made my thoughts known, *"Well ladies thanks for coming to the show tonight. I'll be sure to tell my girlfriend that people don't like me making fun of her dog."*

As I tried to walk away the girl stepped forward, *"You weren't making fun of her dog. You were making fun of HER."*

"Well if you understood it as making fun of her, then I think you understand English about as good as you understand Spanish."

"And if you had any manners you wouldn't go up and say that. Must be easy for a white guy to make fun of immigrants.""

"Got it. Well, I don't know what else to tell you. Guess you had to be there."

Needing to expresses as much patience and politeness as I did in front of a high school tribunal I knew keeping my mouth shut was the next best move. Initially her comment made my blood boil and sparked and instinct to jump down her throat as much as she was jumping down mine. Granted, I'm glad she let me finish my joke and waited to talk to me after the performance. From there I gave a nod of the head and moved around the girl to the right and made my way to the back of the room where a few of the comics stood waiting their turn. Approaching the table I muttered to myself, *"Great time to start comedy."*

"What happened? Your set looked good." - Q

"Not for everyone." - Patrick

"Is it ever?" - Q

"I guess not, just fuckin annoying. Why can't people just enjoy the show?" - Patrick

"So does that count as a heckler...?" - Q

"I don't think so. She came up after the mic." - Patrick

"Could have been worse." - Q

"Always. Well, thanks for coming again man. Appreciate your support."

I went home that night conflicted on more levels than usual. On one level I was angry. On another I was nervous. As far as I was concerned what I said wasn't that big a deal, but the thought of that tape being out there in the hands of someone wishing me ill made it feel like like it could be later, even if it wasn't now. Especially during a time with such a harsh court of public opinion. For the first time I even asked myself if I should keep from telling that joke for a while or if I should stop as a means of not being known as the guy with that joke. All the time wondering, had I not pointed out something ridiculous? Why the fuck is it easier to register my dog than it is a citizen? And who the fuck is ever asking my dog for papers that isn't a breeder? And why am I even talking about this? Who was she? She wasn't there when the joke was a moment of reality in my life. In my experience you can't walk in on a moment and expect to understand it. Imagine if you walked in on a couple experimenting with the sexual endeavors of role playing, would

44

you assume the lady dressed like a nurse was an actual nurse? *That's not how you take someones temperature!* Context totally matters. Uniforms and halloween costumes are the same. Were it not for the context of the moment, shit would be weird. The same can be said for entering a country as a newcomer; you're not going to get it all at first. I've been to Mexico almost ten times and I still can't understand putting spice on lollipops. It almost seems like a cruel joke to play on those with a sweet tooth for candy such as myself, but if availability in the market speaks to the desires of the market, then somewhere out there are a lot of Mexicans who find this treat rather delectable.

As a comedian there's a certain ownership one must possess over their thoughts and their feelings when performing on stage. Although what makes comedy unique is that you're required to get a specific reaction from the audience concerning that which you just said. When you sing a song, you can make some people cry and you can make some people want to sing along, it just depends on how it touches them, but when you're writing a joke you're in a position where your feelings and the situation at hand are required to get a specific reaction as well as the thought, *well that was funny*. Which leads me to something important; the laughter that evening was real. All I know would have me argue that laughter is the hardest emotion to consistently fake, so much so that we all know the discomfort of a polite laugh in a stuffy room. Especially because we all know what it's like when there's real laughter, that uncontrollable laughter that almost makes you expel your drink from your nostrils. It's not just hard to fake, laughter is uncontrollable. If someone laughs, it's funny. So to say my joke wasn't funny is just plain false. Even if only two people laugh, that's what we call an inside joke. They're the ultimate inclusion. It shows that you're family. I've heard hilarious jokes surrounding every topic there is. Anyone who has friends who work at at hospital, as a part of the EMT, or any other sort of *dark art* where one must find a way to address the crazy realities they see every day. Even so, people just have different types of humor. I've had a Peruvian server come up to me and say, *"Dude this table of Mexicans suck right now. They're being so demanding."* Expecting a series of nods or agreements out of me he looked on, *"Come on man I know you know what I'm talking about. You know what. You're the wrong white guy to talk to. I'm gonna tell Trump to make the wall a little higher."* His comment spoke to something else I had learned in my time abroad that I was never able to get across to others;

the racism of non-whites. Truth be told I've found non-whites say some of the most racist things to me, assumably because they see a white guy and think, *"Oh I bet he agrees."* If you had told me when I was a teenager that the worst thing I had ever heard as far as a racist comment would come from the mouth of Mexican talking about another culture I would have never believed you. Now you can't convince me that any form of cultural hate is different than any other. The only difference is that sometimes the splits of color make the division more obvious on the outside. Most of you would never know how deep the divide is between Spaniards and Catalonians, though from ten feet away you would be hard pressed to tell them apart. His thoughts weren't the only ones for me to laugh at in silence as I lived in NYC that spring. By this time people were starting to joke about the election more and more, especially in NYC as Trump was beginning to enter the political zeitgeist.

By this time in my life I had traveled outside of the United States extensively. I knew what it was like to be a member of the group so often touted as having it the best, and as one comedian so perfectly once worded on stage, *it still sucks failing at life even when you're living it on the best setting.* I remember in hearing that it felt like he had summed up what it was to be broke and white in this life. The bills weren't paid any easier because I was white. The parking tickets didn't go away any sooner. I'm always willing to go along with statistics and I'm pretty sure that one goes with it. According to the narrative I'm allegedly free from concern when it comes to my interactions with police, but the 27 times I've been pulled over in my life leads me to believe that's not exactly the case. Though some might say that walking away that many times without being shot is a miracle in itself, but that's not taking into account the fact that about a small percentage of police stops or interactions ever even led to a weapon being brandished.

This girl being mad at me was nothing new in my life. I was canceled early on by the parents of wholesome friends due to negative associations of me and the lifestyle my household could provide. All I had to remember was how not to care. Which is more so to say I must allow myself not to care. The worst that could happen would be if a tape of the performance resurfaced and everyone viewing it somehow felt the same as her. There was a version of me which had been shameless for a while as a younger man, and perhaps that side was needed again for this stage in my life. Although it was still the first time in my life I thought to myself, *"Hmm, why did she feel the need to come up to me? Was it to be seen doing so?"* I couldn't then express how I've now come to see it, but it felt no different to me than the person in a restaurant who starts off by saying, *"I'm not one to usually complain but...."* followed by some set of sentences meant to express how they're disappointed and just wanted you to know for the sake of knowing. Except they hadn't paid to come see me. I didn't quite understand what I was supposed to say or what reaction I was supposed to give. Something I had to remember is that once something leaves your mouth, it's not really yours anymore. In so far as its interpretation by outsiders creates a new meaning of that which you said in the totality of the public sphere. Had she been a reflection of my girlfriend I surely would have listened to her and tried to understand why my words did not sit well with her, but given that she was in no way connected to my girlfriend I just couldn't do myself the disservice of wasting time. They had no idea how much I missed her, nor how ridiculous I found it that it was easier to get my dog registered than it would have been to make my girlfriend a dateable citizen at the time. Sometimes outrageous is outrageous and there's nothing deniable about it. It's not even an agree to disagree situation. Most importantly, they didn't know it was part of the ultimate inside joke between me and someone I loved. Whether with her or with the crowd it's not that I wanna go out of my way to offend anyone. Though I refuse to go out of my way to watch my tongue in-order to protect the easily offended. Something which goes for my time on the stage as much as it does for the relationships in my life.

The term cancel-culture may be something new, but the act has been used for as long as entertainment has existed. Even Aristophanes, one of the worlds first comedians, was taken to court for speaking poorly of his country in front of foreigners during one of his comedic dramas. Going on this long about stage performance it won't be the last time I mention the Greeks and how their culture contributed to what we now see as the modern theatre of life. They might have been one of the first groups of people to look at a wise person without calling him a prophet, accepting them as philosophers in their own time and nothing more. Granted they're the same people who thought that lightening came from Zeus, so let's not paint them perfect. While we'll talk more about the actual stage later, the history of oration itself is fascinating to consider as it was the primary keeper of stories for way less time than it wasn't. Though those stories weren't projected in an arena type setting to our knowledge any time before the likes of Aristophanes. Known as the father of comedy to historians, he was a playwright in his own times which fell around 400 B.C.; regrettably I've never seen any of his plays, but I did manage to flip through a few comedy books over the years so I know how hard it can be to relay comedy with just the written word.

Skipping ahead far from the Greeks I'll bring up one of the first books I can remember reading as a kid was *"Leading by my Chin"* written by Jay Leno as a recount of his life as a comedian with an early focus on his childhood and the funny moments from it. Like many books I bought it as a gift for someone else, my father, and then managed to get it back into my hands to be able to read it. The next comedic type book I can recall touching wasn't picked up until the summer after graduating college. It was *"Too Fat To Fish"* by Artie Lange, the first in a series of books about his wild life in comedy and the existence which that life facilitated. Though I would be leaving out one of the greats if I didn't also mention *"Born Standing Up"* by Steve Martin. Like many books they were inception books about the trail which led these artists to the people we know of today, showing a sliver of their existence and how it led them to becoming the personalities we know, for no book could tell the whole story.

Later that night I kept thinking about what had happened. No matter how many times I went through whether I was wrong or right I still came to the conclusion that there has to be a no-fly zone of sorts for the arbitrators of our cultural existence, a place where people work things out without interruption. If you find yourself not okay with those things or triggered to a level you deem concerning, it should be somewhat a matter of personal responsibility to avoid those places. Like not eating at *Chik-fil-A* if you're allergic to peanuts, or gay. Deep down it bothered me to think there was a group of people in favor of taking me off of the stage for such a thing. The historian in me can't ignore the entire library of first amendment cases brought forth over the years, with 870 rulings being issued from major courts across the country as of this publishing. This should show even the simplest mind something. Examples keep stacking up. The whole thing makes me wonder how many times people need to read some version of Martin Niemoller's famous quote *"First they came for the socialist, and I did not speak out - because I was not a socialist. Then they came for the trade* unionist, and I did not speak out - because I was not a trade unionists. Then they came for the Jews, and I did not speak out - because I was not a Jew. Then they came for me - and there was no one left to speak for me." Now don't get me wrong, I'm not so overdramatic as to think anyone is coming onto the stage and ripping my fellow comedians from the planks and forever banning them from the mic, but it seems every now and then that generations forget the foundations which were put before them. In fact, as of this writing in 2021 I believe the last man to be arrested on stage for performing comedy was George Carlin in the 70's.

By most accounts a humans ability to express themselves freely is starkly greater than it has been in any other time in history, especially since the advent of the internet and in particular that of social platforms which give each human the ability to project themselves to the subscribing masses. Back in Carlin's time they went through a sarcastic view of our freedoms with thoughts like,"*Oh so you think you're free*" where people would cynically poke at the freedoms we believed we had in this nation, each time showing another way we really couldn't do whatever we wanted. There was even a song by a band named *Anarchy Burger* that said, "*If you think you're free, try going into the deli and urinating on the cheese.*" The disgusting point of which is to tell you that you're not free to do just any old thing you want. Though I hope anyone who thinks that's okay just goes and does it so we can filter that person out as quickly as possible.

Being a lifelong writer I've always been a fan of words. One of my favorite words (*fuck*) gained national recognition when proponents of it sought to protect its use, as well as six other words deemed dirty by the current controller of the airwaves. This was done by George Carlin who cultivated an act called *The Seven Dirty Words* which he performed all around the country and was ultimately arrested for. This case eventually made it all the way to the Supreme Court and once again the protection of artistic rights won out. His point at the time was to show that there are only a few words which have no other use beyond that of vulgarity and are therefore banned on T.V. As Carlins act stated, there are words we can't say on TV, but not words we can't say at all.

Luckily I wasn't one of the unfortunate few caught saying one of the only words that is still on the societal list of no-no's in the modern age. Of course I'm referring to the only word I think I'm still prohibited from saying, though not everyone is prohibited from saying it. Still, it's at the top of the list of *at your own risk* as far as combinations to make with your ability to create words. The word which I'm referring to is more commonly known as the *n* word. For the record I'm referring to the version of which would end in the hard *-er*. However, I have different thoughts when it comes to the more commonly used *nigga*. At least in so far as the differences of intention when singing in compared to saying it. As a white person I'm always confused when I hear another race using that word in casual conversation. I'm even more surprised when it turns out to be some Asian kid. I didn't grow up in an area with many black people so I didn't really have people around me using it amongst each other. But it's wild what a dividing mark it can be. There are some who throw it around freely and others that avoid it at all costs. The more I heard it in popular culture the more I started to look at that word the same as *bro* or *dude* would be relayed if trying to understand my culture. Especially considering how music has altered that words meaning from the 90's to now. The way I see it, if I were coming from another country or culture and you integrated me into black society, I wouldn't translate that word into something hateful. It would be the same as trying to figure out what *"Amgio, Parce, or Weuy"* all meant in Spanish. At the end of the day they're all terms of endearment translating into something resembling *bro*. I'll be interested to see the linguistic history that develops around that word as its entering an area of time where soon no one will be able to remember it with an offensive tone without using historical reference. For the record, I don't plan to throw it into daily use or have it attached to any of my greetings, I just want to be able to sing along to the music I listen to without having to worry about being cold cocked when I'm on the subway chanting with my headphones on unaware of the audience around me. Furthermore, I would love to know what percentage of hit rap songs, or rap songs in general had the word *nigga* in it. I mean a majority of the songs I would ever bump to had it embedded in them somewhere. Sometimes in the title, sometimes in the chorus, sometimes in every line. That word has even been in the title of hit songs on the top 40 list. Though even then the host of whatever radio show always awkwardly skirts around the word or title for fear of losing their job. Something which I've understood less and less over the years. Especially if the music is so broadly marketed. If it were only made for and sold to members of the African American community I could totally see where I would be wrong, but that's not the case. I was sold tickets to a *Snoop Dogg* concert without anyone asking me if I had the right skin tone to sing along to the chorus just as simply as I was sold songs with that word in the title by iTunes. Yet, there's still a part of me that can't help but think that this train of thought would find it difficult to find a place in the mind of anyone descended from slaves who was alive in the 1960's to see and hear the evils of the hateful society in which they found themselves a victim.

This topic came up in conversation once with some Africans in America who I learned didn't wanna be called African Americans. As a person who was particularly nuanced with language, the label of African American always seemed like a vague interpretation, as well as conflicting with the reality of the fact that my mother was born and raised in Africa, doesn't even say where on my birth certificate, just mothers place of birth: AFRICA. And it wasn't South Africa like you may be expecting. Anyways, having grown up there I would argue that her *in-country* experience is larger than almost any of my African American friends. That being said, I can recall being a child and going back and forth with myself over whether or not I could say my mom was African American in the times of which it would benefit me on college applications. She didn't want us to nor did she ever raise the notion, but my particularity to language always had me tearing the term and its applications apart. Granted, I couldn't just agree with the terms black or white either. Overall the nuances of color are too much to part hairs over. It also wasn't my place to determine what a group wanted to be called that I wasn't a part of, but calling my freckled ass white seems like it's still lacking in linguistic clarity.

As always, one argument around free speech is often highlighted by the point that you have the freedom to say whatever you want, but that you don't have freedom from consequences. On that part I can agree. It used to be that a fist to the mouth was a fine way to learn that you should be watching your mouth. Somewhere along the way we decided that wasn't okay and as a person needing a lift to reach 5 foot 10, I couldn't be happier. I dare say it has worked to my advantage more than a time or two. Especially that one time with that guy in the parking lot in front of that pizza shop. Though I should have been the one hitting him. Luckily the exertion of my my freedom of speech didn't come with any consequences that time. To my knowledge I'm still allowed back. To anyone who thinks I shouldn't be, my answer to that would be a bit too biblical with the ringings of, *"Let he who is without sin cast the first stone."* Which is what I wanted to say when I was younger and was excluded by local parents who didn't like the reputation of my family or the parties that went on at our house. Knowing all too well that those criticizing me were no angels now or before. I can remember being confused at the thought that the same kids who stole weed from their parents sock drawers weren't allowed at my house because we had parties with kegs. Though now the weed fan in me would agree with their preference even if not their attitude.

As far as consequences go, I ultimately saw none. Nothing beyond her comments that night. Proof to the fact that the level of controversy determines the level of backlash, with today's backlash being more digital than literal. This due to the fact that for the first time in human history we are in a time when an individual can know what it's like to have the entirety of the connected world putting down pressure on them, even when it's not *all* of them, because let's be honest, it's never everybody. I wonder how much backlash someone would feel if they didn't have a phone. As I imagine is the case most of the time. Especially when we consider how quickly that feed can be refreshed and forgotten. I find it hard to take anything seriously when you know how quickly your offense will be freed from their mind. This is not to be a rallying cry to tell others to blatantly disrespect the past, but when no apology for a past indiscretion is accepted then what is the point in doing so?

In this new era the screen serves as a stage and the interruption capabilities of someone who has access to all of your information and personality is truly alarming and without any substantial fortification against it beyond our own will power. Which is a lot to ask when a morning is basically started by a headline telling you, *Hi I know you weren't gonna look at this anyway, but here's something to be mad about it if you haven't already found something for your morning.* Between information and outrage overload I find it hard enough to keep up with who I'm not supposed to pay attention to anymore or from one week to the next. Modern day outrage comes in many forms and meets the public on many levels. Sometimes it's an angry person in a chat room hidden behind an avatar spewing rude rebuttal, other times it's an extremist obliterating a marketplace in the name of one god or another. It seems that outrage is more often than not pushed up on me as opposed to cultivated in my own brain anymore.

Bending more towards a Stoic way of living I find it bothersome that we've become a culture in need of so much new stuff to be mad about that we actually go through the pages of the dead to see what dirt we can bring up now that that victim is no longer around to defend themselves from even the most absurd of accusations. If something doesn't age well, and loses it's comedic efficacy, people tend not to laugh when they see it anyway and think, *"Oh, well that's strange."* So what the hell are we doing? Would you tell your kid to stop painting because the first few drafts sucked? Would we have Picasso if that had taken place? Perhaps it did. I don't know his history, but I do know that had someone inspired a young artist at the right time we might have never had a Hitler, or at least not the one the world knew. History would much rather have another failed artist than another successful despot. Perhaps it's a sign to the levels of the current levels of human success and relaxation as enough of us are now in a position at this moment to wish for the erasure of a person and their entire body of work in a time where there is literally so much stuff out there that the likelihood that some of this stuff would have been seen again beyond twenty years or so from now anyway are nearly zero. Does anyone actually think many people going back to find episodes of *Good Times* in the year 2030 as a way of filling their day with meaningful entertainment? Seems unlikely. By then there will be centuries of other entertainment to occupy their restless minds.

Now despite what it may seem like, I actually do believe there are some things which you shouldn't say in polite company. Otherwise in the most ideal of worlds I would be able to say anything I want to anyone around me at anytime possible, and in that same bubble of perfection they would be receptive to it in whatever manner was meant at the time I say it, not judging me for my words, only seeing that there's something happening between us that I wanna acknowledge, and perhaps even talk about. From there I imagine a lot of conversation happening. I'm not going to bother telling you what I think should or shouldn't be talked about, because well it just sounds stupid and people are assholes who will bring those things up around me just to aggravate me the same as I would likely do.

For those worried about the freedom of speech getting out of hand, it has already been deemed pretty unacceptable and publicly crazy to just stand on a proverbial soap-box and speak your gripes with the world. The only thing out of hand is the idea that discourse in the public forum is less and less permissive these days. More so because the entire definition of *public* has changed and the forums are not capable of visitation without physical presence. The difference this time is that the charge of obscenity is not coming from the government, but rather from the people. Which perhaps is something to eventually be expected in a democracy. I mean that's kinda the point, the people are the government. So, in most cases, the government is just a bunch of people; usually elected, sometimes appointed, but always just people, human like the rest of us. Each one capable of biases and indiscretions. Though now we are in a time when everyones voice can be heard almost at once on public forums like Twitter; a company whose invention has leveled the playing field for free speech as anyones voice can be highlighted in an instance. Which as we all know, can seem like a good thing as much as a bad thing in the same few moments of your early morning scrolling. With the argument always being in front of you that it is your choice to keep the feed as it is or change it more to your liking. In this way one can sculpt the world they wish to see, even though it does not mean it will reflect the reality of the world in which they live.

Truth is, I never had to suffer the same consequences of those that came before me. Something which I attribute more to the nature of progress than anything else. I could be afraid to be blogged about, but unless I pulled my dick out on stage I was unlikely to ever be pulled off and arrested. Even then I might be able to claim I was using it as a prop. This is why people like Lenny Bruce were ahead of their time; honored more for their defiance than for their words. By some comparisons perhaps he should be lucky they were only arresting him as there are some nations in the world where his type of outspokenness would not be tolerated nor allowed to continue. The unfortunate reality is that we are quickly moving away from the days when all we have to worry about is arrest. Our leaders may not like the things said about them on late night talk shows, but at the end of the day Jon Stewart never had to worry about some governor or President making a call to the network and having his show removed from the air or even worse having himself removed from the streets. It is the very ability to make fun of our own institutions which separates us from some of the less fortunate parts of the world. Though an argument can be made for unbridled adherence to that which the state desires when intentions are good, but it's a matter of who is at the wheel that we should be concerned about, and as that position is always changing, our position on speech should not, because speech is just a form of expression. The fact that I can even write this book talking about this is in itself a promotion to the fact that the citizens of our country enjoy a great deal of expressive freedom.

The all seeing eyes of the surveillance state are already in place. It's only a matter of time until you say something which provokes them and are forced to deal with the wrath of their decisions. Making it important to notice at this point that *government* is merely a term we use for the collection of people elected or otherwise who are in states of temporary control, but while we call it control, what it should really be is oversight. The government is supposed to be a branch of the people looking over the functionalities of the nation we are in and making sure that the things going on are within the bounds of the constitution that we have set forth. My issue with anyone from the outside who comes here and hopes to alter any of our constitution; if you don't like it, don't come, simple as that. Truth is I used to feel bad about expressing that, but the older I get the more I realize that we are all a product of our own decisions and if your decision includes coming to the United States of America then you are obliged to adhere to that which we have going on. We may not have a culture in the same sense as nations who have been around for thousands of years, but we are a group of people with more similarities than differences who have developed a system in which we want to operate.

Our nation has an interesting relationship with free speech, especially as paperwork is concerned. Constitutionally it's listed as our number one priority. The protection of that speech and overall transparency are supposed to be a part of our motto no matter where we go. We're so open as a society that we even televise the White House Correspondence Dinner, an annual meeting of political pundits of every sort for a night of shared laughter and seven course meals each year hosted by a comedian of the era. As a comedian and former student of the world of politics, no comedic adventure would seem to interest me less than being the one to host being in that position. Aside from being nowhere near as up to date on the references needed for a successful performance, nothing would seem more socially uncomfortable as an environment in which to perform. First of all, roasting a ton of people you don't personally know though they be public personas is a weird proposal. Now add on top of that the fact that you've gotta sit in a room with them for a few hours before and I don't know how many people could even handle the stress of that moment enough not to forget their act. Then again, maybe seeing their stupid faces all night gives one the fuel needed to go up and deliver when the big moment comes. No doubt they never pick the most controversial of comedians to take the stage. With the exception of that time they asked Norm McDonald to provide the evenings entertainment. RIP to one of the greats, we miss you Norm.

It seems to be no accident that the writers of the constitution knew all five rights of the first amendment to be of equal importance. They knew you can't have authority over discourse without giving up the essence of freedom of thought. That's why people were still coming here, it was the place with the best protection for its people and allows discourse from all sides. As participants in this democracy we have to accept, and I think most of us already do, that an accepted consequence of freedom of speech is the natural presence of conflicting ideas. Which would be present regardless of forced silence or not, they would just be unknown and further internalized. That's part of the package of choosing to come here. I'll even go as far as to say there are times where you'll hear something that's just blatantly false, and to that I say you've gotta take it upon yourself to filter that information for truth or not. Similarly the fan chooses to be a participant in the entertainment, but to what consequences does the performer open himself up? Something I began to ask myself was whether or not entertainers should be subject to the opinions of those who are not participants in the fan-ship? Should those who are not tuning in have any say? Should a team care about those who cheer when they lose a game?

This isn't to say that politicians or the government have always been on the side of free speech as they or their founding documents claim to be. Some of the first examples of outrage culture took place when the conservative forces of the country wanted to stifle performers like Lenny Bruce and his ability to speak freely on stage in the early 1960's. Not that it was necessarily the first time censorship took place, but it was the first time it took place in retaliation of those going on stage to try and get a laugh out of the crowd. Well, that's not necessarily true either, but that thing in Greece was a little over 2,000 years before. Can you imagine going on stage knowing that what you're going to say is going to get you arrested afterwards? Well, early comedian Lenny Bruce did it four times. Each time a combination of either being arrested for speaking obscenely or for performing without a cabaret license once they had stripped that from him as a means of keeping him from performing legally. Luckily he resisted by continuing to go on stage. I guess it worked. I mean it wasn't as if there was some police officer in there waiting to pull me off of the stage and throw me in a cell. I was still in America, not some place where I needed to worry about being taken away in a van and never seen again. Here we at least had a certain level of accountability that we demanded from our authorities. All of which serve to protect the freedom of the people. Which isn't to say our leaders or figures of authority weren't guilty of some flagrant neglects and misdoings in regards to protecting those rights. In fact the first example I can think of from my lifetime was in the early 1990's when rap music started to be censored on the radio waves, early on via sound effects and blank noise during the allegedly crude set of words being strung together. Most notably censored was a group called 2 *Live Crew* who was at one point fined and ultimately censored for performing crude lyrics in the state of Alabama. Though it was later established that there was a freedom of speech in art as a part of the argument over where art ends and obscenity begins, ultimately paving the way for the protection of parody. The same court case stated that adults have the right to listen to what they pay to listen to.

One of the crazier examples of this protection not involving music took place around 1958 when the American Civil Liberties Union, at the time dominated by a counsel of lawyers being largely Jewish[1], decided to defend the right of a Neo-Nazi group to have a public rally. Something which I'm sure would rattle brains today, but shows how important the idea of free speech was to a group of people who had recently learned what can happen when anyone is silenced. I love to picture a room of judges arguing over some of the things they had to say out loud in order to make this case work, but mostly I love how that group of lawyers understood the importance of defending even the most extreme and offensive forms of speech.

By a lot of standards the Supreme Court is one of the most important parts of our country, arguably one of the most powerful, as they have not only the ability of oversight, but the obligation of upholding that law to the letter as it compares with previous judgements made by the same court. Its judges are appointed by the President in power at the time a vacancy in the court exists, and that person remains in their position as judge until death or resignation. Pretty important shit. At the end of the day this was one of the most

---

[1] An actual fact, not a stereotype.

important cases in recent history with regards to free speech. No doubt it normalized and open the flood gates for vulgarity. It also further concreted our nations stance on the stronghold to the freedom of speech. As a person who loves using the word fuck, as my first book would prove with over 200 uses, nonetheless I don't care to walk through the streets shouting it up at the windows. *"There's a place for that. There is, and there always should be."* However, when did we decide that society did not need to have its feelings hurt? Why is that the case and yet we still don't give help for those in need of actual mental help? Instead allowing for record numbers of suicide. Despite not wanting to ruffle feathers of anyone minding their own business, it's not my concern if you're offended, and I don't care if I hurt your feelings. As an ancient saying goes, *"If something offends you, ask is that true? If it is, accept it and move in. If it isn't, move on just as well."* The bottom line is that it's your choice to embrace the feeling of offense instead of embracing your capacity to control your emotions and move on. Even as a performer it was far more likely for it to be something personal than it was something from my stage time. The reality was they can cancel me all they want. As if it somehow bothers someone who is yet to become someone. This brings me to one of the few things I feel qualified to preach to others, and that is the ability as well as the necessity to control your internal emotions even if purposely provoked from an annoying outside source. Which I would argue is on the more than unlikely side of antagonistic triggers one receives in their day.

Every now and then you would have a very NY experience where you had to remember whatever was happening was just part of the agreement you make when deciding to live there. Sometimes you deal with some crazy shit. That goes for America as much as it does NYC. We have certain things we've all agreed to. In a manner or not. That's what civilization is. As far as the hierarchy goes, there's nature, then civilization, then society. Agreeing on a certain life when you come to a country is the same as agreeing to the rules of a gym or a movie theatre. You gotta wear the right shoes and yes you're a dickhead if you forget to turn the volume down before coming in. Some think we're moving towards the way of absolute transparency amongst the minds of humanity, some sort of singularity. I'm gonna right now call the bluff on that one. It's not happening any time soon. We still can't get running water to everyone. We can't make all desert cities run off of solar. So that being said, we still gotta figure out how to live with each other, because I don't see any harmonious universal mind-scape being created anytime soon. So we all gotta live with each other and do so peaceful, while also not bothering the other person in their attempts at a lovely existence. That's the language we need to use to open up our set of rules governing each other. The story of a nation becomes part of the language of that nation, for that matter a nation might be more of a language than it is anything else. Because it is language through which stories and traditions are carried, only maintaining their integrity as the understanding of their words is complete and without the gaps of translated indifference. All of that being said, it is up to the residents of any country to aid in its continuation utilizing the freedom to call-out and freedom to criticize. Often this is exercised most by one of the arms of our freedoms, the press. One of the backbones to our nation is the idea and practice of a free press. Which is why I find it so disturbing any time that the rights of the press are attacked and the public doesn't meet the attacking authority with a vicious resistance. When the freedom of press comes under attack everyone needs to worry, because it is the press who can serve as a funnel to let others know what is happening. A free society is one with free flowing criticism ultimately leading to constructive discourse. Today a comedy stage might be the only place free of discourse. Unfortunately we have become so used to getting rid of the content in front of us on our phone that it has somehow transferred to our desire to do the same at an actual stage.

Through most of the ages it didn't necessarily matter as much if a man could say whatever he wanted or not because in the end his message could only get but so far. The biggest difference now is the extent to which you can broadcast that message to a ton of people before the censors lay the smackdown. Though the majority of the time it is the speaking out against the state which gets someone in trouble. Though at times it was enough to say something against the church to get your burned at the stake. Times at which we now look back and think...*uhhh they thought they were witches*? Now granted, I have no idea what those women were doing. Hell, maybe they turned someone into a toad and I should be glad that the powers that be rid them of our society. History is so hard to decipher these days, but should that not be the case I'm just disturbed to know that not only did a large amount of our citizenry support it, but many did so with righteous encouragement. Even using the first printing press as a means of publishing books on how to spot witches[2]. Truth be told it was probably the witches cats scaring away the plague filled rats which led to more paranoid than anything. In one way it's like being asked on the daily *okay, do you not know you're supposed to be mad about this thing that you had no previous knowledge of? And how dare you for not knowing, and how dare you for being a fan when you didn't know?* Asking someone to keep up with everything goin on in the world is as hard as expecting someone to know every restaurant in NYC. It just ain't happening.

NYC allowed for a certain level of self-expression that nowhere else seemed to possess. I was constantly reminded that I was walking in the cultural capital of my era by all of the things around me. There was always something which could be found to do last minute. It was here where the voices of America had previously come to speak at the microphone of the expanding American world. Whether they were looking for a place to get a message out or just a place to serve up a meal. The cuisine available in this city shows as proof that we are a nation of subcultures all building together, sometimes grabbing bits and pieces of the best made from each group to help enhance the whole. Much like the inter-workings of a city we all have a series of managers inside of us which gauges the things from the outside world that we wish to adopt and express externally. Someone who finds the most amazing thing and puts it where it belongs. If we do it right then someone around us chooses to adopt it. Early on we take a little of this from our mom, a little of this from our dad, maybe this from our neighbor, and so on, all the way down to the celebrities and stars we emulate in our actions and desires. What, if anything, in our lives is not appropriated from someone else? Even enlightened words of wisdom come from the minds of humans previously inhabiting this thing we call existence. That's why it takes a village to raise a child. My thought has always been that the best way to embody a culture we adore is to act within it and to emulate it. If someone is going to carry it on that is what matters. No one gets mad when an outsider learns a language and helps it survive. So why would someone get mad at a person for carrying on a style of clothing or dress not of their own culture? Especially one which feels marginalized and pushed toward the fringes.

Seems odd to me that in a time where anyone can identify as anything they want to that it's somehow seen as not ok if someone of

---

[2] So I've heard.

one culture decides to dress in and or *appropriate* actions or styles from another culture. Is it okay for them to do so if they say they're identifying with that other culture? With how blended the world is becoming there will soon be a time when appropriating is the only way anything will be preserved as a truly pure version of the original will no longer exist. Religion itself is a series of appropriated behaviors stolen from the pagans of ages past, albeit some of them necessary to fall in line with the stories and others needed to convey some deep human truth and make it relatable to the masses. We used to say *imitation is the highest form of flattery* and now it has changed to being wrongful appropriation? That doesn't seem to make sense. Even as I stood there on the street corner I looked at this child and wondered how would he know what *belongs* to anyone culturally speaking after a youth spent in NYC. There were no fucking rules here. At best maybe he would be able to associate certain people with certain things. So is the kid supposed to associate certain races and certain cultures with certain things and leave those things strictly to those people, or is the child to sit there and figure out which things from each area would serve him best? Far as I could see I figured this must be the luckiest kid in the world. I mean, who wouldn't love being exposed to all of this at such an early age? Would there ever be a possible future he finds himself unable to imagine? A place like this could've made me feel better about possibly becoming a writer. Yet, I realized that while this child would know the ins-and-outs of modern urbanization and all it has to offer, he would never know without his own efforts what it was like to take a deep breath of air free of brake dust. He was born in the real world internet, a place where every set of stimulants could enter your nose in a moment and lure you down some far off street to a meal from a place you've never heard of.

If outrage and early cancel culture had worked I would have been denied one of my earliest pleasures of *The Howard Stern Show; a* place with as many titties than sob-stories. Listening to his show was one of those experiences I could remember from the earliest days of childhood when I would turn on the tv late at night as my mom slept and put the volume at level 1 with my ear up the speakers trying to listen to Howard's interviews. This memory came to the surface one morning as I passed the Sirius XM building and saw the studios which served as the house to his show. It was my attention to the show that had given me exposure to most of the comedians I became a fan of over the years.

Exposure in the sense that he provided a platform for them to come and speak their minds and let you into who they were a bit more than they did on stage without the necessity for laughter at the end of each third second. In my opinion the interviews with comedians were some of the best. They allowed all types of people to speak. The strangest of the strange. The sad reality was I had slowed down on my show listening since relocating to the city. Something about the ups and downs of the subway and constantly running in and out kept me from wearing headphones too much. Stern, perhaps the most versatile of all comedians to date. At the very least the most prolific. The man created a show which captured the attention of rebellious minds alike for something close to or over three decades now with original content the entire time. Howard Stern endeared a generation of listeners through his brutal honesty, about himself and the world around him. He did what any great writer would do, he just did it every day for millions of people. Listening to his show it was hard not to look up to him and the people around him. The people who came on his show were always considered the contemporary cool ones in Hollywood for being willing to go on the show and put down their defenses to the best interviewer of his era, and by his own accounts, of all time. A statement to which I must agree. They were always trying to get under the skin of some annoying boss who was telling them they had to be quiet in order to not piss off the advertisers who were hoping for good wholesome entertainment. A part of me even understands why some people advertising in the early morning didn't wanna have their products associated with the conversations he would have, but what I can't understand is why they wouldn't wanna be associated with someone so genuine. As a broadcaster he is more honest and open than any politician you've ever come in contact with and his honesty didn't stop at honesty with himself, but thankfully extended to the likes of those he had as co-hosts for over three decades. The relationship between those on the show is what led people to respect and revere it as much as they did. That and the chemistry between the trio of Howard, Robin, and Fred; eventually adding Gary to the mix of the regularly heard with comics like Jackie the Joke Man Martling and Artie Lange spending their time in the seat of honorary show comedian. Despite all of my listening I can't be certain whether or not he ever considered himself one, but I always thought of Howard as one of the most prolific comedians of our time, and easily one of the largest defenders of free speech this nation has ever seen. As a fan a part of me hates that I'm using Howards name in this book as I get the feeling he wouldn't love that. The number of times he's criticized people for trying to sell things with his name attached is a number that I can only begin to guess, but I'm sure it's as high as his run-ins with the FCC and the wrist smackers of our society and to leave him out of this topic would be ignoring one of its most important figures. Which is more or less why I am compelled to bring him up because by the end of 1994 nearly 2.5 million dollars in fines had been accrued for things that were deemed unsuitable for the air. Nonetheless each time helped swing the pendulum further into the direction of protecting free speech as neither Howard nor his fans would stand for such early forms of cancellation, with a crowd capable of drowning any city street at a moments notice.

All I can remember is constantly thinking how ridiculous it was that others were trying to keep audiences, willing audiences, from hearing that which was being projected. Aren't those who are tuned into the radio know what they're getting into? Isn't that the risk we take? I suppose from one perspective there must have been some good natured people out there who worried that his shenanigans were corrupting the minds of his listeners and instilling the willingness to further test the bounds of our polite society. As I grew up I was constantly reminded of the ridiculous nature of those in charge of censoring, even once recalling the FCC for getting on Sterns back about using the term *spread eagle* which was ultimately bleeped due to the sexual connotation of the phrase. The freedom of speech and freedom of expression in a country do not come without some baggage attached. Along with it comes an intrinsic understanding that you will be subject to hearing statements that you do not agree with, and at sometimes find to be so illogical you can barely stand to hear them uttered. There is a reasonable side of the argument that would accuse me of overreacting and taking this entire situation too far, correctly pointing out that I am at no real risk. However, there's also a side of me that sees censorship happening without anyone even noticing. Example you ask? Gladly. Well, I mentioned rap music earlier, and depending on if you listen or not you may know who *Tyga* and *The Game* are and possibly even a song they did called *Switch Lanes*. Don't worry if you don't, there's only one part that matters to my point here. I remember first hearing the song and being a fan, even remembering the ending. Though the original version of that song is no longer the one which you'll hear if you go to download it today. Lucky, I have the original and therefore I can relay to you the change which I saw happen to the lyrics of that song. In the original there's a series of lines towards the end that go.....

"Maybe she a rockstar, maybe she a sinner,
Fucking with them lottery boys, now she a winner,
I'm all in that Virginia, I mean that vagina,
Get lost in that pussy nigga you won't ever find em,
Eat it like lasagna, Eat it like E. Honda,
Shout out my nigga breezy[3] and beat it like Rhianna[4]

Like I said, that's how they WERE. If you go listen now that last line involving Rhianna is gone. It just goes,

Shout out br-br-breezy, shout out Ri-Ri-Rhianna

Now, if it was *The Game* who decided to change those lyrics, then my bad. It's his song and he has the right to do so. BUT, if that change was made via the influence of music executives, Jay Z, or the influence of Rhianna or Chris Brown, well that's censorship and it's wrong. Technically it's post censorship because it was allowed to be released once and you can still find it online. So it's censorship by extraction and alteration. I'm also bothered by the fact that they replaced it with lesser lyrics. The equally annoying part to this is that though this is my most concrete example of something which once was no longer being, there are countless examples of this I've found in our media over the last few years. Some of them in songs, most in movies, but all done quietly and without any form of disclaimer at the bottom. And as someone writing the words you are reading, I get why people do it, I get how social pressure builds up and one decides to censor themselves. I'm just here to remind you that it's wrong and to tell you that I won't ever be one to do it. Fuck 'em if they got a problem with it.

Growing up in a neighborhood which was slightly more religious than one would deem normal, I was unfortunately used to the idea of seeing my friends mouth washed out with soap as a punishment for saying something they weren't supposed to say, even when they didn't yet know that it wasn't supposed to be said. As a result I always tested the lines of what I can and can't say to the people around me. I one day told my grandmother, a devout woman by any standards, that I

---

[3] Virginia native, rapper, and one of the best dancers alive; Chris Brown.

[4] A reference to an assault and battery charge between the couple many years before.

thought she was overstaying her welcome in the house of God, a statement which sparked many talks. Knowing the sadness of reality I made sure to do the one thing I really wanted to do with my comedy career, perform in front of my grandma. Getting her up to NYC wasn't easy. It was honestly harder to convince my aunt that I could keep her safe for two days than it was to get her to be willing to come up. Of course the reality of having her sit there while other comedians went up spewing their lines wasn't easy to consider either, but I could just tell her to turn off her hearing aid if I needed to. When she came to visit I didn't wanna have her deal with my apartment building so I got a hotel for the evening and made sure to find one as close to the clubs as possible.

One thing about New York is you never know for sure how long something should take, not that there's not a schedule, there are too many schedules. Once they're thrown off the commute times become impossible to predict. I should have taken this into account before I told my grandma we could take the train to my show when she came to visit with my aunt, especially since we needed to get to the show before 11 and I wanted to get her seated well before the crowds started rushing in.

Even I wasn't completely immune to wanting to make someone else shut the fuck up once in a while. Being with my grandma on the subway I was faced with one of the few times I wished I could tell the strangers around me to shut the fuck up. More specifically, I wish they would turn their fucking music off. I wanted her to get the New York City experience, but at 10 P.M. all I wanted was for the boombox 3 seats down to stop playing. Though even in my frustration I had to admit it was hard not to bob my head along. They have their rules about no loud music playing, but it's not really enforced. I mean ALL phones come with headphones. Even if they don't *(which they do)* the phone cost $1,000. You can't buy $20 headphones and keep shit to yourself? Check out *Skull Candy* headphones if you need a suggestion, they're awesome and affordable. I love *Funky Coma Deena* as much as the next guy, but sometimes you just don't wanna hear it. I don't know why everyone thinks their soundtrack has to play for the rest of the world. It used to be that if someone wanted to listen to a certain song they had to call into the radio station and request it unless they were able to not only afford the CD, but also had to be carrying it with them at the moment the mood to listen struck them. Oh how spoiled we've become.

My grandma even had her own side that could be called out if she had ever had a Twitter of her own. I remember my grandma would see people of a certain level of weight and wonder out loud *"How do they live like this?"*, creating one of the few times I was the one silencing her, *"Grandma, you can't say that.."* Worried more about her volume than her statement. Then I would catch myself thinking that this woman worked in a hospital her entire life, maybe she has the right to judge others for not taking care of the one temple they're given from birth. Still not sure how commenting on someones outwardly projected lack of health was deemed rude. I mean, it's rude only if you assume the person knows and doesn't care, in which case they're still your problem. There's only a few things you're not supposed to say, I suppose *"you're ugly"* is one of them. *"You're fat"* is another. Both of which usually are unnecessary due to the obvious nature of their truth. Nonetheless we should be able to tell someone when it seems they're living an unhealthy life. Why is it impolite to refer to someone as fat? I don't think I hate many things more than the modern desire to make fat people feel better about being fat through the denial that it doesn't facilitate a riskier life with questionable longevity. Don't I, as someone who will be averaged out with those who are unhealthy, have the right to criticize those that don't take the proper efforts to up their average? I'm a conflicted individual. If you've not figured that out yet then you have close to no understanding of me as a human, and likely lack a grasp on your own conflicted nature.

Despite my grandmas propensity to speak her mind, I wasn't sure what she would think when I first told her about my pursuits into the world of stand-up comedy. I had a feeling she would give me that natural support one can expect from their grandparents, but she was oddly encouraging from the moment I let her into my world. Enough so that I even had her come out to a show and hear a joke based off of her.

"You ever tell people the same stuff over and over again and it just feels like you're talking to a wall. I hate when that shit happens with family. I never know what to do. Sometimes I can't tell whether my parents are developing Alzheimers or if it's just alcoholism. We all know the truth about grandma. Her bookshelves had more bottles than novels."

Hearing the muffled chuckles of an uncertain crowd I scanned the tops of heads until I found my grandmothers perfectly groomed mane tilted slightly to the right as she processed the joke with the same attention a curious golden retriever gives the clicking sound of its doting owner. To this day it was one of the hardest things to do, performing in front of her. Not the actual performance, but the inability to look away from her. Each time I did I would catch her eye or notice her glance at the people around here almost in shock at the presence of the the the crowd of people staring at her grandson. She had been one of my bigger supporters over the years and an absolute saint as far as the term would go. Possessing a nature so pure that most crowds would have been shocked to hear my grandmother hadn't drank in over 50 years and hadn't consumed meat in nearly 40 as she neared her 92nd year. Growing up I hadn't seen her much after I was five years old. My family moved beyond the distance of a reasonable days drive and the added difficulty of having four kids of varying ages made it hard to get back to the grandparents as often as anyone would have liked. One of the more sad thoughts of reality I must come to grips with is she may never get a chance to see the home I build one day, nor the children I raise, or the people who become my neighbors, but I wanted her to see what I was up to. I didn't want to admit it at the time, and even doing so now is a bit hard, but it was really important to me that my grandmother saw me make something of myself, or at least saw me on a path to do so, maybe showing her effort was enough. I can sit here happily and say I don't feel like I let her down, but I'm sure the life I was living in my twenties had her concerned, more so than she would ever express to anyone other than myself. It was interesting to have my grandma come see me considering the strict household she grew up in. Once I told her what I was up to I felt like I had this new buddy I was able to talk to about anything and everything. Sometimes the complete lack of relatability is what makes a conversation so enjoyable. *"Don't worry about failing."* With that comment I stopped and put my hand on her shoulder, *"Grandma, I've never been afraid of failing, I've been afraid of succeeding at the wrong thing."* Smiling she replied with a simple, *"That's wonderful dear. Hollywood was never the place for me."*

"When did you take your shot at Hollywood?"

"Never, but I did live in Long Beach for a few years."

"When the hell was this?"

"Right after finishing my studies in Antwerp."

"Wow, I had no idea about that. How did you pick Long Beach?"

"Well I decided I wanted to go work at the best hospital in the United States. So I packed up my things and flew out to Los Angeles to try and get a job at Cedar Sinai."

"That's awesome. How did it work back then? Traveling wasn't as easy, did they give you like two weeks to show up for the job or what?"

"Oh no dear, I didn't have a job when I got out there. I demanded a job."

"You what?"

"I told him I wasn't leaving his office until he gave me a job. I was qualified and I had come all the way from Europe."

"And from there you just refused to leave...."

"Well I wasn't joking with him. I had flown thousands of miles."

"I hope you know how crazy that sounds Grandma. That would get me arrested today."

"I don't think so dear. You just gotta stay firm and believe in yourself."

Whether it be your grandma or some random stranger, may we all have that level of encouragement in our lives....

New York City, N.Y. pt 4
May 2016

"How long do you plan to do this?"

Around the time Spring was transitioning to Summer I was starting to feel antsy about my position as someone in NYC long enough to receive visits from the same person twice. I had only been there a few months and somehow it felt like I had lived 3 years of life already, with an ever growing list of people *I'll see later,* another curse of the NYC lifestyle. Most nights were for open mics. Other nights were for work. On the nights I performed I would go from one spot to another with only the running distance between locations serving as breaks. Although I was originally doing this to some comedic soundtrack in my ears, I had stopped listening to anything new a few weeks ago. In the beginning of doing this a lot of it is figuring out which comedians you feel like you vibe with and which ones you feel like you're able to imitate. I had grown up loving a little bit of everyone. Carlin, Pryor, Rickles, they each had something to offer. Then when I was working in construction I would drown myself with angry rants of Lewis Black and Chris Rock as I painted the walls of homes I would never live in, decorating the shell from which the sounds of laughter and love would one day hopefully bounce. Early in the morning I would watch reruns of comedy shows and interviews with comedians hoping to absorb a mood of comedy to start my day.

As time went on comedy became more of a mainstream form of entertainment and branched to create a labyrinth of ways one could consume their favorite funny people. I'm sure to some of the older generation I will get this slightly wrong, but I shall relay this based upon the best of my memory. Comedy went from the silent types of Charlie Chaplin to sketch shows which eventually forked into a series of late night paths. First *SNL*, then *MADTV*. Eventually Late Night shows started to throw their own little bits into the ring, decorating the airwaves with a series of well dressed men with combovers and a set of jazz musicians to complement the improvisation needed at the pace comedy can require. When it came to that type of comedy I didn't have that sort of desire, I never thought about taking this and trying out for

Saturday Night Live. More so due to the fact that I didn't think I could just punch up sketches on a weekly basis, nor did I keep up with enough popular culture. If I was going to make it in any way it was going to be off of adaptations of my own stories. Nothing else would ever have the same staying power, and when you're trying to make it as a comedian I think that's all you can hope for. As I would argue that of all of the powers, the one which is most difficult is that of staying power. Among comedians and perhaps entertainers in general the hardest thing to be certain of is your staying power. Today that is even harder as some hope to get rid of those who have that staying power long before they're done staying around.

When I wasn't making the money it took to stay alive I was doing everything I could to get to mics and hang with the circle of comedians floating throughout the city similarly to myself. On one of these hangouts in early April when it was finally warm enough to walk home, but still cold enough to see the light mist of your breathe, I went to an open mic in Queens. I hadn't been in two nights; a fault of the Hamptons and all they offer anyone who can put up with a 3 hour drive. To top off the night the group headed down to a diner on the corner somewhere in Queens. The one girl with them ran a few mics downtown so I knew not to turn down the chance to sit and talk with some of the funnier comedians I had seen perform over the last few months. Plus, the sporadic nature of the city and my nature to sporadicalness had made it so I wasn't really a part of any one group of comedians. I was never able to be off work consistently enough or make it to ever comedians mic enough to ever land myself as a member of anything beyond the category of city comedian. All which made me more than happy to hang out when one of them was offering up the time.

What started off as a quick introduction turned into a long conversation, and with the clock nearing 2:30 A.M. I sat and tried to gain an idea and who was I was surrounded by. I started with a guy in front of me and I asked how long he had been doing this. He had started two years ago. Next to him a girl named Joan who had been slipping in an out open mics since she was 16. Each one was seemingly younger than the last, and in some cases even more experienced. We continued to sit there talking for a bit. Soon one of the younger comedians informed me that he had recently returned from a trip out West where he visited his cousin and hit up a few mics. I was old enough by now to see the cycles we all get caught up in over time, some necessary, others not. I felt like it was getting repetitive. This city. This mic. This crowd. This difference. It was all a formula. Here in this dinner I could see myself moving throughout the city over the next few weeks, gaining a bit of inspiration here and there. I knew if I wanted to switch it up I would need to get myself out into the world a little more. I also needed to see if I had what it takes compared to the other guys out there trying. Perhaps see what happens is all anyone can ever hope for. But I felt like I had paid too much time to that particular sentence in my life.

"I love New York but this isn't where I wanna be forever. I mean I'm sure it's somewhere I'll always come back to, but there's no way I'm gonna stay here ya know? What the fuck am I gonna do? Raise a family in a one bedroom apartment?" - Patrick

"Plenty of people do."

"That's not what I'm trying to do." - Patrick

"Well, if you wanna be known, this is where you gotta be."

"That's the thing. I don't wanna be known." - Patrick

"Then what are you doing trying to go on stage? You gotta be known if ever wanna make some money."

"Yeah. Maybe." - Patrick

"There's no maybe to it. You're not gonna ever fill stadiums if people don't know you. And to know you they gotta see you. This is where people come to be seen."

As the conversation went on I continued to field some questions hoping to gain some insight from the more experienced but far younger comedians around me.

"How long do you plan to do this? What about you? What's your plan?"

With each answer I saw a slight hole in either their faith or their drive, as one after another I heard a response somewhat in the realm of *"I'm gonna do this a few years and see what happens."* A few years? I was just entering my thirties after having spent my twenties on everything except serious pursuits, I did not have a few years to *see what happens*. I didn't wanna get caught in that trap. I had learned in my time before. Plus I had heard Peter Diamantis once ask poignantly and without arrogance, *"Why can't you do your ten year plan in 4 months."* His ambition was for getting rockets into space, so I figured I might as well consider the same methods for getting my own star into the sky. At this point of the comedians threw my own question back at me.

"So what are you gonna do? How long do you plan to do this?"

"I don't know yet. I'm still trying to figure out if I'm good enough to make a living at this or not."

"You and the rest of us! Yo, we're trying something new tonight. It's a No-Lite Mic. Go as along as you think you can go." From across the table one of the other comedians chimed in, *"Don't have enough people again to do a real show?"*

"Fuck you."

I found myself sitting there thinking, *well sure, staying in Nyc would be great, and I'd get on stage a lot, but I'd be in front of the same type of crowd over and over again.* The thoughts continued down those roads until I woke up realizing that I was already three blocks along my walk home. On that walk I skipped every train stop in sight. For starters, even though it was a few miles I was likely to spend the same time commuting whether I walked or I waited for one train to transfer to another, but that wasn't why I needed to walk. The truth was, I needed to think. It was one thing to have the doubt of an outsider put inside of me, but it was another to hear the voice of actual comedians admitting they had no real idea on what to do or what destination they were trying to get to. Perhaps this was one of those arts without a real destination. Sure there were plenty of places I could stop off at, a late-night show, mid-city tours, hell even one day a guest appearance on *Saturday Night Live,* but what if none of that worked out? What could I do to up my chances of success and lower my chances of living off of peanut butter sandwiches for the rest of my life? In the end if I was happy did any of it matter anyway? I had learned in my younger days how you could get trapped doing the same thing, repeating the same environment on each swing of the pendulum. I felt like I saw the trap I could get stuck in if I continued to make my way through the circuit of open mics provided by the city at large, subject always to a random crowd and always vying for the chance to get in front of the mic on the right night when the right gatekeeper sat in the crowd ready to give me my opportunity.

Walking home the streets around me were a mixture of homes and shops all flowing along one seemingly unabridged block of bricks. As one neighborhood blended into the next I felt a sense of repetition that made me wonder how many different ways I could walk home. How diverse could I made my experience in this city and would the ways ever run out? On this train of thought I began to wonder, what if I went and worked out my act on the road. I was still in the mindset of someone wanting to jumpstart that which I had gotten myself into and a my core I was more used to being on the go than not. Perhaps I could use the road as a place to workout what I was trying to do.

While I felt like the kids I would see abroad were getting a widened perspective by the noticeably different settings they're being placed in I would argue that the kids in NYC were living like someone speed reading their way through life. I felt surrounded by the entire history of a civilization. Each block represented a piece of human ingenuity on display in the worlds busiest city. I've had an old man or two show me how you can handle the city on your own speed, but that involves committing to one block for your entire life. I was always kinda jealous of those people, the ones able to find a content existence with the small world they decide to inhabit, uninvolved and unconcerned with the troubles outside of their visual perspective, I think it was Voltaire who said something along the lines of, *"Tend your own garden, let your neighbor tend to his."* That night when I got home I saw no garden being tended but I did see some liquor being drained. Coming through the door I found Jax hanging out in the kitchen with two airplane bottles and a thumb high old-fashioned sitting on the counter in front of him.

"Watcha doing?" - Jax

"Workin on a bit." - Patrick

"Nice, what's it on?" - Jax

"Just this thing about this girls dog." - Patrick

"Word. Look man, I'm not gonna be moving as soon as I thought. You can still crash here if you want. But I gotta save some more money before I can do everything I'm planning..." - Jax

"What's the plan?" - Patrick

"Well, I got accepted to the Peace Corps, but I won't be leaving until end of the year. You're welcome to keep crashing here on the couch if want. Maybe you can get your own spot? I know some people looking for roommates." - Jax

"Probably, but I don't wanna put down all of the money." - Patrick

Whether through serendipity or a matter of this was going to happen anyway, I received a message from an old friend who wanted to come up through the city and see me do stand-up. Explaining to him that I would love to see him, but that I had no place to let him stay I instead opted for his next idea which was to pick me up from my spot in Brooklyn and head into the city to get some food and possibly hit an open mic.

"How long you planning to be here?" - Patrick

"No real plan. I was gonna come see you do stand-up on my way through. You doing it tonight? If so I'll leave tomorrow." - Charles

"Where you heading to from here?" - Patrick

"I'm on my way up to Albany. You wanna come with me?" - Charles

"I wish dude. Albany is far as fuck. Next time though." - Patrick

"I don't care dude. I'll pick ya up. Can you get off?" - Charles

"Uh. How many days we talking?" - Patrick

"I've got all week, but I can bring you back whenever." - Charles

A few texts later and I was sending him my GPS coordinates and awaiting his arrival with a sandwich from one of the better spots in Brooklyn. When he arrived we cruised on up to Albany and into the mountain towns of the NorthEast. I spent the next five days going with him from brewery to brewery throughout the North East, hitting everywhere from New York's capital to the southern stretches of Maine. I forgot how easy it was to be on the go. There was an odd feeling of a bubble surrounding NYC which isolated it from the realities of the rest of the country, and often the outside world abroad. When it was all said and done I didn't get to perform. Turns out comedy clubs aren't a big thing outside of Boston or New York once you go north. I mean, you can find a few open mics, and Burlington, Vermont is still one of the coolest towns you'll ever see, but overall the trip didn't allow for it the way I thought it would. What it did allow for however, was a chance to remind myself how easy it was to hop around city to city once you just got yourself in the drivers seat. That and the sharing of some good sandwiches and coffee with someone who was equally appreciative. Overall it went well, but it was more of a brewery tour than anything. Might even write about it one day, but for now it'll have to stop right here and drop you back in on a conversation I found myself having with Jax right after my NorthEast adventure.

"You say six more months?" - Patrick

"Yeah. If you decide to skip out and get your own place I totally understand." - Jax

"No. I'm not gonna go do that. Gimme some time to think. Just being real, I don't think I wanna stay on a couch for the next six months." - Patrick

Learning the third roommate wasn't moving I was faced with a pretty big conflict. It's not like I didn't wanna continue staying in the city, but I was really tired of crashing on the floor so much, having to move each morning when the roommates would wake up to start their days only to try and catch a short hour and a half nap later to make up for the lost sleep. Then I would have to go try and get myself moving again. There was no point in staying here. Though building an audience seemed like a smart enough thing to do, but was that what I wanted? What was I looking for? Did I want to be a writer? Did I want to be a comedian, did I want to make movies. I only now as I type these words have any idea as to how 'unrealistic' it was to expect to make it at comedy. I mean, there's so much to it. First and foremost I would have to be funny, create a personality on stage, go up and tell jokes, write jokes, cultivate new material, somehow come up with an act AND then I had to build a fan base. Back in the day a fan base was created by touring, word of mouth, and late night television appearances, now who knows? It seems the only way to gain a following is through the internet and the never ending source of online ears waiting to watch your videos, all hungry for a few more moments of entertainment to get them through whatever lull in their day has somehow been magically created by a lag in their telephone signal. *"I KNOW they say if you can make it here you can make it anywhere, but what if HERE isn't the place for me...?"*

I had once heard in an interview something along the lines of, *"What's keeping you from accomplishing your ten year plan in 6 months?"* a lovely question coming from a man named Peter Diamantis. While there are some obvious objections if your plan over the next ten years is to raise a family of 3 children not yet born, but aside from a few of the pesky limitations of time his question struck me with a jolted reminder to take charge once the day came. I wasn't sure exactly what to do from his point on but I knew that I still had to go and put myself in a place where I could do all of the stand-up possible. Another winter was coming and I didn't wanna do it that way and if I didn't leave soon I would have to wait til next Spring to be able to fully explore the country. I felt like a solo trip across the U.S. was what I needed. I had spent so much time away. Since coming to NYC I'd seen plenty of tourists from all over the nation, but I'd not left the radius or reaches of the Tri-State region in quite some time. I had taken cross country trips before. I had performed in front of crowds. I had stayed with strangers. Why couldn't I do all those things in combination? After coming to terms with who I was as a person I had really gone to embrace the lifestyle.

If I was going to get Americans I needed to see America. I didn't feel like NYC solely represented the country anymore. I think one thing anyone from outside of the city can agree on is that those who live within the city meet certain stereotypes in that they are disconnected from a slow-paced existence being a possible way of operating day after day. Something happens to you once you live in that city too long. I don't know how long it takes to happen, but once you do it becomes a wild adaptation. The summer was the best time for such a trip. Not just for the obvious reasons of having great weather, the towns were a booming. The festivals and county get togethers were abundant and it made it hard not to stay trapped in some small towns like a kid who grew up there. As I told each person it was interesting to hear each of them give me their take on what specific doubt they thought I should have about my trip, most likely a reflection upon their own doubts as the majority of them pointed to the necessary finances for such a trip and how that would drain me within a few weeks. Few actually mentioned how hard it might be to find or get onto mics in different cities, even fewer knew that other than a city or two here and there I had no place set to stay and no friends awaiting my arrival. What I did have was the willingness to ask and the proper neck pillow to sleep in my car if needed. None of their concerns were those that I had, and that's how I knew none of them related. I didn't know a lot of comics in a lot of places but I did know people everywhere and I knew how to make it possible to stay cheaply in any city.

"You think you're ready to hit the road...?" - Jax

"Why not?" - Patrick

"You've not gotten enough practice." - Jax

"That's what I'm talking about fixing." -Patrick

"So what are you doing? Like a comedy tour?" - Jax

"I guess that's what you would call it. Nothing like a real tour, but a road trip to explore the best spots for comedy in the country right now."- Patrick

He was running shows and wanted to keep a flow of comedians coming in and out. Which I personally think sucked, not that he wasn't doing something good, but he was so much better a comedian than I was, and here he was spending his time hosting events and making a place for others. Like a heart surgeon that had decided he was going to devote his time to training nurses instead. I always hoped that somewhere in the hosting of one of his shows he would just let his genius tangents take off and say fuck it to letting anyone else on stage until he had given the crowd the thirty minutes I knew he had in him.

"You wanna come with me?" - Patrick

"I'm gonna stay here for the summer. I can't go running off right now. But do your thing. If you meet anyone really good, try to get them to move here. We gotta get comedy back on track. This cities not what it used to be. Things don't feel as funny as they used to." - Jax

In some ways I was questioning myself as to why I thought that I should leave the city and attempt to do stand-up elsewhere if NYC was the Mecca. Then again, isn't it sometimes better to start off in the small pond and growing your way into deserving to be in the larger ones? At the end of the day my mind was made up. What other choice did I have? Commit to another year here? If I was going to take myself seriously I needed to see what the landscape was like outside of this island. Unless I wanted to live like this forever I was going to need to skyrocket just to catch up to where I should have made it by now. I was nowhere near the 10,000 hours needed, but I needed to go see who was out there. I figured I had five minutes, why wait. I had lived my life by many quotes, why not do so by a few of the ones with a bit more potential for the long-term fulfillment. Fulfillment to me meant doing that which I wanted to do, or working towards that which I wanted to achieve. Whether the goal was achieved or not didn't matter, it was the pursuit of it which did.

Something you notice after being around enough comedy clubs is that the crowds are more often than not couples on one of their early dates. That's how it seemed in NYC most nights, but that cities a hive for dating so I don't know that it is that much of a surprise. That being said, I want everyone to come and see some comedy, but damn it's not really the best place to bring a first date unless you're one of those balls to the walls 3 drinks by noon on a Tuesday for no reason type of people. If you are, then good Lord please don't stay together long, but come see a show. I'm still not sure if that's the best idea or the worst idea. For new couples. I mean, depending on the night, it puts it all out there. One wrong awkward laugh can make for a long night. Though I would argue that's one of the best things about comedy and laughter in general, it can't be faked well enough or long enough to fool many people. That's what I loved about comedy from the get go. The democratic nature of it all. In some ways it was the perfect art because you could get it in front of a crowd and receive immediate feedback without the chance of someone lying to you.

In thinking of the realities I knew showbiz to be a tough place, but with stand up you somewhat control your own path more so than in the other arts. At least that's how I was justifying it to myself. As I had told my friends; I was turning 30. I had no kids, no mortgage, no reason not to take my chances down this path. Especially since I didn't have any better path to pick from. It was quite literally my best and most realistic possibility.

I did everything possible to get my mind in the right comedy mindset. Even then I looked for everything I could find to get my brain on a constant comedy wave. I picked up the books *"Sick in the Head"* and *"Born Standing Up"*. Both of which provided enough comedic inspiration to keep me riding high as I would roam through the NYC streets. Even with all of the studying this was a big gamble on myself. I could have gone to school. I could have done anything. But it was time to get rid of the *I could have's* in my life. I really had no reason to look at my life as some timeline of stagnation. I also realized that no great change had ever taken place over night in regards to the progress of a humans life. Though the gaps and divides between who we are and who we could be can remain open for a frighteningly long amount of time.

THE FIRST 5

Days: 35
Miles Traveled: 2,637
Stages: 10

Richmond, V.A.

May 2016

"What kinda comedy do you do...?"

P reparing for the trip I stood there looking in my trunk at all of my belongings trying to figure out what should stay and what could go in a last minute decision to downsize. I figured I would be gone for the next two to three months and the largest debate I had was whether to bring a bike or not. Driving a hatchback I had the ability to put the seats down and all, but how many times would I really use it? Once? A few times? Perhaps I could park my car in the city and get around all day with just the bike. If there was even one time when I regretted not having it, then the case was made for it to come along. Everything else was set. As far as I was concerned I only needed money for gas and food. There were no other expenses. I was going to drive, tell jokes, and eat.

Before leaving I sent a series of messages to my friends scattered around the country, informing each of them that at some point over the next two months I would be coming through their town to do an open mic and gave them an early invitation to said performance. Naturally some messages were ignored, others were answered, meet-ups were arranged. With all requests for exact dates put on the back burner.

For the first leg of my tour I had decided to do a final set in D.C. and then head down to Richmond. As the miles added up on my way to Richmond it dawned on me that I hadn't had such an abundance of quiet thought in quite a while. Left with plenty of time to think the only thing to make me nervous about Richmond was the crowd I was likely to draw. Richmond wasn't right around the corner from where I grew up, but it was close enough for my friends used to driving 30 minutes for milk to come around if they wanted. Thinking of one of those friends I hit up a few people I knew and found myself meeting up with an acquaintance from my time in Bolivia, another transplant now attending medical school in the states.

As mentioned before I had some problems with my high school and their thoughts on my preferred forms of expression at times. Though I

80

would argue that I won the first case against me by benefiting from the forced exposure to new schools and new friends, I eventually found myself at odds with them again the next year, this time for something much less intentional, though arguably far more regrettable. If it's not clear enough by the fact that I went to a school named after a southern general, let it also be stated that this school was located in a rather rural setting, or at least rural at the time of my youth. The type of place where on the weekends we did outdoor shit; had bonfires, went hiking, associated with people who made moonshine, that kinda stuff. Now on one of those weekends, a moment came about a few hours before a rainstorm where a few friends and I were sitting around a campfire daring another friend to eat a bird which we had shot earlier with a pellet gun. In need of something to pick up the bird and put it in the fire for cooking I ran to my car and grabbed a camping knife I had brought with me. No need to explain too much of the rest of the night, just know that no more birds were hurt and only one persons pride took a hit, but for that he was paid somewhere around $100. Then it started raining and due to a lack of tents and a sudden lack of fire we all jetted to our cars and took off. Throwing my things in the back of my two door car before leaving, I did my best to keep from getting soaked and went about my night, falling asleep shortly after getting home.

Two days later, I'm in the middle of 3rd period when an alarm goes off and alerts the students that we're in a lockdown drill, newly created to prepare for the potentiality of a school shooting, though more so used as a way to let drug dogs search the school and particularly the lockers without any disturbance or warning from the student body. Sitting there on the floor I did like most of the students and rolled my eyes wondering when I would be allowed back in my seat. We would occasionally hear the sounds of a dogs nails on the tiled floors outside of the door followed by the rattling of locker doors. Once the drill was over we did our best to get back to the process and gave our attention back to the teacher. Couldn't have been more than five minutes after the drill ceased that a voice came over the loud speaker in my classroom asking the teacher if Patrick DiMarchi was in his room. Upon hearing a rhetorical *yes* the voice instructed the teacher to send me down to the office, a command which brought about laughter from one of the students who looked me in that *oh boy you're in trouble* kinda manner. Despite the seemingly severity of the situation I listened to the vice principal say my name with a bit of confusion building inside of me. I mean, I was guilty plenty of times in my life, but this was a drug search and although I admitted in my first book to doing a whole host of drugs more than a few times, none of this experimentation started until after college, and I sure as hell never fell into anything considered possession of drugs of any sort before 24. So that being the case I started to rack my brain for who could have possibly left something in my car for the dogs to smell. Then I realized that I drove a black Honda Civic which was the most common car in the world at the time and figured that there must be some sort of mistake, an easy mix-up between me and whatever stoner had decided to hotbox his car that day. A thought which was soon dismissed as I walked outside with the vice-principal and saw a herd of Sheriff deputies around my car, one of which had taught me to snowboard in the days before he had a badge. As the noises in my life started to fade I heard the VP ask me what I had in my car, further elaborating on the fact that they thought they saw something which shouldn't be there. Then about 5 spaces from my car I stopped as it hit me and I blurted out, *"Fuck. You guys think you see a knife don't you?"* To which he replied, *"Yeah that's what it looks like."* And as I meandered the rest of the way I left him with, *"Fuck."*

Turns out that was the case and I was right on all accounts. After a throughout tearing apart of my car I was instantly made to leave the school and charged with bringing a weapon onto school grounds. As policy goes I was not allowed on school grounds within the county for the next ten days, and would likely face expulsion after a school board hearing which was somehow scheduled for four days after my ten day suspension. Which in turn meant that I was allowed to attend school for three days in-between being *caught* and being sentenced. As I saw it that time allowed back in school spoke to the hypocrisy of being considered *too dangerous* to be allowed back in school for the rest of the year. The teachers all knew what I was in for, the ones with especially hard homework even advised me *not to worry* about completing my assignments until after the hearing, a silent way of telling me I was fucked and they knew it. Having had only the one run-in with the academic authorities before I tried to rest on my academic record and got in touch with a few teachers hoping to create an argument for not expelling me and not forcing me to re-take my grade, disrupt my life, and put my future applications to college at risk of being denied. You could say the pressure was real. Unfortunately I wasn't able to get the support I thought I would. I mean, I got the support, being told in quiet corners that they *wished they could help* but that their jobs were on the line and they couldn't go against the school board. One teacher was even blunt enough to tell me he didn't have enough seniority in the system and he couldn't risk not getting his tenure, an argument to which I held the deepest sympathies and unfortunately had to accept. I tried to talk to some teachers afterwards and get in touch with members of the school and found myself at a loss. Not that I didn't have support. I had the silent support everywhere from people who couldn't go against the school board publicly. That's what sucked, no one was able to say that they were wrong or that the rule shouldn't apply in this situation because of context or circumstance. I admit I felt entitled by the fact that I was a good student, by the fact that I was trying beyond all reasonable efforts to get good grades, and most importantly, I had no previous record to indicate a history or future of violence.

I felt so helpless, and even more so I felt angry that this one moment could potentially put me in a spot where I wouldn't get accepted to college next year when I started applying. It was here that I used the power of the media for the first time in my life, though admittedly in a haphazard and unplanned nature as I spoke to a local reporter and did my best to get my side of story out there. See, it wasn't really about story though, it was more about circumstance and context. I couldn't say it, but it was 2:15 in the afternoon when they found the knife and I hadn't killed anyone yet, and the knife was in my fucking car, it wasn't on my person or in my locker. Two facts of which the school seemed to pay no mind. I guess they thought I was going to go on a parking lot stabbing spree. Gosh, how many tires could I have slashed before they stopped me?

When the school board hearing came I had accepted my fate based off of recent precedent and did everything I could to negotiate a deal where at least I wouldn't have to fail my final exams and put my GPA at risk. Even though I knew I should just play nicely, it was hard not to be myself during a few moments of the trial as it were. I remember the lawyer saying, *"Don't talk too much...don't say anything..."* A directive to which I replied, *"Fuck that."*

"No. I don't need you to..."

"Look. I'll stop you right there. I'm not gonna say NOTHING. That's not my way of handling shit, and this is the only time I get to go on record. So

fuck all of that. Don't worry, I won't dig my hole any deeper, but I'm not gonna stand there and look all quiet and sad. This whole fucking thing is stupid. You know it, they know it."

Despite my confidence, deep down I knew what was going to happen. When the trail came it was kind of a closed court because I was a minor which was great. Though I do wish I had an official transcript from that day; anything to relay to you with the same vividness how I remember that day. So many details stick out to me. Once the trial got started one of the Sheriffs was asked to display the weapon for the court to see. The knife in question had been put in a manila envelope and labeled as evidence. As opposed to lightly placing it on the table for the court to see, the Sheriff held the envelope a little over a foot above the table and turned it upside down allowing the knife to fall out and land on the table. I remember the thud of the knife and thinking, *you dramatic fucking bitch* with only a few moments between that thought and the presentation of the first and only real question I was asked that day, *"Mr. DiMarchi, what exactly would a knife like this be used for?"* Knowing the methods of a good debate I decided to disarm him immediately. *"Well, what you want me to say is that this is a knife that would be used to produce harmful or deadly actions against another human being. However, the reality of it is as I have stated from the beginning, it was a hunting knife used on a camping trip, a regular occurrence in this type of area, and due to a heavy rain it was also a knife mistakenly left behind which would have been removed from my car the night I got home had I not been in such a hurry to get inside of my house the moment I opened the car door in hopes of rushing inside before the torrential downpour left me without a dry spot to speak of. The annoying part is that it wasn't even hidden; nor was it brandished. All it did was exist on the wrong set of state owned property. The same place that a few years ago used to give us gun safety courses."* Now I know that might seem a bit far fetched, but I was a fiery motherfucker back then and I loved nothing more than the chance to tell authority where to shove it when I felt they were being unreasonable, while also understanding the need for the rule as it was. At the time we were only a few years separated from the tragedies of Columbine and the nation had taken a swift no-tolerance policy on all who violated any type of weapons policy. Which was a strange shift for all of us in our area because before then we used to have gun-safety courses available through school and typically had kids show up with shotguns and hunting rifles displayed in their back windows during hunting season, something which brought no alarm to anyone at the time.

Something I remember doing to no joy was visiting the office of the dean of admissions of our school mid-way through the summer in order to speak with him about the possibility of getting reinstated at the beginning of the year due to a rule based on the right to reconsideration upon the arrival of a new school year. I basically had to go in there and spend five minutes explaining how I had learned my lesson and how I would never do it again. I don't know if there's ever been a moment in my life when I had to bite my tongue more, because while I had come to appreciate the fact that I had an extended summer vacation, I still held animosity towards the cunts who were *just following orders*. Never respected the man at that desk that day. He was no different than every lying officer, academic, and authority figure I had faced before or after. Just a paper pusher happy to have some power.

I often wonder if that was the catalyst which led to me feeling so defiant against authorities at large. Perhaps that was the last straw because after that point I would forever have to explain to people what happened to my life in high school and how that set me on the path to where I went for the rest of my life. It's fair to say that had it not been for that event I would have gone on to be accepted by my first college choice, but that's not how it went. Truth was if I could somehow have just been great at engineering or great at math, or had that knack for selling things I woulda taken any of those paths, but it seemed like this was the one I was built for. You'll notice I tend to focus on the idea of the *how it could have been*. It's not a matter of regret, but a matter of awareness and intrigue about futures that could have been if I had only known sooner. A matter of pure curiosity. How could I have done if I had had my way at a different time in my life? There was a moment where I wanted to move to Richmond. Now I walk through this city, sit here and think, would anything about this city be different because I had been here? I guess that's the thing about life, it's the decisions that make us, not always the goals we think we're pursuing. Well, for that matter it's our underlying motivation which then causes us to make the decision.

This knife event also led to a change in my schedule which had me start working the graveyard shift at a local truck stop. Being it was such a small area I couldn't hide the fact that I was suddenly available a lot and my boss was happy to put me on one of the harder to cover shifts. From behind that counter I got to have a series of conversations which people who had been exploring the world as paid drivers for decades. You got to see the most ridiculous characters at a truck stop, and often you worked with people even more interesting than the guests. I spent more time fucking around and just getting to know this country than anyone else you know. A few of the people who may have a better understanding of this country are truck drivers, traveling salesmen, and maybe historians. Before the trip I looked and tried to map out where I would go, meeting with a few friends a time or two to discuss the best routes possible. Once I had googled to see that open mics existed I knew we would be good to go.

One of the largest dividers isn't always the distance but the path of travel between two places. Most notably a challenge in mountain heavy regions with few passes and unfavorable pitches. This is probably why early man did most of his trading via waterways and the naturally moving highway of rivers each continent has in one form or another. As those paths created links from one group of people to another, still the places that are harder to reach always receive the information last. Sometimes it's the gaps in information that serve us the worst.

Cruising down Monument Drive I rode at a comfortable 25 MPH and made it calmly through the roundabouts decorating the route. In the same neighborhood I picked up my friend Drea and we started to make our way towards a buddies place downtown. As we left her house we took a left and then a right, planting ourselves two lights away from the main drive. *"What next?" - Patrick*

"It says turn right on Arthur Ashe Blvd." - Drea

Thinking of the tennis racket stowed away in my trunk amongst the other summer toys decided to ask her...*"Do you know who that is in Bolivia?" - Patrick*

"Who?" - Drea

"Arthur Ashe." - Patrick

"Well we're in Richmond so probably just another racist they decided to turn into a statue." - Drea

Now if you didn't laugh at that a little. I need you to go use google right now, and then come back to this book. Literally laughing as I said it I responded, *"You're kidding right?" - Patrick*

"No. Why?" - Drea

"Okay. Well Arthur Ashe was the first African American to be selected to play in some major tennis tournaments and the only one to ever win the

singles at Wimbledon...and he had AIDS. I think. He did. Yeah yeah, that too.
But truth be told I don't know about his feelings towards race, so maybe
you're right. He's also from Richmond. Which is probably why they decided to
dedicate a spot especially for him." - Patrick

"Oh." - Drea

At this point she started giggling as we drove down a few more
streets to grab some tacos at a local bodega.

"Okay so ONE of them isn't racist." - Drea

"I'm sure a few other aren't, but yeah. How that fuck does some South
American end up here? I mean get larger cities like D.C. or NYC, but why
come here?" - Patrick

"Money. Those places are hella expensive." - Drea

I didn't tell her in the moment, but my friends first reaction
bothered me that day as it spoke to the knee jerk reaction that humans
tend to and are at times pushed towards in our current state of
alertness for the offensive. Especially since she was in a city that was
filled with far more numerous instruments that could be called relics of
racism if she wished to do so. Though it was yet to happen, the city was
already in discussion about possibly removing some of these
monuments at the time of my visit. Something which held a conflicted
place in my mind. When I first entered high school our mascot was that
of Stonewall Jackson in his General uniform and as the mascot he rode
on a horse and carried a sword as one did back in those days. Then the
Columbine school shooting happened and all of a sudden, everyone did
anything they could to preemptively cover their asses with regards to
projections of violence. It was one of those breaking points in our
society where a handful of fingers were pointed in all sorts of
directions. Some people looked towards the video games, others at
Marilyn Manson, and a couple plenty at the idea of an entirely broken
household. Though ironically none of them pointed towards any
comedies. At this time the school decided it was best to change one
seemingly violent aspect of our mascot by removing his sword.
However, as one might expect, a general on a horse by himself looks
kinda weird, it's like *where you going man?* So instead they decided to
place a flag in his hand, and this being the South and Stonewall being a
southern general, they put the confederate flag in his hand. A decision
to which I remember thinking, *hmm, that's weird,* as I would argue that
particular flag represents more violence than a single sword. This
decision of course came to bite them in the ass again as eventually the

reckoning ways of the woke 2000's caused them to change their mascot and school name after a flood of outside pressures and threats to make them a viral offense if alterations were not made. I'll say it now, though I agree that the flag he was carrying should have been removed from the situation, mainly because as an American it's an attempt to wave a foreign flag within my country. We have decided to be one nation, and that nation flies one flag, ours, and only ours. I don't look at it and think anything hateful, I even kinda like the look of it if you stamp it on top of a Chevy, but I don't think it belongs as an instrument of national representation. Still though, doesn't mean I think that the pressures from those who are not part of the community should be considered on a matter of my alumni. I remember being asked by someone from back home about this shortly before the decision was made. I told him that I was on the side of not changing it. He said, *"Yeah, but we're gonna just do it now so that we don't have to hear about it again in the future."* I said, *"That attitude is the very reason we shouldn't change it."* In reflecting on her thoughts I've never really thought America was as hateful a place as it was portrayed to be at times. With no thought to it when compared to any of the other times in written history that I've skimmed through.

The more I went on the more I was filled with questions regarding my validity. Some from the outside and some from within. The woes of imposture syndrome hit harder at some times more than others. The feelings all went in one direction or another, but at the end they all circled around the same important concern, which was, *do I even have the talent it takes to make this work?* If I do, how do I get people aware? I hadn't grown up in artistic environments and felt like I had no reason to be able to testify to my own talent. It didn't help when even my friends would see me and within minutes be asking me something like David did.

"Hey, can I ask you something?" - David

"Yeah, what's up?" - Patrick

"The last time we talked you said you were talking about going to grad school, now you're doing this? Thought you already got the travel bug out of your system." - David

"It's not about that. This is nothing like that." - Patrick

"So you just HAVE to go on a road trip doing stand-up comedy to see what exactly?" - David

"I don't expect you to understand man. I'm just giving this my best shot.

Trying to do a whole bunch of things at once." - Patrick

   "I hope it works out for you." - David

Feeling defensive and in need of justifying my actions with more logic than planning I responded, *"Look. I got no kids. I got no one at home waiting on me, and I got nothing else going for me right now. Honestly, what's the difference if I try to do this a year and get one last thing out of my system?"*

I saw the same curiosity that was inside the eyes of those who had looked upon my travels with this weird envy. I thought back to a duo of friends I had from college who sat around and smoked weed while watching *HBO*. A lot of times I sit back and think I wish I had spent more time sealed to that couch with them instead of working behind the bar. Which is just one of the many things I may have done with my time had I not had to work so much throughout college. In some ways I had missed out on those times by taking on certain responsibilities along the way. A result of making my life too busy each time I was given the chance combined with a necessity to constantly work. Perhaps if I had been able to have some more free time I would have even dedicated a few hours to some of the lesser prestigious branches of academia as I was now choosing to do ten years post graduating.

   "Dude. Just help me understand. Why are you doing this? Have you ever taken a comedy class?" - David

   "That's about as useful as a bartending class." - Patrick

   "How else you gonna learn?" - David

   "I didn't know Spanish before I started living around Spanish people, that changed, this will too." - Patrick

   "Comedy isn't like that. You're either funny or you're not." - David

   "So are you saying I'm not?" - Patrick

   "No, I'm just saying. It's not like people just become hilarious late in life." - David

   "You never heard of Rodney Dangerfield?" - Patrick

   "Who." - David

   "Google him, you'll know who I'm talking about. He didn't make it til he was in his 50's. I've got plenty of time to find my voice." - Patrick

   "Yeah, but where did he START? My guess is he was pretty funny from the beginning." - David

   "Not funny enough to have to re-brand himself. He started as a comedian named Jack Roy. Then went off, became a siding salesmen, and then came back to become one of the best comedians ever. Ask any comedian." - Patrick

That made me think of something people often say when you're stating out, *"I never thought of you as funny"*. Either that or *"So you think you're funny?"* That's one of the most annoying question you can ever get as a person attempting to do comedy, it's like duh, of course I fucking think that. If I didn't do you think I would be doing this? Sadly I heard that one a lot when I first started doing stand up. *"I agree."* I would always say. I can't remember ever being seen as the funny one. I was just the one who was told to go talk when the group had to present their project, and that kinda spoke to me as far as qualifications.

I wanted to be mad at my friend for doubting me but I couldn't be. One of my biggest problems with getting mad at someone for being the way that they are, either now or at a previous time in their existence, has to do with how I see the individual evolution of a person dependent on the circumstances of life in which they entered as well as the messages they received about how to see that world from the beginning. As that beginning started to shape their language around how they perceived the world and their place in it, forever on the path of struggle to take us away from the damaged versions our parents left to the world, all while going through a series of layered existential crisis's filled with self-discovery to self-loathing. My point is, every person can only be as they are in this moment, no other way. With change of that version only coming through a series of situations all of which hinge on a persons belief that they can change and the desire to do so with an understanding of how that might affect their personal narrative. I guess what I'm saying is that it's a lot more than we think it is to ask someone to change. Which is why I wasn't mad when my friend decided to ask me about my decision to go into comedy considering the fact that I wasn't a funny person as the so eloquently put it. *"You're telling me this before I go on stage?"* - Patrick

"My bad dude." - David

"No it's cool. I appreciate you being real." - Patrick

"Here. This will take your mind somewhere else." - David

"What is that?" - Patrick

"It's a VR system. The HTC Vive 3. Here, come into this room." - David

As we walked in he moved away a few things. Though I saw a few things, it was ONLY a few things. The entire room was practically empty, hardwood floors everywhere and nothing in your way.

"Well I have a dog, so I've got a constantly reminder to take my attention somewhere else, this little fucker is the reason I built shelves."

90

Walking to the kitchen for a moment he returned with a trash bag bulging with coiling, *"Look, all fucking chewed through."*

"I'm not surprised. My sisters dog hates her phone."

I'll be real, I didn't realize we were this far along then, and I've not checked back since then so God only knows how far we've gotten since.

"Nah dude. Video games and drugs, those are the only things where they call the people users." - David

"So what are you saying?" - Patrick

"I only check it there a few times a week. I'll sit here, take a hit from the bong, set my alarm for a few hours later, and fucking dive in." - David

Watching me laugh he gave me that typically intense serious face, *"I"m not joking dude, you can't stay in that world all day, shit's bad for your brain." - David*

"Don't you program this stuff for a living?" - Patrick

"Exactly. I know what the fuck I'm talking about." - David

My assessment after using it was that it was really cool and the educational applications of this seem endless. Even the artist side of me found love in the thought that I could paint a *masterpiece* in the air around me and walk around it and within it as if it were living piece of art. The man in me who loved shooting guns saw the many ways you could teach someone safety and precision. Even doctors could benefit from a completely realistic experience. Could the texture not too be replicated? Surely it's all possible. All of the things exist, it's only a matter of combining them. The further I stayed in there the more I began to wonder how long would it be before we could be fooled into thinking that an alternative reality, one projected by a computer screen, was actually the reality which were experiencing? If inside of the simulation long enough could you learn to ride a motorcycle? I don't know why but flying seems more viable. Something like a motorcycle requires a certain feel. If people are worried about the coming of the robots. One should always ask oneself, am I the decider of where my attention is going?

"You'll be able to do VR comedy shows one day." - David

"I rather not." - Patrick

"Why not? You never gotta leave your house." - David

"Why the fuck would you want that? I wanna be surrounded by the people hearing my jokes. LITERALLY surrounded, or in front of. Plus comedy needs walls for the laughter to bounce off." - Patrick

"You'll be able to hear everyone laughing." - David

"Have you heard multiple people laughing on a computer screen before? I promise you it's not the same." - Patrick

"It's the future bro." - David

"Maybe for some stuff, but not for comedy. Some things are meant to be experienced with others. It's not the same when it's virtual..." - Patrick

This was the largest group of people to ever come see *just* me. I hadn't seen this many people that knew me in a crowd since I stepped on stage to rap with Matt. Then I hadn't been aware of it, but this time I saw all the adult ridden faces of the friends from my teenage years staring back at me. The situation in itself made the idea of what's funny and what's not funny seem completely different. I felt looser and as if I could be the realest version of myself in front of them, even throwing in an inside joke about life growing up in the Valley. Until now I was still at the stage in my comedy career where the crowds in front of me were just there by a combined set of chances. It wouldn't be until many years later before I would be walking onto stage with a room full of people waiting for me specifically. Which in some ways makes me think that I have a broader spectrum of people in my audiences now than I will in the future.

After performing in front of so many friends I started to think of questions related to who I was as a comic and what I was doing with the voice I was putting out there. As member of society we all wear masks. When you do it as a person we call it the ego, but when it's done as an entertainer it's called a brand. If there's anywhere that a majority of the audience knows a thing or two about branding I'm gonna guess it's amongst my fellow Americans. We all do it. Our country does it. Our neighbor. Our roommate. Each one sharing the story of *me*. As an entertainer you have to brand yourself at some point in your life. If you don't, others will. I had to decide who I was going to be on stage. What version of myself was I talking about? Am I a stories guy or am I a gimmicks guy? Did it matter what felt more natural or what got the most laughs and how could I know if those two things would be the same? Even before I had a chance to wonder about my story I was faced with my first problem of getting my friends out of the mindset of what they had seen me as before. Which was no easy task because that image was different to a great deal of them. For the longest time I had been directing the minds of those around me into the idea that I was trying to do something more serious in life. My academic past had been impressive enough to create a level of

expectations for those who knew me in college that was far from a
smokey basement and a Tuesday night open-mic. Being a Political
Science major in college. I enjoyed the classes, but it wasn't the world I
wanted to dive into further. Thought I couldn't blame my friends as I
had done just enough to bake in the false perceptions of the future I
was trying to obtain. Their reaction to my new path spoke more to truth
than it did anything else. The people from home saw me one way, and
the people from NYC saw me another. The ultimate question that I
hated to ask, but needed to know, was, *how are you branding yourself?* In
a lot of ways as a comedian you have to rebrand at some point in your
life. I wonder who the first brander was? Was it nations or was it
religion? It was once just a story told around a fire. Then it became a
drawings. Then books. Eventually we started making films. To those
alive today, none can recall a day when the film industry did not
dictate the information seen and spread, a group commonly referred to
as *the media* or *Hollywood*, both vague labels meant to attach an aura of
suspicion over the keepers of the airwaves.

Having a bit of my goods and information to spread I opened up
my phone and decided to post a video from my most recent
performance as a way to drum up some publicity and comments in
hopes of getting a bit of feedback and encouragement. Neither of which
came in droves. Despite the lack of immediate feedback I still found it
useful to post my clips as they did more to say *"Hey I'm doing this"* than
they do anything else. In the old days true fans had to wait outside of a
hotel or on some street corner hoping to see the people in their favorite
bands, instead we're able to schedule everything to never have to waste
a moment, and while that type off type of efficiency seems to appeal to
many, I never understood wanting that. Now there was so much noise,
so much static, but we all deserved our shot, and for once we were all
getting it. Like many of us I originally hated the idea that everyone was
seemingly important enough to have their thoughts and views
expressed on a video to be watched by all. Perhaps that stems from the
part of us which wishes to invalidate the ideas of others to make room
for our own. The truth should be that the audience decides, but in
recent days it seems like it's the algorithm that decides. Though as far
as I can see, word of mouth is still the most important thing we have as
far as a tool for effectively communicating our ideas. If we move from
that, we are dead in the water. I hated self-promotion, especially in this
instance. More so because of how much went into a post and how little

you got out of it. A small stacking of this and that for the people following you to look at, never sure which parts they love and which parts they could live without. As an artist you have to eventually realize and come to terms with the audience you're able to reach. It's not always as big as you hope *(That's what she said)*. Which I'm sure to some has led to great disappointment. It's because the act of publishing has become too easy. That's the actual problem. It's not that the barrier has been removed, that part is good. The thing that's the issue is that the difficulty of publishing has been removed and that hurdle used to include editors and people through whom you vetted these ideas in order to explore their marketability. Self-publishing used to be the thing for the last resorter, now it's the regular. I also assume some of them aren't looking at the metrics, and the dislike button being removed makes it so you can no longer see the tally of the issue as it is at that moment and in bulk.

Traveling down the I-95 corridor the next morning the feeling of the steering wheel in my hand became the only thing I could focus on. It was the steering wheel after all which had sold me on the car. The dealer never understood that, but he could have stopped talking the moment I put my hands on the leather wrapped masterpiece Volkswagen had made for that particular model. When I first got in it I didn't feel like a driver, I felt like a pilot. A car and the proper roads allow for a level of exploring unlike any other time in human history. The car was the definition of independence as far as my youth was concerned. Sure a bike could get you around, a train would have been nice too, but at the end of the day it was only a car which would allow you to explore without any concern for time or distance. The further I got from Richmond the more I felt invigorated by the idea of this exploration and the thought of getting back on the road to see my country again after spending so much time away. Tucking my hand behind the passengers seat I pulled out a map that my friend Stu had given me before the trip. Sometimes the gifts one gives you are more of a reflection of their generation than their generosity.

As much as the roads on this map were outdated so was the image of America in my mind. What we call America was not always as we see it now nor has it ever been one thing for very long. There have been many versions of America all stemming from the product of increased connectivity. What will we evolve to next? We're already a series of broken up regions and cities operating like mini-nation states. I wonder in an era where cities get increasing autonomy, what will they do to attract people to their municipal borders and how will places beyond the cities wall compete?

Before the internet, it was through roads that ideas and goods were exchanged. The highway created a passage of information and furthered the passing of the American story, allowing a sense of cohesion along the way despite being separated by 3,000 miles of differences. Originally open lines of communication were supposed to help liberate the world from intellectual darkness, but somehow they've managed to fog the truth enough to drive those with the real stuff mad, and make those with the fake stuff famous.

The cultivators of this nation understood that expansion itself was a multi-faceted task to take place over a series of stages. As the story of America grew that expansion took place through many conductors of connectivity but few more so than that of the interstate highways. Somewhere around 1893 the Department of Agriculture started working with cyclists on the *Good Roads* movement as a means to explore the routes most likely to serve our country and those attempting to travel around it by creating a true free flow of goods and ideas one town at a time, in a time when wires and a bridge were the biggest of connectors. As a part of this decision our country cherry-picked one of it's most notable features, borrowed by Eisenhower's appreciation for the German *Reichsautobahn* which he had observed in his time during the first World War. Something which made an impression on him as a result of one of his earlier military outings when he was assigned as an observer on a trip meant to further study and observe the terrain of the United States. A trip which took an astounding 56 days. I could do this trip these days in reverse and not take 56 days. Now in fairness it's not like he was traveling alone. The convoy itself consisted of 81 vehicles and just under 300 personnel. Overall one of their largest complaints was that of narrow roads and bridges that often lacked proper clearance. No small problem to the convoy which broke a total of 88 bridges along the way. As a matter of addressing a few notes from the trip, it was said that California was on the higher end of good roads in the US with mostly paved roads. Meanwhile Utah and Nevada were the most derelict with trails and dirt memories of tires leading most of the way. Though not everything ended up perfect, this project led to every 50,000 person cluster being linked via a web of concrete and asphalt sprawling across the nation and creating 48,440 miles of highway. That same highway later serving the wheels of the vehicles driving comedians and performers from city to city where they would poke at and criticize the very government which had made their transcontinental road tripping possible.

As that highway grew it created another stage of evolution in the American story. You see, what happens to people the moment you spread them out is they immediately want to reconnect. So this time the technologies finally caught up to the desires and eventually this led to the World Wide Web. A place that would eventually defined by one word, access. Access to information, technology, and a better future. The story of the internet is going to be one summed up by how connected the world has become and what the ultimate consequences of that are. Humble as its beginnings were the internet now serves as the global information highway ready to replace all types of print media with digitized information. In the future the networks and platforms which have emerged have to take on some responsibility in their newfound position of power with a finger on the pulse like never before; combined with an ability to direct that pulse to levels that we've yet to see. Given that the internet has turned into this funnel for messages we now have to wonder if it has turned into something open to being called a communications commodity.

As someone who grew up without them being a part of our daily lives, I wish we could go back to a time where we didn't live on our phones, back to a time when we didn't need everyone and everything around at one time. I remember a day when the term *at your fingertips* wasn't so literal, but it has sure developed a new meaning over the years. So much so that they even make gloves that make sure your pointer finger can remain capable of typing away while the rest of our fingers enjoy the warmth provided by fully encompassed fingertips. That's how much connectivity and communication matters to modern humans. Somewhere some poor programmer had to spend his afternoon writing the code to prompt you with a warning on your screen when it becomes too hot after excessive time in the sauna or sun. Again, put a human anywhere and they wanna find someone to talk to or something to do. I'm sure we'll do great on Mars....

If we're going to maintain this level of communication, the topic of *content neutrality* is one that I would pay attention to as best I could over the next few years. Especially as it applies to social platforms which have now moved themselves onto the inter-web. As a creator so much of me wants the internet to remain an unregulated community, but another side of me understands that something must be done from a security perspective to keep an army of bots from stirring up the pot in a way never before experienced during human existence and likely to the levels of which you could not imagine. With the battle against these bots being most easily done through a series of blanket restrictions and regulations to be handed out by our algorithmic masters. Whether or not online speech can be regulated by the Supreme Court could set the tone for the rest of history. The future of free speech is clearly online so it's not something which can be ignored. All with an important question, *Who is responsible for content posted, the platform or the individual?* This is another one of those issues I am really conflicted on, because, as a standard I don't think that our ability to express ourselves should be stifled or regulated by anyone anywhere. I also don't think Facebook or any social media platform can be liable for that which is posted on their site. A lot of it comes down to the humans who need to be doing a slightly better job at educating themselves about what is and isn't real, or at best what is relevant compared to what's not. Then again, we're living in an age where we've all been trained to rely on the quickest purveyor of information to distribute the facts to us at their will. All part of a worldwide race to increase communication and connectivity. Ultimately with the question, *how far can your volume reach?* That's what it's about. I might exist in one of the few times when I can get my message heard far beyond the projections of my voice by broadcasting on the wires of the web. The difference now is that unlike in the past when highways and connectivity took forever to be built, with the technological pathways information can be transported in a moments notice. Even a highway has to be driven to and transversed, but what does it do to us when something new can be introduced at gigabytes per second? To what extent do you need to be held accountable with information coming in at those speeds? How liable are you for how far your words go and what they do? In the end, I don't think it's reasonable to expect any organization to regulate the content their users put up. Even with AI led algorithms you're going to have mistakes happen and the amount of appeals will soon be too much to manage. Though not every barking dog need be acknowledged. Part of what we need to do to taper this problem is teach information literacy and the skill of regulating ones own personal mental traffic. Because the early attempts to curb this issue were simply done so through regulatory hours. Though I am not of a generation to remember such things there was a time when the hours for decent vs indecent programming were separated as if all children would be asleep by 10 P.M. Of course this was back in the day when late-night access to the outside world was limited to the receptor of broadcasts stationed in the middle of the living room. Now the world is at our fingertips on a non-stop basis. I often found myself awake until all hours of the morning watching *The Tonight Show with Jay Leno, Saturday Night Live,* and occasionally *MAD TV.*

The furthering of broadcast and the availability of airwaves is what made one of my younger pranks possible. One which only recently became something I could legally speak about. The short story is I had some friends I was visiting one week in a tiny mountain region of Virginia. Somewhere in a town is surrounded on all sides by mountains where the townspeople live scattered throughout the hollers and up and down the main thoroughfares created by the local topography. Somewhere towards the end of my visit we all sat around a fire one evening reminiscing on our younger days of mischief and pranks. Upon talking we realized that if we had gone to school together we probably would have done some pretty epic stuff. Then at some point one of us made the suggestion that it was never too late. Now in the center of their town was a small high school with an oversized football stadium situated at the top of a hill next to the school. Earlier in the week I had heard a midday testing of the stadiums sound system which sparked a series of thoughts and actions. Recognizing the central location of their school I decided to combine a few forces and see what we could project from the speakers in the middle of the night. This was in the earlier days of the internet and downloading music wasn't as easy as one might have needed. To give you an idea of when this was, I needed to go and buy a portable CD player and a stack of blank CD's to make the next part work. Having found a collection of sounds I burnt a few copies of the same CD and made sure to include 12 minutes of blank space onto the front of each playlist. Which by the way, was incredibly difficult to do. So from there I had to go to a Wal-Mart far from the area and buy all of the necessary supplies. The CD player, CDs, gloves, an AUX cord, plumbers glue, flashlights, some duct tape, and rubbing alcohol. Everything else we needed would be back at the football stadium. Which we knew because we went to scout it out a few nights before to make sure that we could get inside of the control room and take charge of all of the electronics. Well, turns out we could. Thanks to the fact that one of the guys with me had been an early audio visual geek at school.

When the time came, a Saturday night, me and the guys drove to a neighborhood near the school and parked my car near a fence linked to the schools property. We hopped the fence and then went through the same motions we had nights before and hooked everything up. Once the sound system was on I cranked it all the way up and tapped the mic once to make sure that everything was a go. With the sound of a quick pop echoing through the stadium and out into the town I knew we were good to go. Taping the CD player to the back of the equipment we plugged everything up and then quickly used plumbers glue to seal the door shut as we pressed play and ran. In leaving we were spotted by the flashlight of a janitor who had heard the pop while making his rounds. Although we got away I still got fucked on our exit. So did the guy going over the fence before me. The night before it had rained a little bit and I suppose some of that moisture got on our shoes and caused us both to slip at the top of the fence. A fence which was narrowly serrated to discourage such crossings. One of those lovely pieces of metal did its job and ended up deep in my palm, creating a scar that I still carry to this day.

Despite the pain and the very real concern that I might need stitches, the whole thing was worth it. Sound takes roughly 5 seconds to travel over a mile, so that means we were ten seconds behind when those closest to the school heard the first sounds I had burnt onto the CD. Sounds that would soon be breaking their way into the ears of every household within a few miles reach. I had decided that the one thing that might wake up people in the middle of the night but also might not, was the sounds of sex. As you might imagine, those sounds were only available via porn and therefore rather graphic. The first was a woman doing some solo work and moaning in a very high pitched manner. This sound only took a few moments before it had inspired a series of dogs in town to wake up and start going crazy. One by one I watched from the top of a hill with my bloody palm laughing hysterically as one back porch light after another turned on in varying parts of town. Next came sounds of more mutual enjoyment. After those were a few random noises I had found of a nonsexual nature; wood being banged, a chainsaw, and even the sound of a cars tires screeching. By now every cop car at the local gas station had its lights on and was speeding out of the parking lot and on their way to the school. I watched as they all turned into the school and drove around frantically looking for the perpetrators. It took a surprisingly long amount of time before one got out of his car and went to check up on the control board. This is where the plumbers glue came into play as I watched the officer pull at the door to no avail. Though he seemed satisfied once a flashlight search showed him that we hadn't stuck around. Within 45 minutes the CD had played out all of the sounds I had put on it and the town slowly went back to sleep. It took me several hours more before the high and the blood had stopped flowing enough for me to do the same.

As I came up on the exchange for I-85 which takes you down to Raleigh and then onto I-40 over to Charlotte or down to Atlanta. As the state of my mind remained slightly altered I debated taking the exit which I had taken for so many years before directing me to the Raleigh triangle. As I googled and found no options for mics that night I opted out of my desires and continued down I-95 with my eyes set on Savannah. As long as I didn't stop and I didn't get disrupted by traffic I could make it there by eight and get onto an open mic advertised as the best in town. Taking this gamble, and I do mean a gamble, getting there on time required that I only make one stop for bathroom and gas and also that I manage to make all of this distance without any delay of traffic beyond ten minutes at its peak. I sent a text to the number listed on their website, but a good two hours later and 100 miles into N.C. I still hadn't received a response. Truth was, a part of me worried that I was wasting my time. Not just with today but with this entire thing, but if I am I've gotta do something worth doing. Or is life about doing what you want to do? This was the time I had some sort of measurable view of success which I could use to determine if I should continue doing this as a habit or whether it should be pursued for immediate economic gains.

On a final note regarding that which we can and cannot say; I won't sit here and lie or fool myself into thinking that we live in a society that allows for 100% freedom of speech, there are some obvious exceptions. One subset of exceptions we've created are called gag-orders, a grey area of the court systems where one can be legally bound to stay quiet about that which they've seen or experienced as a result of a court order or a previously signed agreement normally known as a non-disclosure agreement. In a few cases I would argue these to be necessary, such as in instances where what you're precluded from speaking about somehow interferes with an ongoing court case or directly disrupts the peace enough to warrant needing silencing. In this level silencing would be keeping visual evidence of such things as animal slaughter houses and environments of that nature. This is a topic on which I have many thoughts, but at the end of the day I've watched enough wildlife documentaries and if there's a *polite* way for one animal to kill another I don't know it. I would dare say that the majority of deaths in the animal kingdom are unpleasant to the most extreme sense. I mean, imagine being pursued by a herd of lions and then running away as you hear them bring down one of your own, that in and of itself must be pretty damn stressful. Not to mention those motherfuckers who have to spend the final moments of their life sprinting away from a zigzagging cheetah. For those living their lives in the ocean, I don't think there's such a thing as a natural or peaceful end to your existence. Which is why I thank God everyday that I am not a fish.

Savannah, Georgia
May 2016

"Like Kendrick said, B*t*@, Stay Humble."

S omewhere just before the sun had fully set I pulled into the thickly cobble-stoned streets of Savannah and turned at one corner after another until I came upon an address and a tiny entrance to my right which opened up into a dive bar with an outdoor game area and a giant window facing the breaking waters. Finding a spot to park and walking inside, I gauged the crowd of locals and the stage set for any performer willing to go up for a crowd of forty or less. After signing up, I was told I would be number six to perform so I knew not to worry about missing my spot. Doing as I usually would I found a seat somewhere in the center of the room and tried to feel out the crowd via the first two comedians. As I sat there waiting to go up the coordinator of the night came walking to me with a bit of purpose in his step and leaned in to explain his readiness. *"Hey man. We've got someone here who's gonna go up before you. Plans to do about 15 minutes. I'll introduce you after him."* With no say in the matter I said, *"Okay"* and went along my way waiting to see who it was I had been temporarily displaced by. Moments later I received the news when I looked to my left and saw a familiar face from the world of the recently famous. Remembering my one buddy to be a huge fan of his I immediately sent a text to him to share in my nervous excitement about it.

"Dude. You're not gonna believe this. I just got bumped by Hannibal Buress."

"Shit. Good luck following that."

"Uh...Thanks."

I came to find out that he was in town for the night getting ready for a large show the next night at the local arena. Needless to say he killed it. He made me laugh so hard at his jokes that I could barely remember any of my own when the time came. It sucked going on after him. On all levels that suck can suck. Other than the ability to get a photo of the two of us on the same stage for a moment I would call the night a bust for me. That and the fact that I got to perform knowing a true genius was watching my work. While that sort of thing happened on a regular basis in NYC, this type of setting was much more unique as Hannibal was not then shuffled off to some backstage where his disappeared from the club. The whole time I did my set he was just standing off to my right watching me. The same place where he remained for the rest of the show.

After the performance I felt a sort of high from the situation even though I knew I had done terribly. Having plenty of reason to hang out and meet some people from the scene I introduced myself and went from one hello to another. Noticing a small swarm around Hannibal I decided to hang back and give the crowd a few moments to die down. Afterwards I made my way to his area of the bar and tried to stir up a conversation. I got a chance to say what's up and if I were to be honest there were maybe thirty words exchanged between us before I blurted out the phrase, *"You mind if we get a photo?"* An annoyance to which he said, *"Sorry I'm just trying to chill."* Afterwards I felt like a complete asshole. Not that I asked. More so the schoolgirl like way in which I waited before I asked, seeking my moment to insert myself into his experience. I like to blame it on the fact that it was my first real night out and I felt excited about the hype I could be building with a photo like that amongst my own circles. I needed to build a stronger online presence. I guess I had been taken in by the power of the possibility that they might think, *oh shit, somehow he made it into this circle, maybe he does some other cool shit.* I also just thought it was one of those moments of fate, but then I shouldn't be the one thinking that. If anything I shoulda been the one in the room with the least amount of star struck sickness, I had just come from NYC. The same place where I saw Andre 3000, the lyricist of lyricists, twice in the same fucking week. Not to mention bumping shoulders with Kevin Bacon (*does that make me a new degree of separation?*) My favorite one though is probably the one which sticks in my mind the most and also sets myself up for an expectation of positive interaction. This happened a year or so after college. I was walking down through the city, my first time in the city actually, and the group I was with was cutting through the less shady alleyways here and there to save some time in our journey to the nights drinks. Near the end of one of the alleys I noticed this dude sitting on a windowsill just texting away in the days before that was everyone you saw. He had on a blackshirt, dark jeans, and some really fresh shoes. I remember walking by and thinking, *"Man, those are nice shoes for a bum,"* taking no real consideration to the fact that he was also holding a cellphone. Around which time he looked up at me, locking eyes for a moment. I lagged behind for a second as my mind scanned through a catalog of faces previously seen. Running to the corner I caught up with my friends where they were waiting for the green light to cross the street. *"Hey guys, I think I know who that guy is over there."* At which point the two girls with me looked hesitantly down the dark alley at the shadowy figure going about his evening. *"No I mean it. Just gimme a second. Follow me."* Luckily for me the crosswalk was not in our favor the the traffic was intimidating so the group had no issues in turning around to venture with me back to our mystery guest. Finding myself standing in front of the figure who was seemingly undisturbed by the proximity of my approach I looked down and said, *"Tracy...."* At which point comedian, actor, and overall funny guy Tracey Morgan flipped up his head rapidly and said, *"Yeah what's up??"* - Tracey

"Yo, what are you doing?"- Patrick

"Just chillin." - Tracey

"I see that. I mean like, what are you doing here on a Saturday night all by yourself? No parties to go to?" - Patrick

"Nah, all of us famous people go out on Monday's, when all ya'll gotta work." - Tracey

Thinking to myself, *"That's fair."* I nodded my head and started talking to him about comedy and some of his characters from *SNL*, even mentioning his recent appearance on the *Stern Show* in which he talked about driving his convertible around in the rain with the top down. Knowing that our clock was ticking I decided to take advantage of the moment and use my new Sony camera for something better than a set of clouds.

"Hey, before we go, could we get a picture?"

"Anything for the fans." - Tracey

"Thanks."

At that moment we saw two men walking down the alley in our direction. *"Perfect, let's ask these two guys here. Hey guys, you all mind taking a picture for us?"* It was at this time I experienced that New York City rudeness I had heard so much about as both of the guys quite literally ignored our existence in a stroll that turned into a fast walk. They didn't acknowledge my question, or even give me the decency of looking in our direction, they just kept walking. I quickly learned that I wasn't the only one in the circle that evening who didn't appreciate their attitude as I heard Tracey's voice project loudly from my side, *"Hey fuck ya'll!"* Which managed to at least get their attention and gave them a reason to grant us a moment of attention, at which point Tracey continued by yelling, *"I hope you all fuck some nasty bitch tonight and get chlamydia all on yo dicks."* Not sure how to react the one man paused and started to turn, an effort quickly defeated by the other man grabbing his arm and re-directing him forward. I remember thinking, *"Oh shit, if we get in a fight with Tracey Morgan and two strangers this is gonna be the best night ever."* Unfortunately, the men didn't seem up for a brawl and I was robbed of the opportunity to have an even better story than the one I lived. Afterwards we all calmed the fuck down and took turns getting photos with each other before slowly slipping back into our night with a brief message from Tracey before we left. One which I've continued to use to this day, *"Travel well ya'll."*

Ft. Lauderdale, Florida
May 2016

"Who needs a spotlight?"

S ome dreams take us to new unexplored places, others seem to take us back to a place our subconscious wishes to revisit in hopes of correcting some faltered moment in the occurrence. The rest, well I don't know. I'm not a dream expert. I know it seems unrelated, but do you know how thick your average windshield is? Not even an inch, around 5 millimeters actually. At that thickness, with no tint, it takes less than an hour for the sun to heat your car up from 80 degrees to around 120. Which is hopefully useful information for more than just the owners of dogs. Sitting there as this happens is a lot like feeling the lights when you're on stage bombing. Which is how I was starting to feel around 7:15 when the heat from the rising sun induced a brief nightmare of that very first terrifying incident and caused me to wake up. No longer able to pretend to be okay without turning on the A.C. I got out and stretched for a minute, using the intensity of the morning sun to bring my eyes to the party and wake myself. Driving down 95, more awake this time, I was reminded of the one thing that always stuck out to me about Florida; how flat it is. One large sprawl of 65,000 square miles with the highest elevation only reaching, 345 feet making it the nations lowest *high point*. To give you an idea just how not tall that is, the Washington Monument is 555 feet tall, making it not only taller than any other structure within the District, but also any landmass in Florida by OVER 200 feet. Another thing about Florida, at times when you're driving there are more than a few spots where if you were to blindfold me and somehow disrupt my perceptions of time and distance it would be totally possible to take off that blindfold and tell me that you had taken me to somewhere in Latin America.

This place was the escape for most of the United States during my life-time thus far. A state with relatively year-round beach weather and approximately 1,350 miles of shoreline to enjoy. In this country there are people willing to drive places and people who are not. People who are not don't live in Florida. There's no place more crowded where things are further part. If your family thinks visiting you living in

Miami and taking them to Disney will be no big deal, think otherwise. 4 hours. Easy. It's for this very reason that car culture is so large in the United States. Not to say that Europeans don't enjoy their cars, but car ownership is nowhere near as important abroad as it is in our own country. Car culture may be one of the more uniquely American things, first of all, we invented cars, which is an awesome start, and they're arguably one of the largest contributions to the world to ever come from America. Driving is such an American thing that it's created subsets of fanatics surrounding the act as well as the watching of it with cars and motorcycles having their own specific obsessors.

This wasn't anywhere near my first time in Florida, but I hadn't been down there for the reasons of Spring break as most of my friends had been at the early urgings of the *Travel Channel* and their top 10 of this and that. I think that's something that only high schools a days drive from the beach end up doing. My first time in Florida I was just entering my teenage years and I went along to attend the Daytona 500 at the Daytona International Speedway where the race is held every February. While there I remember being left alone with my moms car keys all day while she and whoever the hell else went to the Daytona 500. Given the span of nearly 11 hours I found myself wandering around the town and into the mall. I browsed for a while, but eventually went back to the car. At the time I wasn't old enough to drive. I think I was around 12; and though my memory is usually pretty great with such matters, as of this writing it can't yet recall how I met these two girls who ended up walking around with me for a while that day. If I remember right the one was a year older than me and the one was a year younger. I think they were in town for some type of volleyball tournament. Anyways, it was this type of thing which led to the stacking of my reputation as a social butterfly early on. Especially with my family who found me hanging with them in the truck a few hours after the race under the promise that I didn't see why my mom couldn't drive them home.

Even though NYC comes off as the entertainment capitol of the world, I would argue that Florida is where more Americans think to go to be entertained. The place has everything; sports, parks, beaches, and about everything else you could want, even alligators. Despite an assortment of differences between the people and the types of entertainment or sport they demanded I still found it that no matter where in the world you went you would find a great deal of people looking for an event to go to in hopes of killing some time. At the end of the day it's the crowds who demand entertainment in the first place. Surely we've all heard the quote, *give them bread and sports and they'll never riot,* or something of that sort. This is probably a lot of why sports became popular. For it takes the encouragement of the crowd to approve of sports in order to provide the justification to others in playing the sport. Doing so in front of others is what makes it matter. For those unable to find their own way of expressing oneself there has always been sports. Not to say sports can't be individualistic, but an individual is not a team. The olympics were one of the most unifying things back in the day, and even now the bubbles are known for everything if not mingling. The sports which are popular say a lot about the nations who enjoy them. Though not spoke about enough I would say the possibility of a tie will always cause soccer to fall behind in the eyes of Americans enjoying competitive sports with a bit more roughness and a bit more certainty about who's winning. I remember the first time I saw a soccer game live, they tied, I felt so robbed. I had spent the last two hours watching these guys in the burning sun only to see them walk away with both sides exhausted at a 0-0 ending. Why the fuck aren't there penalty kicks at the end of every game? I think if soccer could fix that glitch they could get a lot more Americans on board. Goal differentials are a great way to make your crowds watch the next game, but maybe the idea of victories could be enough to ignite broader viewership. Oh, and stop pretending to be hurt every time someone scuffs your cleats, a message I would also deliver to the NBA. Ever notice how you never see someone faking an injury in the NFL?

After a morning of driving through one coastal city after another I finally found myself at the proper address in Ft. Lauderdale where I saw a series of two-door sports cars in a variety of bright colors, all indicating a house full of dudes. As I had been told before arriving, the one part of the house was for this guy and his girlfriend and the other was for my buddy. A knock at the door and the sound of a dog rushing to greet me caused me to put my book bag in front of my legs in preparation for whatever four legged creature was about to bombard me. Somehow Camilo managed to beat the creature to the door and used his legs to hold back a tiny blue Shepard with a curious look to his dark eyes. Eyes much different than Joes which now looked well rested as they sat on a face tanner than the day before.

"So this is the castle?"

"What's good brah? Yeah dude! This is it. Come check it out man."

We got the the back porch and I was introduced to a series of guys sitting around a team of candles attempting to stem the onslaught of mosquitos sure to come. *"Guys, this is my boy Pat I told ya'll about."* From there a series of hellos and handshakes led to the parting of bodies to create enough space to fit myself and my small backpack amongst the crowd. Here I met Loki, the most manipulative thing on four legs I've ever encountered; an Australian Blue-Shepard with a black patch on his left eye and a set of ears that stayed perked up and only exaggerated his constant smile that much more. His face, though narrow, was able to portray more emotion in a few moments of confusion than any of the human kind of seen, and most certainly of the dog kind as well.

"I started making surfboards a while back. Do you surf?" - Camilo

"Nah. Never learned. How long does it take to make one?" - Patrick

"Couple days. I wish you were gonna be out there later this summer. I'm moving to Cali in August. You should just stay here and drive out there with me when I relocate." - Camilo

"What am I gonna do with my car in this magical arrangement?"

Tipping his eyebrows up and clasping his lips together he caught the major hole in his plan, *"True."* - Camilo

"Yeah. It's all good dude. I'll come visit you again after you get settled. Where you planning to live?" - Patrick

"I don't want think about that yet. Everything out there is so overpriced. Do you know what I paid for this place?" - Camilo

"Don't make me guess. I went from living in the third world to NYC. I have nothing but warped views on property pricing." - Patrick

"Two-hundred and seventy-four thousand." - Camilo

I looked at him kinda nodding, still unsure how great that was. *"Did you hear me? I have a full fucking acre here."* Noticing the unchanged look in my stare he decided to change the topic, *"Fuck it. You ready to do some comedy? Lemme hit my up friend Jazmin. She's from here, she knows everyone."* - Camilo

"Awesome."

"I can't believe you don't have more friends here."

"Yeah me either. All my trips down here were back when I was younger. Like pre-driving age. We didn't keep in touch the same as we do now. I don't often say this, but I wish we had Facebook back in the day. I woulda kept up

with everyone."

On my first night I took advantage of being with a friend and used the passenger seat to rest as Camilo took me around to introduce me to his local favorites. Most of which were in a a cluster of food trucks next to a little Cuban bodega. Getting out I started to read the menus and saw that I basically had my choice of chicken styles from Peru to the Caribbean. Still staring down at my menu I heard Camilo from across the table, *"Get whatever you want. It's on me."* After ordering Camilo told me about a girl who was friends with a local comedian. *"Yeah. He runs the shows. She said you should hit him up."*

Next we got connected and he invited me to an open-mic he was running after a comedy class he taught at a local improv. *The Improv* was located in one of those city centers that is kind of an outdoor mall, in Florida this might not help anyone in their distinction for directions, it was close to water, would that help? Finding a parking spot was easier than usual and when I got to the door I did everything in a slow manner hoping not to fling open some door and break in on a new comedians performance. Which wouldn't have mattered, because the closest door I could find to the stage was a lengthy hallways distance away separated by a room lined with tables and chairs all in neat little rows for the audience to find their place in a quicker fashion. At the end of my view there was the stage and just before that two tables holding somewhere between 10 and 14 people, one of them resembling the Santos I was shown over a text message earlier in the day. Directing my attention and steps towards him I introduced myself and stood there while he took a moment to interrupt the group and announce me to them. Having had no expectation of this I stood there hesitantly as he explained to the class that I was his comedian friend from NYC and I would be there to perform a little tonight after class. Apparently she hadn't been joking that she had her ways of influence. I was someone who used to think that it was ridiculous to think that you could teach people to be funny. Maybe it still is, but he was providing a safe space for them to practice and do so in front of people they knew they were equal to. Sometimes teaching is merely allowing the opportunity to learn more so than it is the lesson. Santos was teaching some classes and I decided to take this chance to hear his advice. First they did an improv lesson where they were supposed to start talking about things off the tops of their heads, followed by a chance to work from the punchline backwards. Before getting off stage he reminded them once

110

more, *"Remember, they're there to escape. Take them somewhere."* Truth was I was still a student, as much as any of them sitting there that night. I had plenty of questions. I felt somewhat fraudulent even going up in front of them. I had only been doing this for six months. When he asked how long I had been doing it I told him 2-3 years, something like that. I wasn't trying to impress him, I was just trying to make him not ask for me to send him a clip to my videos or something. That was a fate worse than death.

I sat there watching as they all went up and told their first few jokes. One of the guys was a man in his early 70's on stage for his first time. This reminded me of the time I drove with my grandmother and she spoke to me about things she had never seen before; a story shared after I questioned her on why she was being so quiet after staring at this particular tree for a while. Next was a girl named Jackie. A string bean of a girl with a late 90's emo look and an act that was legitimately funny. So much so that I had to ask her if this was was just to tighten up her act or if she was really a student. Before this I used to think comedy classes were a waste of time, but the more I watched the more I realized he was facilitating people getting over the fear of being on stage. When my turn came I went up and gave my best five minutes, more so charming with my stage presence than my act. Afterwards I was welcomed back and told that there were a ton of mics to hit up during my time in Southern Florida.

As I went to say goodbye for the evening I was made aware that there was another mic going on a few miles away if I had nowhere else to be. Being that this is the purpose of my trip I agreed and decided jump at the opportunity. This jump led me to *The Funky Buddha* which was more of a lounge than a comedy club with a hookah set-up that made for a really comfortable environment where attention was easily paid as the MC started the show. He introduced himself as Jordan, a 28 year old from central Florida with almost ten years in the game and a two-bedroom apartment he shared with his grandmother. His spiked hair and shiny white teeth reflected the crowds of Floridians ready to hear his monologue as they got settled into the tiny dark couches surrounding the stage. His command of the audience was something to marvel at, and anyone sitting in the first few rows soon realized that they were just as exposed as he was.

As a performer you can't let a heckler take over the crowd at any point in the show. You can't allow any interruption for that matter as it's all an interruption in the flow which you're trying to create. Similarly, I think our society has to address something which, if ignored, is likely to snowball us down an even worse path. See, the *crowd* used to mean something. An angry mob used to actually exist as a group of people with pitchforks and torches at the castle gates. Recently however, it appears as if the same labels have been applied to groups within an internet chatroom. As if a few keystrokes are enough? It's kinda fucking crazy what we used to let the crowd do. I mean they used to throw fucking vegetables, tomatoes specifically, at those who performed poorly. At one point it was enough for us to just be entertained. Then at some point someone said, *"Oh come on, we've heard this one before, I'm gonna go listen to that other guy..."* I always like to think about the times when there was a story teller in every village, someone in charge of the oral history of the community and it's people, essentially the worlds first living community board. Acknowledging I am somewhat of that person in my own group of people it should be no secret that I took every chance to talk to people when I was out and about, sometimes selling them on the possibility to come see me tell jokes and sometimes not. It was depending on the person, sometimes the talk of a road trip was enough to incite a conversation. One time in particular which sticks out was one day on the boardwalk when I walked inside a tiny store hoping to buy some postcards to send back home to the family. Fumbling through the mini portraits I met a man who told me his family had always wanted to take a cross country trip and never had. Then he got kinda sad looking down. As if I was doing it with such ease. One of my earliest memories of the Cuban people can be encompassed by the reference to Elian Gonzales, a name and face any from my time will remember. The other memory we have of the Cubans was done so through a drug laced portrayal of the American Underworld by Al Pacino and Miami's hottest of the hot. That film helped drive a culture in the 80's that made Miami the newest global hot spot.

We spent the first few days hitting the gym just after sunrise, cooking during the afternoon, and then oddly not going to the beach in the evenings despite the fact that I brought it up almost daily. Though I had scheduled to meet a few people along the way, I had nowhere to be at any particular time. This of course led to conversations starting off like this, *"You wanna go down to the keys?"* Now on a long list of questions that don't need much thought, that was one of them. We ended up driving down the next morning, probably an hour later than we should have if we wanted an early arrival. Nonetheless we were able to make it down there in time to find a boat still at the dock and with a few open spots available for an afternoon snorkeling trip.

Panicking wasn't the right word, but as I looked and saw the depths around me dropping into ever more darkness, I froze. Then suddenly my mind shot me above the water and into a sky view of the surroundings with just me and this stupid group of tourists bobbing up and down in this endless spread of aqua colored horizon, graced periodically with a mound of sand to remind us what land looked like and how far we were from it. I wished I had just stayed behind, but I know I woulda ruined the mood. The people here in the keys didn't have a true island life. They had ready access to all modern conveniences, but without the crowds.

By the time sunset was near neither of us could justify being tired enough to press paying for whatever overpriced spot was still left. On our drive home I couldn't be sure if it was finally the availability of food which added to the taste, or if this had become one of my top three burritos of all time. With another favorite to be mentioned later in this book. Mind you for a moment, that's a title not easily contended with when you consider the amount of time I spent in Latin America. This is one of those areas where I assure you I know what I'm talking about.

The next day Camilo and I went to an outdoor set at this beach style bar set up in the Boca Raton area. There I saw some of my favorite street art in the country, only describable as an assortment of brightly colored pipes and street signs all combined together to make an angry looking purple Gorilla. Beyond that Gorilla we found a bar and at that bar was an open mic unlike the ones I had been going to until now. The whole environment was weird to be honest. I mean, I love doing comedy, but there's something very weird about telling jokes when the ocean is breaking behind you. You never really got an honest reaction. Bombing wasn't really possible, at the end of the day these people were 100 yards from the Caribbean. It was smiles and umbrella cocktails all around. Oh and boats. This entire coast serves as a friendly reminder that boats aren't just for the rich. When I usually look at boats my mind tends goes to the idea of lives I've never gotten a chance to experience, and of which are still unobtainable to me. Boats are just like horses, except they don't literally die one day. They are both dumbly expensive and a luxury to even be able to own, they're both such a long term commitment to creating a certain level of financial means to maintain them. Hell, while I'm writing this I realize that though I don't have the numbers in front of me I imagine a horse has got to cost more in different way, it's not like you can put off the maintenance. You literally gotta feed that thing every day. Perhaps it depends on the size of the boat.

Growing up you hear about Miami in the reference of south beach. Though the locals want you to know that's not all there is to the area. As opposed to those in Vegas happy to leave out how cool their city is beyond the strip. However, for those looking to move there it should be noted that as it has been described by insiders, Miami, is an area with, *"third world infrastructure and fourth world government."* Currently facing similar issues to the ones that plagued the scene of NYC for all of those years when my dad was growing up there. Only now the sellouts are for billions and the city doesn't get the random benefits of public transportation projects.

One morning about a week into my stay I woke up on the back deck somewhere within a few moments of the sun peaking beyond the horizon. Served with the luxuries of not having to pee and feeling rested I woke up and went on a walk. A few neighborhoods away I started to get my mind in order for what the plan for the rest of my summer was going to be. I needed to stick to that which I had set out to do. I had been doing a good job of saving money, but an extra week here would put me back another hundred bucks or so without much progress along the way. I finally had to leave. I had to be careful not to get caught up in the enjoyment of life on the road. Such things were possible each time I gave myself enough rope. I didn't wanna get caught up chilling in Florida. It was an easy place to waste some time. Hemingway had. I understood why those ready to retire often choose this state as the final spot to grow old with the artifacts of their existence. The reality is that there's a lot of hours to fill in the day. It was easy when I was at Camilo's and I could just relax, but it's getting harder to fill in the time.

Although there was a good amount of opportunities to perform here I still needed to get my ass moving in order to continue the narrative of being on the go and trying to get a fanbase going across the United States. Both for the continuation of the mission as well as the limitations set on me by budgets. On the way through I decided to

Google how far out of my way it would be to drop by Disney. I didn't really have much interested in the park, but I had become ever more curious about the place as a result of ultimate creativity after listening to Walts biography during my time in the NYC subway system; filling myself with a history of art and entertainment all at once. By the time I made it that far up the only thing still open was Downtown Disney so I took a quick detour through and did a walk around a series of bars and restaurants filled with tourists from around the nation. As someone who spent my time living in NYC I would call this the next closest thing to seeing a little bit of everyone our nation had to offer. No matter how reluctant one member may be, each family in the country has some draw to this magical land.

New Orleans, Louisiana
May 2016

"Where's that sound coming from?"

On a road trip this far anytime before 1803 you would have had to have asked yourself if you had the proper visas for visiting the territories of Spain, France, England, and even Russia depending how far you hoped to venture. As far as histories of lands go, never before has a nation or land been sprawled in so quickly a time, and by so many different people at once. In the beginning it wasn't just *us*, as if any of *us* even had anything to do with it. It was a little bit of everyone in the who's who of Europe; the French, the Spanish, the Brits, Germans, and even the Portuguese were exploiting this land long before Americans were considered a group of people. In a lot of ways that's kinda the story of civilization. Things seem to get recycled every few generations with a new group of pioneers finding their way to the top of some sort of mountain, be it social or economical. I sometimes wonder if that's what happened before the natives were considered native. Who might they have fought and kicked off this land? Would we care if we knew it was just the Neanderthals? In looking at the grand scope of history and the tendency of humans combined with a natural limitation on resources there seems to be a certain inevitability to the emergence of people considered colonizers at tipping points in history. Especially colonizers originating from certain parts of the world where a limit on resources is strictly placed by the borders of an ocean surrounding an island nation. Whether it be Japan or Northern Europe, both places of harsh winters, high populations, war, and limited time and space to grow and distribute food. The nature wanderer in me hates aspects of this more deeply than the humanitarian at times, for even the best of people are never as loving as trees, but the realist in me gets the ways of the world and what happens when stories, technology, and the indefensible foundations of nature meet; I just don't like it.

In continuing on the topic specifically of the Native American side of American history I feel like people outside of the U.S. think we don't learn much about the Natives here, or that used to be here. All I know is that I come from what would be qualified as a redneck area and we learned a ton of stuff about the Native Americans in school, we even visited a few spots with cultural centers surrounding their way of life. During none of these times would I say that the lessons at these places did anything other than paint the Natives as the group who got the bad end of the deal at every end. Which is why we must be a place that protects the right to talk about the undesirable sides of our history. I don't think we're currently aware what a privilege that is these days. Unlike countries which wish to wash away the ugly sides of their past. As far as the topic of ignorance while in school no one taught me that the trail of tears was anything short of awful. In-fact, I had more than a few teachers suggest Howard Zinn's, *A Peoples History of the United States of America*, a great read if anyone wants an account of some of the lesser taught facts of America's history. It'll fill you in on the gaps that some of your teachers may have missed or willfully ignored as well as tell you that the majority of the travesties in the US have taken place at the behest of big business and those silently protecting them from inside the chambers of justice.

In my mind no place so consistently embodies the most recent past more accurately than cemeteries. I dare say one of the stranger habits I've developed over the years is a love for walking through such places. They've always been an incredibly humbling place for me. There's something comforting about the fact that no matter how much we argue with one another while we are here, we will all end up in the same six by three space (*actual height may vary*) at the end of the day. New Orleans was a famous city for cemeteries so I was thrilled to accidentally park near one of the cities more famous ones when I first rolled up into the *Big Easy*. Within only a few moments of walking around I quickly saw that *Louis Cemetery No. 1* had to be one of the more diverse ones in the nation. Walking through I saw names from West Africa, Latin America, France, the Netherlands, and combinations of those not listed. Each tombstone casting a light on the fact that all around me were souls buried possessing genes from each end of the world. Leaving there I continued along and found myself next to Congo Square, the first place where a blend of local and slave music created a new type of sound that would eventually led to one of America's most famous musical cultures. Though many of these people had never seen Africa and were now more Caribbean and West Indy than they were anything else. This place had one of the craziest blends of music you'll ever see. The Baptists brought church music and hymns. Then the French brought some classical and at one point the city even had two symphony orchestras. Keep in mind most major cities barely have one if any. As time went on each style of music found its blend and place in the local culture of grand weddings, parades, and carnivals which flood the city streets from one day to the next. All of this making it the most musically inclined city in the country.

In my opinion New Orleans is the most uniquely distinct place in our country. By that I mean, when you're here, you know you're here. Even though it may have evolved as a result of how to handle death, I would have always looked at New Orleans more as a place for entertainment than tradition. Growing up I remembering seeing Mardi Gras on the travel channel with elusions to beads being thrown and yardstick margaritas being chugged between the two-storied downtown with a balcony from each holding day drinkers and onlookers to the parade which matches below. All in the name of a celebration which I believes serves as a great example of how humans need a few days to let loose once in a while. I think it's fair to say an assessment of the holidays around the world would indicate that; given that a major party holiday falls every three to four months no matter where you are across the globe. We're social beings and we're meant to socialize, and what better way to do this than to party? Parties are what brought me and my friends together when we were younger and showed us who was a part of our tribe in ways that a class schedule couldn't cultivate. In a lot of ways these streets of New Orleans reminded me of a frat house, mainly a result of the overwhelming stench of beer and piss that hit me every time the breeze came in from the south. Between that and the drunken fools stumbling about I felt right at home just a few years separated from that version of home. At these parties there's a chance for the individual to dress like someone else, to put on a mask for the world and pretend to be some other being for the day. Unfortunately we've begun to cultivate a world where someone can keep their mask on forever by continuously projecting falsehoods of their lives and their inner-beings from a trusted handheld and fancy login name. This group of people having forgotten that we should only keep on those masks for so long. Even as a real performer we can't stay on the stage forever.

Humans have always needed to huddle around a circle once in a while and just shoot the shit. I often pine for a day where that's all we did. Despite being in touch with the reality of how lucky are we that we don't need to spend our days with the only concern being from where food is coming next. More than ever I yearn for a society without phones or signals, a place where we focus for a moment on a moment. A desire only created by the constant urgency to read, react, respond, and regurgitate. The further the future unfolds, I become more worried about our attention spans than I am anything else. It doesn't seem like it, but it doesn't take terribly long to rewire ourselves in that manner. I even find myself wandering the kitchen sometimes looking for what to eat with my phone in my hand and my headphones blaring and every once in a while I'll stop myself and say,*"Okay, do we need any more stimulation right now?"*

In the same way that humans need a place to go and let loose, they also need a place to sit, be quiet, and listen. There's a reason we have two ears and one mouth. To be fair, the reason probably has a lot more to do with the necessity of auditory symmetry, but let's pretend it's so we can listen more than we speak. In that same way, the purpose of stand up comedy is to give people a place to sit where they can listen to interesting, unusual, and sometimes uncomfortable, thoughts. With the venue of a comedy show performing a different function for both sides of the table, entertainment to some, practicing of the act to others.

After enough time wandering through the crowded and overly humid streets I did my best to make a beeline for my car, only making two wrong left turns and twice almost making the wrong right. Having never been to this city before I decided to take a drive around some of the areas I had seen on the news over the last few years and take my own assessment of a few situations. The first stop on my list was that of the 9th ward. It was so sad to see a city of such historical importance ignoring its people when they needed help so badly. The place wasn't completely screwed, but I did and still do have some dire fears for its future if things remain undone. The city itself has experienced more than few tragedies, and the impact on some specific wards is more than enough to warrant some special attention. No more is it the fault of those currently living in New Orleans. That city was built in an area bound to flood. Same thing with D.C., Houston, and most of the Netherlands. As a general flaw humans just love living by the water no matter how uninhabitable the surrounding land reminds them it is. With some parts of the world even placing floating communities along riverbeds, at ground level, or straight up in the flood zone. I couldn't get this thought out of my mind when standing there at ground-zero of the 9th ward a few minutes into my visit of the surrounding neighborhoods. From an uncomfortable closeness, I looked around and saw the hull of a ship coming towards me. All around the homes were a scattered assortment of brand new and still wrecked, some fixed up by the Brads and Angelinas of the world, all looking starkly different from the dilapidated houses on either side. I looked on concerned for the future residents of this town and all that would be lost if the civilization within were to be suddenly engulfed by the powers of the ocean. I wondered how many times have societies been washed away through the history of humanity. How many times was it something devastating for everyone in a kingdom and how many times was it just some small town that never went exactly noticed as it was washed away, sailors passing by and saying,*"Oh, that's weird. I thought we used to pass a seaside village about now..."* all the while not knowing that they were floating over top of it. This is a fear that I don't imagine many people living on the beach talk about, but I couldn't be one of those people comfortably without a reliable boat and a mastery of the seas.

Upon leaving the ward I made it to a street side coffeeshop with a deli and a small white barn look to the outside, outlined in red and lined with a black fence holding in a small set of tables for those desiring the comfort of an umbrella and a dip in the Louisiana humidity. Sitting outside after getting a sandwich I made the pick of the afternoon for a photo to post to my followers and did all of the appropriate tags to show where I was. In posting a picture I did all of the proper tags and went about my walk, discovering one street after another, awing at the sights and finding myself surprised to see so many colonial-Spanish markers on certain street corners as my previous base of knowledge would the led me to believe this city was French all the way even thought it was as Caribbean as Miami.

While wondering around this cultural complexity a text came in from a character I had not heard from in quite some time. We had a touch and go relationship ever since college when her boyfriend at the time became quickly uncomfortable with our friendship after seeing a few text messages between the two of us at hours he didn't approve of. And no, not those kinds of messages, I mean, they were about sex, but not between us. I was just telling her about this girl that I had finally hooked up with after all of this time and I made the mistake of sending the text at an hour that I suppose seemed unusual to him. How am I supposed to dictate how late at night someone has me over and why was I to alter the hours by which we had started our relationship as late night workers and bookstore buddies after said hours and how was I supposed to know when that transition was doomed to take place? I had a lot of odd friendships in my life. But the ones which have caused me the most headache have been with really good 'girl' friends. I don't know why, but I've always just preferred the conversational company of woman. Or perhaps I found that easier to come by. I mean, how many guys can I just walk up to and start chatting with without experiencing some sort of awkward reluctance? Usually two guys approach each other with the same hesitation of soldiers from countering armies checking out the situation. So I was happy yet confused when I saw her name attached to the following message.

"Hey! What are you doing in New Orleans?" Giving her the explanation I awaited a response hoping for some suggestions on where to go and what to do. Oh yeah, she's from here. I should have mentioned that. *"I saw you're doing comedy now. Where are you going next?"*

"Texas, then off to California and then up the coast. Hopefully back home by July."

"When are you going to be in California?"

"About ten days to two weeks from now. Depends on a few pit stops. Probably stay on the West for a month or so though."

"That sounds like so much fun. Well, I'm actually gonna be out in Los Angeles later this month, let me know when you're out there, maybe we could get a coffee and catch up if we're there at the same time."

"That'd be cool. Let's see what happens...Til then, any suggestions?"

"No. You're not a foodie. I don't even know why you bothered going to New Orleans."

"Okay hater."

Truth was, part of me had no interest in seeing her, but another part of me was eager at the thought of meeting up with a friend who had taught me so much about myself, sometimes with her presence as much as her absence. She had always been big on being herself and in that she taught me a lot about being myself. I would argue it was her that first helped bring me out of one of my shells in college. I'm not sure what it was, but she cultivated a group of people who were there own breed. Which is why it surprised me when she let herself fall prey to the wishes of someone else, but that's another story for a time when I'm feeling more bitter.

It just so happened that the deli where I decided to finally grab some dinner was around the corner from the spot I had found to do a set for the night, a small club called *The New Movement*. There I searched the front for some type of entrance only to be led down a narrow brick hallway which dropped me out into a courtyard and a back door. The show took place in the basement of the building, a dark room with a few foundational poles splitting up the room and a tiny chair by the mic as opposed to a stool. Facing the stage was a set of fold out bleachers going about 4 rows high with room for a classroom of people. There wasn't any particular place for the comedians to stand so we all sort of stayed off to the side keeping from blocking the entrance, dipping outside to catch a few moments of conversation. I was somewhere close to number 10 to perform. The room was full when I started. Then about a minute in, just as I was pulling up to a punchline, the room slowly emptied as some sort of outside commotion took charge over the moment.

Once my act was over I followed the crowd to see what was up and immediately understood as I encountered some dude free-styling while another played the saxophone. They were really good. At least I think he was. I can't really tell the difference between good jazz and bad jazz. Either way he literally stole the crowd from me. The attention a musician receives is so much different than that received by a comedian. Someone can dance, flirt, drink, and somehow bob their heads the whole time with no interruption in the listening of the music. Meanwhile, one word missed and an entire joke is lost.

If there is something for which I need to apologize in this book it would be my lack of jazz knowledge compared to the amount of jazz knowledge I will attempt to convey. I still can't tell you what good jazz is. Is there even bad jazz? Seriously, it all just goes, and how can anything that's meant to break the rules be seen as good or bad in terms of execution? Its very existence is a representation of its desire to break the rules as an art form. There's seriously just so much to learn about jazz and so much to study up on and I would have needed this to be delayed by at least a decade to make up for my lack of knowledge. The only thing I'm sure about is the timelessness of the art form. Though I can't imagine what it would feel like for anyone who heard jazz before the 1900's. American made is how I would describe Jazz. Not just in that it was made here, actually more so in the fact that it was made as a result of the process of living in America. Few things highlight so accurately that sentiment in the early 1900's than Jazz does. As it has been explained to me Jazz was a blend between the classically trained and the musically rebellious. That blend created a mania for horn and trumpet playing which was said to have taken over the city by the late 1800s. This mania evolved and around 1917 the original Dixieland jazz band became the first group to record a jazz album. Only able to do so after the first real musician turned down the chance to make his own album out of the fear that his unique quality would be stolen as it ultimately was.

Prior to getting into comedy I was only accustomed to hearing jazz when I would be out at a coffee shop somewhere. Through much time in those coffee shops I've taken a surface level curiosity about jazz and the more I look into it the more I've come to see comedy as being pretty similar to jazz in that it's an improvised situation done with an instrument and a crowd no wiser to the end result of what you're doing than you are. The two arts are even similar in the ability of the performer to work together or alone and start on any note they please. Jazz music was the first wave of musical counter culture in the states. If you ask me, and let's face it, you're reading my book so you're at least curious about what I'm saying, America really started to find her modern identity somewhere around the 1950's when names like Duke Ellington and Louis Armstrong became part of the lyrical lexicon of the American lingo. In the North they had helped begin the bonds of friendship with African Americans while fighting beside one another during the civil war nearly 100 years prior. Then by the 1950's though nowhere near perfect, race relations in the United States were beginning to make some progress. I know it doesn't seem like it, hell, it wasn't even til the 60's that we had real progress on a legislative level, but what was happening was a shift in the culture and the conversation. That is to say the conversation had truly started. Our country was fresh out of World War II and ready to take charge on living up to the *liberty for all* side of her agreement with the people of the United States. As it was first recognized by some that the *powers that be* were not doing what was needed to make sure for an equal opportunity for the masses coming into this country. Even as I type that I can't really believe it because I know it's not true. It's not to say that some don't have a much better starting position than others, but how is that different than any other time in history?

Jazz music and comedy both found their times in the courtroom and for jazz it was given the highest honor of being called a national treasure when Democratic Representative John Conyer's of Michigan introduced Congressional Resolution #57 which stated, *"Jazz is hereby designated as a rare and valuable national American treasure to which we should devote our attention, support and resources to make certain it is preserved, understood and promulgated."* Can you imagine if that ruling had gone differently? Would we have ever had rap? Would comedy have stood a chance? Think about how you used to feel when you would get a CD and it was unknowingly censored and you would hear the version the studio was cool with and you were like *"WHAT THE FUCK IS THIS? I MEANT TO BUY THE EXPLICIT VERSION!"* As a whole we usually gawk at the past censorships of life and dismiss them as being ridiculous and from a different generation. Given that I came from such a family I totally related to the idea of being told you're not allowed to listen to this music or that. Which was a shame because growing up in a majority white region of the state I found myself first having to explore other cultures via whatever external medium I could find. Black culture was far more available through the arts than it was in any reality I could walk into near my actual life. Though in this musical case I am speaking more so about rap than jazz. I like them both, but I wasn't cultured enough at 12 to be listening to Jazz. As far as rap goes, if I had to guess I first came in contact with it at a skating rink or something of the sort and became an instant fan of what I was hearing. To explore the history of culture I had to go into books, but to explore culture happening at the moment we had to go to a music store.

As my first book should make pretty apparent, I am a huge fan of language and the ways in which humans use it to play and to evolve. Which has a lot to do with why I've always been impressed by someone who could come up with clever lyrics. Someone who could make you hang on the edge of your seat from line to line. I'm not sure which part fascinates me more, the neural connections which carry you bar to bar, or what sparks the synapsis to ignite the first words. This is one of the reasons I came to love Andre 3000 so much, that and how much he lived up to his reputation for awesome outfits the two times I saw him wandering around the Lower East Side as mentioned before. Once draped in a classy blue trench coat with a screaming orange coming from the lining and a gym bag to match. The other time sporting a throwback with a white-t and a pair of baggy overalls.

Driving on no sleep is something I have become far too used to over the years and certainly no stranger to during any of the time I was on this trip, but each time I did it I felt the same sort of jolt through my body as my nerves would do their best to keep me from dying in some roadside ditch forgotten by the world. Of course there's also the side of you that somewhere around 4 A.M. can't tell whether you're looking at a weather balloon, if the aliens are landing, or if you're just driving straight into the stars. It's around this time that I suggest pulling over, though if you don't you might make it til the point of daybreak at which moment there are few things the human body is less likely to do than sleep.

LONE STAR GRINGO

Days: 10
Miles Traveled: 2,377
Stages: 4

Austin, Texas
May 2016

"Lets hope the laughs are bigger here too..."

Early in the morning I brushed by the outskirts of Houston, Texas and caught a glimpse of the first bits of traffic which held one of Americas largest populations in its grasp around the 9 A.M. hour. The rain from the night before had been replaced with a blanket of humidity. With nowhere to go I stopped at a Panera just off an exit to use the bathroom and brush my teeth. By now I was going on practically no sleep. When you're traveling for this long and across so much space and time you begin to lose any sense of normalcy with regards to an internal clock. I hadn't really had a good nights sleep since Florida two-and a half days and some 1,100 miles back. This is the part of the road trip, about two weeks in, when you start the really appreciate a comfortable front seat. Or any comforts you've added to make that seat more than bearable. Were it not for the outrageous price of gas and the short amount of miles each gallon got you, I would happily be cruising around in some sort of SUV.

Depending on where you're from, this place is most likely known for Cowboys, some with lassoes and others with coke-fueled linebackers. From outside of the United States and perhaps the outskirts of most other areas, it is seen as the hub of American conservatives and more or less regarded as a rogue state who flies their flag above that of *Old Glory*. I think it's fair to say Texas is a place suspicious of government, and I would say rightly so. The citizens of this area went through 6 passport changes in 26 years back in the late 1800's. On top of that they've been everything from abandoned to entirely backed by the same government in even smaller amounts of time.

Another area in which our nations protection of free speech is conflicted is with regards to our history of attacking musicians. There honestly could have been a very extended version on this when I was talking about Jazz earlier. I went with this example however because the idea of censoring country music seems more absurd when we consider who the early censors were. My case here is that of the Dixie

Chicks with the first set of attacks being on what they were saying as people using their entertainment as a podium to broadcast a message, meanwhile the second time was an attack on the very utterance of the latter half of their name. They were cancelled by the right for being too left anti-government, then the left cancels them for being too far right. Ultimately ending with a name change that was less reflective of the Civil War and therefore less likely to trigger those who might see their name on a playlist somewhere. Then they criticized Bush for getting us into a war. Once worrying about their opinion on something, and another time about their decision to keep the name or not. All the while not changing a damn thing. Speaking of which, that's a word I want back into play, Dixie, that and retarded. Because sometimes there's just no better word to describe how stupid someone in traffic is being.

As an American abroad you often have to answer questions about certain parts of your country when you're out there on the road; few things bring more of those questions than guns. Guns are probably a counter-culture to the rest of the world, but in America they're a never ending topic. As I do abroad, I won't make my opinion on the topic vague, though I would argue it's as nuanced as most of the stances I take. In short, if you don't understand the reasons or motivations for gun ownership then you're too optimistic about the realities of the world and the ability of humanity to correct itself through some altruistic miracle. As it has once been said, history is a constant race between innovation and disaster and if you think governments are the only institutions which should possess weapons, well you're just not very good at history. Because any government is nothing more than a representation of the people in charge at the moment; and my how those seats and moments can shift on a dime. But it doesn't take a quote beyond this one *"God created man, Samuel Colt made those men equal"* to help get the point across as to why they're important in maintaining the most free society possible now that they exist at all. That's the thing, for the honor of war and the safety of all I wish they just didn't exist, but they do, so here we are. I wish we lived in some altruistic society where not only was there no need for personal defense, but any concern for future offense, but that future doesn't seem likely. I look at collective ownership of guns as more of an insurance against the government ever doing anything incredibly stupid, compared to them just doing the regular stupid. This is kind of something we have a reputation for though we forget it once in a while.

We as Americans were the first to successfully refuse the imperialistic past which had ruled the world for as long as time can tell. Some may say we replaced it. We had come to a new land and we were going to do what we could to live as we wished. Granted I would need to read more journals to really speak further on this part, but even then they had to fight their way across the West. They decided we're not going back, but we're also not gonna stop pushing forward, and we will do so at the cost of it all. Not to insult those who first welcomed their presence, but if those natives had been more like the warring tribes of plains, its likely history would have turned out a bit differently. I'm conflicted as a man who loves the wildlife by thoughts of what this nation must have looked like a few hundred years ago when it was first discovered by outsiders. Let it be known I'm aware that *discovered* is slightly inappropriate as a term here as the nation was not undiscovered and far from empty. Though the discovery was not just a discovery but a link between two eras of operation. A true proof of what happens when two cultures of two very different forms come across one another for the first time. I hate to think of the amount of history and culture that we've missed out on as a result of that interaction. How much could have been transferred over for the good. How great could it be if we as people just took the best from each side and did it that way? Combined all the good. Then again, that's the sad story of every library ever lost.

I can't tell you how much I wish we could go back to the days before this country, maybe even the world, was industrialized and explore the American countryside. As a white dude it's unlikely I would enjoy the realities of wandering through Comanche land back in the day, a people so brutal in their tactics of war that even the Apache were afraid of them. So much so that they once tricked the Texans into battling the Comanches by leading them into a battle that they themselves were supposed to be fighting, leading to the Massacre at Santa Ana. All of this is to say it should at least be noted that they weren't exactly living a peaceful existence here. This place was run by a combination of plains Indians which came from raider societies, each with a nomadic nature to their existence, something almost as relatable from their culture as their willingness to go without shoes. They used everything from the buffalo, and they seemed not to want more. Or perhaps they only didn't want more because they weren't aware that more existed. The journals of history from that time lack no consistency of young Native American boys using every chance they could to barter or steal to get a hold of the shiny new objects brought into the wilderness by their recently displaced European neighbors.

Entering Austin I went to a few places I had not been on my initial visit a few years back; first stopping at Z-Park where I walked around until I had worked my way to the center and up to a rock formation and a cluster of trees providing shade over a span of a dozen or so picnic tables. From that spot I had the unpredicted but much appreciated advantage of sight over the park and was able to do as much people watching as downtown Manhattan. The flocks of humans walking their dogs and tossing frisbees reached that of a day at the beach in the widest of sands. Standing there these two guys started to smoke a joint after finishing up their bike ride. Then of course they offered, and of course I accepted. This was not the Texas I knew by reputation. The zoom of responsibility and paranoia which suddenly shot through me was almost too much to bear. What the fuck was I doing and why was I on this rock? Why was I at the highest point possible literally putting up smoke signals? The longer I sat there the longer I wondered if something in particular had naturally led me here, something in my nature, to the same place where everyone else would want to smoke and hang out. Perhaps my bright blue hammock waving in the wind sent the right type of signal to let the others know that they were amongst friends. It made me incredibly paranoid as I stood there dwelling on the fact that I was in the center of the state that has a relatively zero tolerance for the indulgences of marijuana. In fact, they're so committed to the idea that they were even willing to arrest Willie Nelson, for his possession of such things while cruising across the state in his tour bus. Granted, it was no small amount with which Willie was cruising. Still, I had nowhere near the financial ability to get myself out of prison, and I was even worse on the guitar. With no guitar and no real plan I sat there atop the park until my paranoia eventually left me and I could start untying my hammock and gathering my things.

Once back at the car I changed my illegally odored clothing and then got myself back downtown where I would soon perform. Finding myself in the heart of the city I started by taking a walk around 5th and 6th street. Unsure what it was I was trying to relive, what it was I was hoping to grasp onto for a moment. Going from bar to bar I questioned each bartender about what he knew regarding stand-up in the city. A few of them had something useful to say about an open mic at their bar, but none of them had it going on tonight or tomorrow. At the help of one kindly barkeep at a rodeo style bar I got the name of a local comedian who then answered me later on a Facebook message about a mic happening down Chavez Street later that evening. Getting the name I scouted out the area and decided to park close to the venue and explore the surrounding area. Finding a spot to sit down and hang out before the show I was soon approached by a waiter. After a brief pitch I found myself ordering a salad of sorts with a mixture of watermelon, almonds, and watercress; a delightfully refreshing way to stem off the central Texas heat.

After college I had some friends move to DC because it made sense for government jobs, and others than went to NYC for finance, some who headed towards the mountains, but the ones who wanted the most hip upcoming city at the time went to Austin. Certain cities had a particular function, or an overwhelming reason for which people move there. Washington had the government, NYC was TV and big business, Los Angeles was Entertainment, but then places like Austin were just the new destination because for some reason they had become cool. There was a time where *cool* was enough to make me wanna drive 21 hours to check it out. The first time I did I looked around the city and I saw so many things I liked. Despite not having the largest comedy scene at the time it was still a city which largely promoted live entertainment.

The other thing the city had was a sense of identity. Austin has this thing where they like to say, *"Keep It Weird"* as a way to say, *"Don't Mess With OUR Weird."* Because I don't think they would like Portland, Oregons version of weird. I'll give it to them, the things that they do differently they do really differently. Paying for my juice I asked the girl about how far it was to this one park I had heard of before. Giving a concise set of steps she handed me my change and then as I thanked her I said, *"Hey I love your city!"* To which she responded, *"Thanks, please don't move here like the other 1,000 people a day do."*

"Uh. Yeah. No problem."

"Thanks. Do you need a receipt?"

"No. I'm good."

"Okay. Have a great day!" she said excitedly waving me off to my next destination. Walking outside I was met by a broad glare coming from a white based building across the street. Standing outside I looked

up at the apartment buildings across the street, each modernly designed with spacious corner windows and abstract bulging to create the biggest feeling possible. Do places ever stop? Why don't we make our own places cool?

"Bringing money, but boy the traffic is terrible."

Harboring sympathy for her strife I thought about how it sucks to see cities like this start to blow up as a result of other places drowning out others. Or because they're abandoning others instead of changing them for the better. In some ways it makes sense, especially at the beginning of the change. Can't blame the herd for leaving when the waterhole has dried. Some people stay through the troubles, some people migrate, that's just how it is. Some people will want to be rooted and want to make an area their own. The jump from being a small town to a small city is odd, but the jump from small city to big city is felt all around, with real estate prices jumping for miles around. The thing which comes to harm the surroundings the most is the weight on the surrounding infrastructure. Granted I don't think someone should be able to invest in an area that they are not willing to live in and be a part of, if you don't wanna be a part of a community then you're not really trying to do anything other than profit off of its existence. Especially if in doing so you make that area increasingly less affordable for those already residing in it. In that case I struggle to see how you're doing anything of virtuous use.

When I got to the show I signed up and put myself down as 7th on the list. Just before my set the show runner came up to me and told me that it was going to be a few more minutes before I was able to go up. This happened again after two more guys went on. This time I was told I would be next. Again, my name wasn't called. I stood around looking for a minute wondering if I had done something wrong or somehow offended someone in my innocent moments of standing around trying to stay out of the way. By this time I had gone through three rounds of adrenaline preparing myself to go up and then being let down by the announcing of another comedians name. I didn't even mind the slight of the situation as much as I minded the constant fucking with my emotions. As the show went on I was teased once more and then finally put on right before the last guy, finally able to let loose all that had been building up in my head over the last two hours.

I don't have much else to say about my experience doing stand-up in Austin except for a note about the surprising demographic with which I was performing. I don't really know how else to say it other than this, but they had a noticeably higher volume of more gay stand-up comedians than I had come across in any city. Perhaps only noticeable by the additional information that Texas is labeled as one of the most conservative states in the nation. To those outside of Texas, Austin is known as that drop of blue floating in a sea of red. If they knew how big Texas really was, I don't think they could even call it a drop as it accounts for only 271 of the 268,597 square miles which is the state of Texas. Speaking of numbers, I didn't realize nor take note of the fact that college graduation would be going on this weekend. The University of Texas houses no less than 25,000 kids and this particular graduating class was nearly 8,000 members. That's 2-10 extra people in the city per student, plus 2 extra cars, then factor in the extra security and speakers, all in all I knew I would be looking at a more difficult parking issue than normal. Though I could probably use it to my benefit and blend into the surrounding cars way easier than I had before. Plus my out of state plates wouldn't raise any flags in whichever neighborhood I decided to park my car. It made sense tho, this is why there had been no AirBnb or couch-surfing availabilities. This would absolutely change how I planned the rest of my trip. Graduations were done, but I needed to consider local events a bit better if I was going to keep things on track. Walking down 5th and 6th street I did my best to keep my shoulders to myself as I moved through the crowds of new graduates. Seeing the reflections of faces from my younger days scurrying about I tried not to lock onto any one glance for too long for fear I may miss the capture of another memory in a face only passing for a moment. One face in particular brought me back to the memory of a girl from back in my younger years. One I used to take trips for, always sidetracking my life in order to see her, even if just for a moment. Our relationship had started back in the days before it was normal to make friends online. Back in a time when your parents were still warning you about doing such things. We met in a chatroom, she was the only name I didn't recognize. Which obviously led me to engaging her, though at the time her screen name said nothing to let me know she was a girl. She was one of the people I thought about when I first wondered if I could ever do this as a career, I'll never forget the times I heard her say, *"Patty people don't talk like that."* Which at the time confused me, but as I got older I began to wear it as a badge of silent honor. I sometimes worry they would both be painfully ashamed to see where I was at this point in life. I had only ever really had affairs with either of these two women, so it's not as if I can even say whether or not we would have worked as a couple when it all came down to it or if they saw me as anything more than a little bit of fun.

In a lot of ways this trip was stating to feel like the one thing I was doing that was related to my major since I graduated college. I had taken plenty of political campaigning classes never realizing how applicable they would be at this time in my life. What I was doing felt no different than the versions of the story I read growing up through the likes of Hunter S. Thompson and Lyndon B. Johnson. Falling in love with the stories of a future president who used the promise of connectivity to help gain votes in the furthest reaches of the Hill Country in his early campaigns before becoming a Senator. Granted, in an ideal world I would have done a tour the way the famous comedians did, a jet, flights, racking up airline miles, and writing jokes in a plush seat as I soared through the air.

Ninety miles later while entering San Antonio I reached out to a guy I used to work with across from the golf-course during my summers in college. We were both movie fanatics of a particular nature and during our time working together we bonded on our love of the obscure as well as the foreign. Yet the thing which got me to this conversation is how his roommate in college had moved out to Los Angeles a few years ago. Supposedly taking a job at some comedy club in the city. Sadly I hadn't done my research so when I was probed about the name of the place it could possibly be I had nowhere really to draw a name from. My mind was already in Mexico. I needed to find somewhere to get supplies. I needed somewhere to shape up and get my shit in order.

"Nah, we don't really have many comedy spots here, come on by though, I'll get you some food."

"You gonna stay around for the night?"

"Yeah. Plan to do some sightseeing and then go on my way."

Once I got to him we continued to talk as his restaurant sat in an afternoon lull. Towards the end of our conversation he went out of his way to apologize for the fact that he wasn't able to extend an invitation to stay at his house tonight. Apparently he had recently earned custody of his daughter and didn't have the room for a guest in his two-bedroom apartment, nor could he arrange for a last minute baby-sitter. Not that I would have asked him to do so, I had accepted the duty of this journey with full knowledge and willingness to stay in my car any and every night if needed. This situation would also serve to a sad reality that I would increasingly see as my thirties went on.

Scrolling through the spots downtown I found it odd that there was a comedy club hosting known comedians and yet there was seemingly no open mics advertised no matter how hard I looked. Aside from that I was mostly surprised by my visit to the Alamo; and not surprised in the good way, it's in front of a fucking movie theatre. Literally one of the most iconic Western landmarks in existence, and it's right in front of a Cineplex. Though despite the lack of formality the surroundings call for, a sign on the outside still reminds visitors that *"In Texas, we take our hats off before entering the Alamo"*. So a brief history to consider when thinking of the Alamo and the evolution of Texas. According to even the best of Mexican historians the lands of Texas were sparsely populated with actual Mexicans back in the day, and for the most part the government in La Cuidad de Mexico had little concern about the Northern Territory beyond the pure possession of it. In fact, at the time of Western expansion the entirety of Texas was populated by less than 6,000 Mexicans. Which is an average of one person every 44.7 square miles. A number if applied proportionally would be proportionate to about 10 people living in an area the size of Los Angeles County. Surely a dream for any Southern Californian, but not nearly enough people to defend the land from an invasion by the exploratory forces of the early pioneers, which was a mix of people beyond the English speaking Europeans, though they ended up being the ones to ultimately win the influence over that land, once trappers and gold seekers had made their way through.

Leaving the Alamo I got online and booked an AirBnB, taking a room in a guest house off the side of this lovely home sitting along a lakeside subdivision. There a woman named Betty introduced me to her husband, a truck driver with an apprehension to guests in the tiny-house they had in their oversized backyard. Though he took more of a liking to me the longer we spoke about our time on the road; both sharing a liking for talk-radio over music for the longer trips. Sitting there he walked me through some of his favorite things about the comedian and recited many things which I could recall hearing before. He took the path of many of us, starting first with the internal workings of his existence, eventually branching to the introduction of characters which have aided to the contribution of his character, and now expanding.

Somewhere around 5 AM I woke up feeling antsy. I tried to keep still and fall back asleep, but to no avail. Quietly leaving the house I went through an opening in the gate off and backed my car out of the driveway before turning on the lights. Exiting the neighborhood I took a wrong turn and wound up driving around a cookie cutter subdivision for a good ten minutes while I tried to navigate my way back to the exit. The place was growing in every direction. That was the story of America, it does its thing until the outsiders find out and come along to take part. Cruising the main roads of the city I rolled by the Alamo again, seeing the glow of the local mall radiating it with the occasional flash of red.

Before this day I had never actually left a car at an airport. As I arrived something about the fenced in parking lots surrounded by the vastness of the Lone Star state lead my mind to concern for the future of my belongings more so than the gates assured me of their safety. If it went missing how would it ever be found? With such paranoia I did my best to position things in the backseat as I collected my supplies for Mexico. The energy of an airport is much different before a redeye. Two hours before the flights take off there's a large hum about the terminal. I was going from one airport to another, across a border, less than 300 miles and under two hours, to one of Mexico's coolest cities; a place sure to be known by many more after the 2026 World Cup, but for now I'll do my best to give you a first impression in the following chapter.

MONTEREY, MEXICO
May 2016

"Can I call you Gringo?"

S omewhere driving through Louisiana I got an idea. In short that idea would lead me to buy a ticket taking me down to Monterrey, Mexico for a four day trip to visit some friends of mine in the culinary world. That friend had once lived in the United States and was one of the first Mexicans who was truly *only visiting* that I had ever met in my country. At the time she was once an au-pair to a rich family who lived around the corner a local watering hole with the best Mexican food in town. When we first met I'm sure I was just this odd overly friendly American talking to her and the group at her table, never did either of us think that years later we would be reconvening in her home country. Luckily the connectivity of the world allowed us to maintain that friendship. Here's how she responded to that message about the idea to take a flight and visit, *"Are you serious?"*

"Well that's why I'm texting you. Wanted to see if you're free first."

"Of course! You've got to come! I have a friend here who does comedy."

"In English or Spanish?"

"Spanish."

"Cool. I'd love to see a show in Spanish."

"I'll check his schedule! Are you driving here? We're only a few hours from the border!"

"Yeahhhh, but I don't really wanna risk bring my car down there. No offense, I just have everything I need in it, and last I recall it was you who told me about their friend getting carjacked and left on the side of the road on Christmas Eve right?"

At her silence I sent a text back, *"Exactly."*

"Well, I just got done with school so if you want to come I've got the time to show you around."

Part of me didn't really plan to go through with it until a search for tickets showed me some for under $200. Then I saw that the overnight parking at the San Antonio Airport was going to be less than $30 for an entire 4-day weekend. Then it was just a matter of finding a spot to stay. I knew Ana had plenty of family down there, but I didn't wanna make such an intrusive first impression, not after knowing how easy it could be to find a willing participant in the game of couch surfing. Upon my first search I found a girl majoring in journalism who was more than happy to have a traveling comedian stay at her downtown dwelling, a label which continued to open arms across the land.

"Alright, so looks like I'm coming. My flight lands Friday morning."

"OMG ARE YOU SERIOUSSSSS?"

"Yes."

"My last exam is Friday morning. I can't get you from the airport :(Want me to ask my dad?"

"No no. You're cool. I'll take an Uber, it's no big deal."

"OMG I'm so excited. You're going to LUV Monterrey!"

Before 9 A.M. my flight had landed and the stewardess began handing out papers to be filled out for the customs officials. The airport was on the far end of the city, completely hidden from view. Once through I called on an Uber, a decision which to this day continues to bring me Spanish language advertisements and promos on my phone. Being picked up I gave up all autonomy and sat in the backseat with the highest of hopes that I was in a legitimate Uber. I soon realized the airport was a little bit outside of the city and that a conversation would be needed to get myself through this drive. My driver was a neat guy named Ernesto who was from a few hours outside of the city. He had come here as a teenager and was allured by the same big city fun any of my country friends had experienced at one point in life or another. Through a series of texts coordinating with Ana I had the drive take me to a coffee spot near the local university. Sitting there waiting for my drink I looked around puzzled at the crowd making it's way through the door. Then, I gave my surroundings a glance and compounded my confusion. Asians. All around me. Which I know doesn't sound like some profound discovery if you think of the global odds, but in this part of the world it was somewhat odd. I walked outside expecting to see a tour bus of some sort, but no, just the same parking lot I had seen moments before. Not knowing a more polite or linguistically accurate way to say it, I leaned in to the barista and inquired, "Una pregunta. Que esta pasando con todos los Chinitos?" (An unpolitically correct way to say "So what's up with all of the Asians here...?") It was then that the girl explained to me the creation of a plant by the KIA car company which had recently taken place in one of the surrounding towns resulting in a slight influx of outside workers, most meant to do the training for

139

future KIA workers to be stationed in and or originating from Mexico. A conversation with one of them would further explain to me how much easier it was for Koreans to learn Spanish than it was for most other Asians to do so, Filipinos excluded. Apparently there were a great many sounds which the two languages shared, and the vocal recognitions made the adaptation fairly simple, ultimately resulting in a plethora of unique accents in the room around me. Already in love with the idea of language and culture I opted out of staying outside and instead sat in a booth on the second floor of the shop where I got to absorb the oddities of the words being used in my surrounding directions. My surroundings were another example where I saw how the powers of industry more often than not had to do with human migration than anything else. From that cultures share and spread, usually the favored wins out. It was also the first time I found myself wondering if there was a term for what was going on around me. When used with a blend of the two we label it spanglish, so was there a word for what was happening around me? EspanKorea? Koreancito? Maybe that's a Korean baby? I've since wondered the same involving Amharic and English. Amglish?

When I was twenty I couldn't speak a lick of Spanish, and by thirty I was practically fluent. Which brings me to something I'm conflicted on; and that is the idea of America having an official language. I took the time to learn Spanish. I'm even aware of that *"We didn't cross the border, the border crossed us!"* mentality which sits in the minds of some of our Southwestern towns. All of it makes sense. However a nation of this size must have a unified language as it's the only way that culture really works, spreads, or stays. On some levels I don't see why we can't be a cross-cultural multi-lingual society. Countries like Switzerland serve as a fine example as to how a country can operate with it's citizens embracing an idea of multi-lingual operations, but this seems to only work in so far as the people are willing to all learn these languages. Which in fairness I must say seemed to be a thing of normality here in the North where a fair amount of people spoke English. Not just spoke, understood and could articulate to a level that was nearly native.

When Ana finally picked me up I was filled with a joy that I hadn't felt in a long while. To explain how close I felt to her as a friend feels impossible. She was like a sister in another language. In maintaining her friendship I had alienated at least two ex-girlfriends and their requests to have her become one of the items of the past in a life only moving forward by the removal of each possible threat. Seeing as neither of those women are longer in my life, I feel ever more confident that I made the right decision.

"OH MY GOD. I CAN'T BELIEVE THAT YOU'RE HERE! When you told me you were in Texas I thought okay cool come over. But you actually bought a ticket! I'm so excited. I can't wait to show you my city." - Ana

"It's good to see you too hun." - Patrick

"OH MY GOD. Patrick! What is your life these days? You're trying to be a comedian?" - Ana

"Yeah, that's the plan. Working on it the best I can." - Patrick

"I can't believe you go up on stage like that, I could never." - Ana

"You serious? You're not shy! You do those cooking videos!" - Patrick

"That's different! I get time to edit." - Ana

"Technically I get plenty of time to edit before I go on stage." - Patrick

"Still not the same." - Ana

"So what do you wanna do?" - Patrick

"There's so much to show you! Are you hungry?" - Ana

"I can always eat." - Patrick

Departing the coffee shop she took me through the city, parts the cabbie had, parts he hadn't, ultimately bringing us to the cultural downtown of the city.

"Your family excited to meet me?" - Patrick

"They're very interested that you're here." - Ana

"What is that supposed to mean?" - Patrick

"Let's just say my mom is very suspicious as to why some American man is visiting me. They all think you and I had some type of affair they just won't say it out loud." - Ana

"They sound like like my ex-gf. She was always on that with me and you. It was annoying. The only time sex was even a topic with us was that one time you asked me to take you by your boyfriends house and you took forever finding your things." - Patrick

"OMG I remember that. I swear I just grabbing my sandals." - Ana

"You don't have to stick with that lie." - Patrick

"It's not a lie!" - Ana

"Well if we just told them that story I'm sure they would understand our friendship a bit more." - Patrick

"I'm not telling them that story." - Ana

"Even though it would show them that we never..." - Patrick

141

"I don't care what they think honestly. Victor knows the truth and that's all that matters." - Ana

"I hope I get to meet him too." - Patrick

"You will. He's busy today, but we're gonna all go out tomorrow." - Ana

"So what's the plan for today?" - Patrick

From there her plan consisted of heading towards a riverwalk in the city center and going around to a few local attractions. Ending our journey at an Argentinean themed pizza shop we were enticed by the combo of a half-off deal and 100 degree heat to get a few pitchers of sangria. After crushing more than we planned to order we realized that walking was the new challenge of our day and this led to the decision to take an hour long river tour through downtown Monterrey. On one part of the tour Ana started to look at another boat approaching us and started to speak what I initially thought was nonsense. *"Mirra! That's El Bronco!"* - Ana

"El Bronco? What's that mean?" - Patrick

"He's basically the Mexican Trump." - Ana

Confused I looked at him for a bit more confirmation,"How so?"

"He's not really a politician. He's just good at getting attention." - Ana

"Well, that's the market these days..." - Patrick

Mexico and America were both going through a similar thing at the moment. Granted, the politics and the history of Mexico are so broad and crazy that I'm not gonna try and sway you all into any sort of understanding. It's a lot like NYC, except a Mexican version. Other cities can claim to be multi-cultural but none are so to the extent that NYC is is. Bronco was an independent, the first to win an election in Mexico's history.

"You have any good Trump jokes?" - Ana

"No." - Patrick

"Can you say something like him?" - Ana

"I'm not good at impressions." - Patrick

Truth was, despite being a Political Science major in college it was never my desire to be political in my comedy. I feel like it isolates you and more often than not puts one side of the crowd against you. Even if not against you, they might just not wanna hear about it. I mean, who can blame someone for wanting some reprieve for a moment from a world that won't stop shoving politics down your throat? Often times doing so around topics that aren't even political, they're just made to be as a means of drawing in an audience and creating a firm hold on

142

this side or that side as the group to blame for this all encompassing problem. I tried to even avoid topics that were political in nature, climate change and that type of stuff. Perhaps asking people to think about long term consequences as opposed to short term gains is a bit much to do with all consideration given to human nature. As a teller of jokes I wasn't that political and the one time I tried to be it fell completely flat. It was the one area in life in which I had more of an interest to remain serious than joking. It was like if you didn't say something they would wonder why you didn't, and if you did you could only take once stance. I never wanted to bring it onto the stage unless there was a DIMARCHI 20XX sign below my name. Trumps ridiculousness was so obvious I felt no need to comment on it. What could I add to the madness other than*"Oh hey, me too!"* All I could do was nod in agreement and wonder if he was reflecting what we were? As a national character he definitely divided us and would continue to do so over the following years. The things he said were so extreme that those who latched onto him were thought to be the most inconsiderate of individuals. But how responsible can the masses feel to their actions when those actions are created by the ultimate jester?

As a message came in she looked down at her phone and let out one of her characteristic laughs with an unhindered smile that stayed on the face long after the noise of the reaction had left.

"Omg look at what my little bro said." - Ana

"Who the fuck is that gringo? Where the fuck is Victor?"

"He seems angry." - Patrick

"He just don't know you. And he really likes Victor." - Ana

"Well shit. I hope I get to meet this Victor guy." - Patrick

"You will, he's gonna join us for dinner tonight." - Ana

" Awesome. And your brother is coming too?" - Patrick

"No. He's got plans with his girlfriend." - Ana

Later that evening at dinner I got one of the questions I had expected. Uncomfortably from some people on the other side of the wall.

"What do you think of what is going on in America. Think Trump will be your next President?"

"I don't know man. It's weird. I wouldn't say the ones that are are actually for Trump are FOR Trump as much as they are just ambiguously against the other options. It's weird. I don't know that I've ever seen anything like it."

"So you would say he's a bad choice for President?"

"Yes. He's a bad choice for President. Wonderful T.V. personality, great on the radio, wouldn't really want him in Congress."

"Or the White House I hope either?"

"Lets hope his hotel is the only bed in Washington for him for a long time."

"You know, everyone said that Bronco wouldn't win, that he was only loud and talking."

"Yeah. A lot of people think that back home too. I don't know yet. It's weird. I don't think people think he's qualified, but I also don't think people hate him, I'm not sure."

"But people are voting for him?"

"Well they might. We don't have the best turnout rates either."

Later we went and sat down in the town square. Walking around I saw that I was the lightest person in the area with my freckles sticking out more than anything else. Despite an influence of Spanish blood in the region I still stuck out more than the average pale skilled man in these parts and the ones who held similar features than my own had a distinctly different Iberian influence amongst their faces. In my moment of hyper observation Ana spoke up with some plans for later.

"Wanna come to my house for dinner? My parents want to take you out."

"Uh yeah sure."

"Aye okay. We'll take you to anywhere you wanna eat."

"I think he's going to ask me to marry him."

"That's fun. Excited?"

She looked down shyly and then the left side of her face lit up with a grin, "Yeah. I'm really happy with him."

It was no surprise to hear that her family was a fan of him or he a fan of them. They were beyond nice, even the grandparents embraced me. I had no idea then that this city would become so special to me over the next few years. Maybe one day I'll even write a book about it, but for now I'll just tell you that my first visit there was amazing. It was off the beaten path. It was cool. I shall do my best to relay memories of a first impression, though now the city has left a much deeper mark on me. Something about me blended in. It was one of the few places I had heard about but never visited. It was on my list for a long time and somehow I always put it off.

I met the family. They took me out to a nice restaurant named *El Hornocito*. I suggest giving it a look. Sitting inside with her family I looked around and tried to adjust to the setting, feeling the eyes of the family on me and the words bouncing around conversations meant to be too fast for me to hear. I always loved Spanish. One of the things which I loved most about it was the culture of the people. They weren't afraid to call each other names which represented exterior labels. In fact, from what I could tell they were pretty wide open with one another, uttering such thing as, *"Oye pelon!"* Or *"Hola Gordo!"* (baldy and fatty for those who don't know). When called that, neither the baldy nor the fatty are offended, just aware that they're still noticeably either quality. I don't have the best head of hair, one might even say I have a rather noticeable forehead which is why the first of those hits me so hard. I'm not one to normally watch what I say, but you could mess up speaking Spanish and no one would be mad at you.

"You know how my grandma is. Feeds me too much then asks why I've gotten fat. Or asks me why I've gotten so fat and then feeds me the whole time I'm there."

"Sounds about right."

From there they insisted on taking me up a series of back roads which eventually got us to the top of a mountain, the name of which I'll never know, but one which gave me a view on the city that showed it for the first time in all its grandeur.

The funniest part of the experience was the ride home. Her stepdad insisted on being the one to drive me and then seemed uncomfortable the entire time. When he finally found it in him to ask, he fumbled his question and had no recovery. *"So you know my daughter well?"*

"Uh. Yeah. I guess." Driving along I watched his eyes dart around as he realized he had blown by his mark and would need to make a u-turn. He was not the confrontational type despite his aggressive appearance, and more so he seemed uncomfortable in the phrasing that he had been told to tie into his queries. Upon this notice I lightened some of the burden and tried to do what I could to dispel his concerns and the situation all at once. *"Uh Señor. I get if you and your wife don't understand the situation. I'm a strange dude from the states down here visiting your daughter. I know how that might seem. But I promise you, it's nothing."*

"The family likes Victor."

"Wonderful. So do I."

"So we are on the same page then?"

"Yeah. All respect. Just visiting friends that live in cool places. Ana's

been telling me to come here for years, so here I am. Love the city. Big fan."

With crows feet deepening on his right side I watched as his brow too sunk slightly as he searched for a response, never having had to say any of what he had been told to say, with many gaps left unfilled, intention not being one of them, *"Okay. So you're Ana's friend. Where are all you traveling to?"*

"Well for now just across the United States. Maybe up into Canada, depends on the amount of time I have."

"And the whole time you're doing stand-up?"

"Well, definitely not the whole time, but in each place yeah."

Shaking his head he continued to show his uncertainties both for me and my future, with thoughts now far from his daughter in law. *"Well, I wish you luck. That sounds like a confusing road."*

"Yeah. That's one word for it. There's no real road, there's just doing. I kinda think of it like working out and staying in shape, you just gotta keep doing. I've not gotten to actually do as much as I should lately. I thought I would do a lot on the road, but truth be told I woulda done so much more if I were in NYC this whole time."

"You're from NYC?"

"Not FROM, but yeah, I've been living up there the last few months, just working and doing stand-up."

"Ever think about doing a road trip through Mexico?"

"If I could find safe passage..."

"Lemme know when you're ready. I could give you a few routes where you won't find much trouble."

"My experience, there isn't much trouble in Mexico that can't be solved."

"Mexico works how Mexico works."

The next morning I was up having some coffee on the patio when my host came out to say hello.

"What are your plans today?"

"I'm gonna go with my friends to some lake up in the mountains."

"Oh, probably Presa a Cuchillo. Don't get in the water."

Happy to give up the wheel, when they arrived I got in the backseat and crawled into the middle where I got a panoramic view of life coming at me through the windshield, with Ana in front of me to my right, and Victor fastening his seatbelt in the driver seat to the left. For the first time in a long time I got to sit as a passenger as he drove us away from the city through the mountains. They took me to a far away town. All in all about two hours outside of the the city. From there we parked and walked around a cluster of colonial bodegas and churches made of old stone and half completed bricks. They chose this town because they ran a YouTube show and were trying to visit a few spots to show, with 34,000 viewers and counting. I imagine each time this book is republished I will have to revisit the numbers and reformat this entire paragraph to keep up with the mounting zeros which will soon add up. I saw why they had so many people interested, they were putting in the work.

"You wanna be on an episode of our show?"

"Fuck yeah. What's the show though? Gonna be real, I see you post them but I've not really seen the videos, I'm not a big foodie so I never think to watch people cooking ya know?"

"It's not JUST the cooking. We're trying to show more of the local places here in Nuevo Leon. It started as a cooking show we made of little restaurants we found throughout the region on our road trips when we first started dating. He always had a camera and I always wanted to go places to eat."

"Sold before the story. Just tell me what you need me to do."

"Great. We'll treat you to something good. Victor! Aye Que Padre, what is this town again?"

Giving his light laugh he quickly replied with,*"Se llaman China."*

Bringing out the camera, *"Okay, he were are on the streets of China. The pueblo not the country. Oh My God Victor look at that car!"*

Looking towards the right I saw a tiny VW with a convertible top as Victor yelled,*"Cut! Redo!"*

Looking somewhat guilty at her gaffe Ana asked, *"So you hungry yet?"*

To which I reliably replied, *"I can always eat."*

"Awesome. We found a restaurant that specializes in some local specialties and Birria."

"Whats that?"

Here they introduced me to a red meat called *birria* which I still seek out at every food truck I visit. I'm not great at describing food so I'm not going to start here.

"Okay, so you're sure you're comfortable doing this in Spanish?"

"Fuckin' let's see I guess."

Victor pulled out a GoPro and started to film, handing me a mic in the process. As I clipped it to my shirt Ana moved in closer and got within the frame. At this point I was well beyond the days when someone could trick me with food or an unknown menu item, but as I looked down I wasn't certain that I knew what I was being asked to eat. Taking a look at them I was positioned to ask, *"They're what? Say that word again."*

"Chapulines. Uh how do you call them? They're the tiny bugs that jump and fly. One of them lies to the little boy with the wooden nose."

"Oh you mean grasshoppers!"

"Punta Madre! YES! Those!"

"Uh okay. So how do they prepare them?"

"We fry them. They're seasoned so you'll barely taste them. Trust me."

"Honestly I don't care, you all are making a bigger deal out of this than I am. I have had a worm burger before."

"That sounds gross."

The duo turned on their camera and started recording an introduction to an episode that would soon be dubbed, *"El Gringo come'lo"*

"Hello again hungry people, today we have a special guest for you today, my friend, and comedian, Patrick DiMarchi."

Looking into the camera I gave a nod and took another sip of my mezcal as the shot went back to Ana who had positioned a perfectly scooped glob of guacamole on a blue tortilla chip, *"Es Buenisimo!"*

After a series of weekly updates and a spiel about the restaurant and ingredients they shut off the camera and repositioned themselves for the arrival of the waiter.

"See what I mean about the editing? If the audience saw this I would die. Oh, Victor wants to know, does it offend you when I say gringo?"

"No...Should it?" I asked, almost half in jest and half so she would elaborate.

"You don't know where it comes from?"

"It's how I introduce myself when people ask where I'm from in Spanish. I say, So Gringo. It's what they called me everywhere. Even a few people in Spain."

"Oh. Well, when American soldiers first started coming to Mexico the locals would point at their green army uniforms and say 'Green' and then point out and say GO. GREEN GO. GRINGO."

"No shit? That's interesting. Can't believe I've never heard that."

"It's true!"

"I believe you, but no, I don't care. Plus it sounds way better to me than blanco or pelon. I'll be Gringo all fucking day."

Upon leaving the tiny town we continued climbing up a series of narrow mountain roads until we came upon a parking lot indicating the beginning of a trail which would take us to the waterfall on the map. We toured the area and looked at the falls. Falsely named as to attract more tourists. They were more of a place where the water happens to come down the rocks, rather roughly I imagine after a great rain, but barely creating a mist at their speeds on a normal day. A few photos later we were making our way back down the trail and into the car.

Continuing away from the falls we meandered a bit more up the road towards a villa of sorts with signs advertising an overlook to the valley below somewhere ahead.

"What do you think of bungee jumping?" - Victor

"I'm not against it." - Patrick

"But, you've never gone?" - Victor

"No." - Patrick

"Oh it's set. Your first time bungee jumping will be in Mexico!" - Victor

"Uh, okay. Yeah! That'll be awesome." - Patrick

Despite the giant lump this thought put in my throat I had taken a vow a long time ago for any time a situation similar to this were to come up. My theory had always been to view oneself like the fat kid at the top of the diving board. Once challenged, sure, you could back down, sure, you could even reverse on the decision to jump. Or, you could jump. Much like going to the gym, I've never regretted jumping at a new experience, not even when the experience ended up being way more uncomfortable than I had planned on.

We arrived at a large parking lot and drove by empty lane after empty lane with our windows down taking in the locals sounds. One of which was less pleasant than the device from which is came. If you've never heard the loud shrieking of a peacock you wouldn't believe such a terrible noise could come from such a beautiful creature, and if you're not sure you've ever heard it then I'm pretty certain you haven't. Google it. Turn the volume on low. You're welcome.

From the top of the mountain we looked down and saw the city as it snaked its way through the mountains. It spoke to the sides of me that loved mountains, the sides that appreciated elevation, and the tiny part of me that was missing the view of a sprawling city such as the one I had just spent my last couple of months. Though this city did so in a much different way. There were no skyscrapers by the standards of any super-metropolis. Still the scattered nature of the buildings provided enough volume and presence to make you feel like you were in the middle of some place serious. Which is good, because the city itself serves as Mexico's business hub and is home to a little over a million people. I wanted to tell them that no part of me wanted to do this, but I couldn't find it within me. Forever shall I wonder how much that had to do with them having a camera in my face.

When Ana went off to get a drink I took a second to pull Victor aside and try to escape the music enough to let my words come out unobstructed, *"Hey man. I'm really glad to see she found someone like you. I couldn't be happier to know you're in her life. Pleases let me know if you ever make it to my area and I'll show you around."*

"Thanks man. That would be really fun. You're in D.C. right?"

"That's funny, I haven't been asked where I live in a while. The real answer right now is nowhere, but whether you go to NYC or DC I'll make my way there and show you around."

Something inside of me told me that I would not get a trip like this again, at least not with these friends and not in these lives. It was the first of many stages of transition that I was seeing in the people around me the further I went along in years. After college the majority of friends kept in touch with their excited updates, but obvious differences in career and geography of experience soon take over in the prioritization of who one decides to hang out with. Then kids come. That changes everything. Perhaps I would one day come here for her wedding, and perhaps another years later, making a stop off to meet her and Victors first child. Over the years my own life will take over, and I'm not sure how or if I will be able to maintain the close binds of friendship I have built over the last three decades of my existence. Mere matter of facts about time and the limits one has in using all of his 24 hours, it just seems that eventually there will be unknown last goodbyes, and eventual fading offs of the connections I spent late hours trying to make.

It was here on my last day in Monterrey that I first learned how to properly iron a shirt at the ripe age of 30. Odder so is the fact that the one to teach me was a mid-twenties dude named Ernesto from Chihuahua in town visiting his girlfriend at the next apartment. Apparently he had become friendly with my host over occasional smoke breaks and was sitting inside the apartment waiting when I got home that evening to pack and get ready for my departure. After learning to iron my shirt we sat around shooting the shit until the topic of comedy ultimately came up and the trails of conversation led to asking if I would be performing in the city.

"Is there a club here you can perform at?" - Ernesto

"Yeah. Ana, where did you say it was?" - Patrick

"It's downtown by the Iguana Bar. Lemme call them and see." - Ana

We checked for an opening, but there was none. Not that there wasn't a spot, the club just flat out wasn't open certain days of the week and this happened to be one of them. With all of my love for Spanish I pretty much started thinking about having an act in my foreign tongue from the moment I started doing stand up. That doesn't however mean that I had yet to procure one at the time that this group of kids asked me if I could do some jokes in Spanish. Not just asked me, but encouraged me, practically begged me. I should have just said *no*. As it turned out to be hands down one of the most embarrassing thing I've ever done. I don't know why I didn't just say no. That woulda been way easier. They might have given me hell about it once. Maybe twice. I had hoped to be funny in Spanish many times throughout my twenties, but I had never deliberately done so. This time I found myself struggling hard. Struggling to translate it, struggling to relate it, just all around struggling. As I knew before and the moment reinforced, comedy doesn't always translate in my own language, how the hell was I supposed to turn it into Spanish? Especially since so much of comedy is predicated on the knowledge of the circumstances or context put into the joke. Which means we are largely fighting a battle of knowledge. Your job is to find the point at which knowledge starts and then fill in the gaps quickly. In some ways I knew more what they thought of me than the people in my own country. I could see my act falling flat on their faces. The hope and smiles fading away into confusion. Wondering themselves whether or not this was a moment lost in translation or a matter of obvious delusion. The fact that her friends saw me as a fraud was almost as bad as her seeing me as such. Well, perhaps not as bad, she actually knew me to be legit in other areas of life so why should she assume I was lying now? It sucked that my friends had to see me like that. Especially those who receiving their first impression of me. Unlike the crowds which I would never see again, these would be the friends who may forever feign interest in that which I claim to be doing. To add to the factors against me I was in the worst of places to try and be funny. Worse than a stage was a sidewalk, it's why I was never a street act. Seriously, if you don't think that takes balls as the old saying goes then

I don't know what you find difficult.

Comedically some things are truly universal; someone stepping on a rake and having it jump up and unexpectedly slap them in the face will generate the same reactionary laughter in nearly all cultures and people; even if only rooting out a feeling of regrettable relatability. Music translates better than anything else. But comedy has its hits and misses. Even the British style of humor is sometimes lost on my fellow Americans, with our American edge lost on those on the other side of the pond. All a means to showing that comedy isn't just about funny, it's about the context of the funny and the mental relatability of the audience. A joke about the Bill Clinton scandal would likely not be as funny to someone hearing it back in 1600s, for or many reasons, most of which is that they wouldn't know him. You would have to explain to them the concept of a President, who the fuck an intern is, and why he can't get blowjobs from them. That would be a lot of linguistic ground to cover in only a few moments on stage, probably best to make jokes about the feudal system if they'll let you. Though it's unlikely any of the surrounding population would be able to read anything you wrote. Nor would it have been as easy to get something printed back then, ink and paper were as big an issue at obtaining as water and rice, and dare I say, far less important.

PHOENIX, ARIZONA
May 2016

"Maybe it's the heat...?"

I f you can live without the usual conveniences of modern life
and you like the peace and quiet I suggest going to places like
West Texas; like somewhere an hour and a half outside of El
Paso. Places like that are a different type of isolation and you'll never
see stars as bright as from the view looking up at that sky. While I may
have somewhat over exhausted the topic of borders in my first book,
it's hard not to take a moment while driving and notice the fence off in
the distance to my left and consider how many people might be using
these same night skies and stars for comfort tonight as they make their
way across that line quietly and with a combination of anticipation and
apprehension, seeking some sort of better as it is defined within their
desires. Though it was easy living in NYC to pine romantically on the
migratory past of this country with a daily view of the Statue of
Liberty, this area paints it with a much different brush. In many ways
the two messages being very similar, I mean, how different is a barbed
wired wall from an island not quite in the country yet? They both tell
you there's a system to entering here if you wanna start this journey
playing by the rules. Rules which even I can argue are sometimes
unfair. Where I was, I still had a full days drive before I would arrive in
Phoenix; not needing a footnote to tell you it would be another 2 hours
before I even got out of Texas and into New Mexico. A state no less than
5 hours wide. Which was fine because I would need that amount of
time to come down from my time in Mexico. Driving along I soaked in
that certain feeling of home the desert has each time you're there. For
that matter the whole SouthWest had this quiet comfort I couldn't quite
latch onto. Of all the places I have driven through it has probably been
the most surprising as far as its ability to keep drawing me back
despite being so far away.

If you've read my first book then you'll know that I was twenty
before I took my first flight, though I neglected to mention at the time
that it was one which connected me via Minneapolis on my way to
Phoenix. From that first flight I was exposed to a whole new way of

life. One that made me wanna travel and made me realize that I had missed out on a good share of the potentiality of life already. When I had come here on that trip I stayed for two weeks visiting a friend of mine and was struck with the thought that I would have gone to school and moved here if I had known about this place sooner. Of course I had already paid for my current semester and any alterations to that path would have been more than complicated to change. Not to mention the lack of logic in moving somewhere for school just because they have hot girls and great weather. Granted, great is a matter of opinion. To some the heat in Phoenix may be far from ideal. I enjoyed the lack of humidity and the inevitability of walkable nights that came with the steady temperature. Nonetheless I found myself a bit discouraged a few times by the level of heat radiating off of the sidewalk when I attempted to run outside and grab something that I had forgotten in the car. That being said, Phoenix always had this oddly nostalgic association in my head as one of the coolest places I had visited in my early days of exploring this great land and in many ways this place had many fantasies left to feed me.

Phoenix was also the first place to put me in the situation of needing a fake ID. I can't speak on its current situation, but at the time Arizona State University was one of the main party schools in the nation and a large part of that party scene involved the downtown bars, none of whom would let me in as I was still 8 months away from being 21 when this trip took place. Going through all of the usual channels I sent the creator of my new adult pass an updated picture against a blank wall and all of the information needed to match with my drivers license information in Virginia, only replacing the birthday by a year and giving me an Arizona based address. The whole thing worked perfectly and $150 later I was having my first *legal* shot at the Sky Harbor Airport. The next ten days or so were awesome and no matter where I went I never saw any problems. Even though the restaurant worker inside of me panicked when I noticed that their ID's didn't expire for 50 years, a trait which turned out to be no flaw of an uninformed fake ID maker, that's just how the state did things. I imagine it being a way to attract retired people with the alleviation of ever having to deal with the DMV again after doing it once. I can't be sure, I never got to ask, but I had a feeling that such a detail would lead to a lot of questions once I got back out of Arizona. Regardless the trip went well and weeks later I was still using the ID with no problem.

Then one day I went into a local grocery store to grab a case of beer for my friends, a 24 pack of *Natty Lite* if you must know. Confidently placing my future purchase onto the conveyer belt I let it float down while I casually removed my ID from my pocket knowing that I didn't look like a twenty-one year old in the eyes of anyone with eyes. I bring up eyes because that was the part of her that seemed to widen as she first scanned my ID. Staring back at this bright eyed girl all I could rudely think was, *"Okay, there's no way this ditzy teenager knows this is a fake ID."* An internal thought to which she replied with external excitement, *"Oh My God! It's not often I meet someone from my hometown!"*

Again my mind wandered with expressions as an internal voice wained, *"Get...The Fuck...Out of here..."*

Before I could respond she placed her smile in my direction and attempted to engage me in conversation, *"Don't you hate the winter here?"* It currently being sometime midway through a Virginia winter I responded with something vague to buy myself some time, *"What? Oh yea, its fucking terrible, I hate it."* To which she further inquired, *"Where did you go to high school?"*

Having little experience in the city itself I drew together a few facts and decided that someone working at a grocery story on the other side of the country was unlikely to have gone to a private school and so I decided to go with naming something generic. *"Oh, I would have gone to Scottsdale Prep but my mom moved us to Tucson before I started, I just use my dads address still."*

"Oh okay, Did you know Stacey Davies?"

"Nah, I don't think so."

At this point I was saved by the graces of another customer hoping to move the line along and pay for their produce. Needless to say I never went back in that store again despite my promise to *"See you again soon Sun Devil."*

Arriving in the real Scottsdale the only thing which I could be certain of was that I was going to eat at the best breakfast spot in all of America, *The Breakfast Club*. There I would buy a breakfast burrito. Beyond that, the rest of the day was without plan. There was a weird lack of meaning in the concept of time at this point in my trip. The only time that mattered was what time the mic started and how many hours it would take me to get to the next one. When I first arrived I tried to mark off the two important things needed in each city and from there figured I would go about my day. When I got on *Couchsurfing* I found a few responses waiting for me and fielded a few of them as one in particular caught my eye. A woman named Debbie living near Mesa with her husband said she could put me up for the night as long as I was cool with sharing the house with a set of dogs. Which of course I managed to manage given the fact that I was miles away from the city and more in a hurry to get that settled than I was my open mic.

Despite the fact that you see a good bit of solar energy used in the Phoenix area it's still surprising you don't see even more. It felt like everything else was built around living in the sun. I know that sounds simplistically obvious so let me elaborate, I know it's a desert after all, but anywhere you go has a pool. In fact, having a pool isn't even a sign of luxury or high living, it's just a sign that you know you need the option to cool off when the temperatures reach somewhere above 120 degrees on a random Thursday in August. Most restaurants have misters outside. These neat little things hanging up above entrances putting mist out into the air to help give you a bit of reprieve from the solar torture. Despite the ability for a few feet underground to provide cool air not many homes have basements. There's an obviously false nature to the plants around you. Even the grass has a false feel to it, probably from the dryness. Grass is supposed to have a light fluffy nature to it, wet, but sharp. This felt as if it had just been in a toaster. The air itself is noticeably dry too. Most of the green looks forced, clearly contrasting on an unnatural level with the rustic orange and sandy browns that make up the majority of the areas rocky geography. The whole area as a city is generally easy to get around. There's an intelligent grid system to everything and their version of beltways interlink in an arguably more useful way than the ones I am used to. They do a few things really right. I just wish they did a few of the right things even more. I feel like the places most qualified to deliver solar energy to the rest of the country or surrounding region should be doing so and yet the topic doesn't even feel on the table. Overall the idea that climate change has gotten political is ridiculous. First of all, going back to my idea on not carrying generational guilt, none of us started the industrial revolution. Aside from a few quietly existing people here and there in minor pockets of the world, we all use tools of that revolution and contribute to the overall perpetuation of the issue at hand. I've never even understood why this was an issue. I mean, if you're rich and you want your beachside house to not be flooded one day by the rising waters of the ocean isn't that enough alone to inspire you to do the few things you can do to help the issue at hand? Even if only through incremental change? Much like walking around with a few extra pounds around the waist we are all a walking example of the decisions we've made over life and the society we live in is a living example of the consequences of society compounded over years. Only now things are compounding much faster than you realize as our societal and human desires have impacted our surrounding nature in such a way that it now threatens to impact us even more harshly.

Having a room for the night I set the alarm and went out driving around the outskirts of Scottsdale looking for a park or something to kill some time. In my meandering I went for a walk through the Boyce Thompson Arboretum where I got a text which warned me, *"Watch out for hornets. They killed a hiker yesterday."* - Debbie

"Uh. Wow. Okay, yeah. I'll keep my eyes out."

"Don't wanna worry you, but I had to tell you!" - Debbie

Hmm...kinda wish she had kept that one to herself. *"Thanks, I appreciate it. Oh, also I'm gonna be late getting by the house, probably after nine tonight. Is that okay?"*

"YEAH! Take your time!" - Debbie

Phoenix had an impressive comedy scene at the time so I figured finding an open mic wouldn't be hard based off the number of mics I had seen advertised on the local facebook. It hadn't dawned on me at first that their proximity to Los Angeles would create the type of environment conducive to performers jet setting around the SouthWest to get in front of any crowd willing to come in out of the year round sun for a few laughs. Of course getting there and getting up were always two separate battles. That was the weird part about this entire experiment. I was constantly facing the battle of being a man who brought on intrigue by being the guy willing to drive thousands of miles around the country for open mics, yet I was simultaneously viewed as a man who might be a major bullshit artist and thus looked at skeptically by those arranging the open mics.

When I got to the mic it looked like no other I had seen before. A wood planked picket fence surrounded a dirt filled property and the appearance of a frat house backyard. I know once a professional you should be able to do your job whenever and wherever, but there is what I would call a right time for comedy. It's not a specific hour per se, but it is AFTER a specific hour, and I've decided that hour is somewhere after 8 PM. Just seems like it all comes out better after the sun goes down. That's why even the places which granted you the favor of a 5 p.m. open mic did so behind a set of thick curtains to trap in as much darkness as possible; putting you in the mind of the comedian and the mind of the room all at once. As always once I found the person running the show I was met with a few questions, first and foremost, *"Do you know anyone here?"*

"Nah man. I messaged you guys on the Facebook page for the show, but I hadn't heard back from anyone yet. If there's no spots it's cool. I'll be in town a few days."

"We got room for one more. 3-5?"

"If you want 5 I can do 5."

"Perfect. Where you from?"

As the conversation continued I was introduced to another comedian who came to tell me about how he was doing a similar cross country trip but in a remodeled VW van. Seeing the comfort with which he traveled I became instantly jealous at his exceeding levels of comfort. Despite what he tried to lead onto I doubt he banged many girls in his van. Which is a shame, cuz he had it decked the fuck out and the bed had a surprising amount of headroom. There was even a mini-record player built into the wall. I always wonder what happened to that guy.

The first time any new comedians saw me I wanted to be remembered as funny. Especially those who saw me coming in from NYC and expected anyone who would have the idea to drive cross country would be doing so with a pretty tight set prepared. Eternally afraid that these guys would think of me as the guy from NYC who had no idea what he was doing. Once again the internal voice continued to creep in with a frightening thought that perhaps I wasn't worthy of that which I was doing. As if I would be remembered for succeeding or failing only. With succession only counting to some people if you made it to the highest levels. Although comedy was unique in this manner from the inside because there was never one best of all of them comedian. It's not like boxing where we can go against each other. There's plenty who are obviously better than others, and the elites of laughter, but no one agrees on a universal greatest whether considering it immediately or over time. Yet, how many comedians had I seen that I no longer remembered or barely considered on a daily basis? The trip was becoming more about making sure I was making a good impression than actually learning. It was like studying abroad. I was learning some lessons, but they weren't always the ones I could have hit by making sure to be on stage 20 times a week in some dark NYC basement. How would I know if I were chasing the right thing at the right time? Floating through the comedians and audience members gathering before the show I eventually got to talking to a guy named Daniel who was being featured tonight.

"Where did you say you're from?" - Patrick

"Sacramento." - Daniel

"How long a trip is that?" - Patrick

"It's usually a two hour flight. I drove though. Spent a few days in Vegas before." - Daniel

"Nice. I've been debating going up there or not." - Patrick

"You won't get on any good stages without planning ahead." - Daniel

"Good to know." - Patrick

"Yeah. You new here?" - Daniel

"First time performing in the area." - Patrick

He wasn't known, but he was seen as worth while around here. I knew as much as anyone a lot about being taken seriously is pretending like you know what the fuck you're doing. Making it to the rooftop of the Roosevelt hotel had taught me that long ago. After the show that same guy found me, "Hey I'm about to run, but when you can go up with me in Sacramento if your road trip takes you there. Can you do a clean set?"

"Yeah totally."

"Like PG? It's for a small town."

"Yeah."

"How much time you got?" In that he asked me the only question that really mattered. While quality of time is then to be assessed and measured, it's a matter of volume needed to entertain for large crowds.

"How much you need?"

"Can you stretch it to ten?"

"Of course."

"Cool. Send me a message, here's my info."

"I'll throw you a couple of bucks. You can crash at my place so you don't have to spend money on a hotel."

"Awesome."

After the show that night I made it to the address from earlier and parked at my final resting place for the day. They lived in a modest home with a pool out back, typical for most Phoenix area dwellings. Going in I was introduced to an assortment of four characters spread out around an island in the kitchen which poured over into the foyer that linked the front of the house with the living room; a place with an old school big screen television and a series of expired iPhones being used as cupholders and paperweights holding unstapled documents collecting dust.

Taking me down the hall she showed me a dark room with a fan and a noise canceling machine. I quickly dropped my things and followed her back out into the living room where I was met with an extra body that I swore wasn't there before. A slender girl with an Indian background and long silky hair to match. Through a few moments of conversation I came to find out that she was the ex-gf of the woman's son who was hosting me. I know that's confusing. Let me restate that. Her son had dated this girl for years, and somewhere recently he decided to break up with her. However, despite this separation here she was, maintaining a friendship with his mom. Which is fine by me, but it did seem a bit awkward and in some ways devious in nature. With no room to judge those housing me I sat around with them for an hour or so getting to know each other and eventually was invited to a pool party the next night.

"Where did you say it's at?"

"Oh just down the street. You should come by after your show."

"I might do that. Haven't had a chance to get in a pool in a while."

"Don't try and get in ours. We've not taken care of it in a while. Don't look at it during the day."

The next day I killed some time driving around before finding the next location for a performance. I was glad to find that the open mic for the night was taking place in a coffee shop. I was a fan of such places long before comedy was a requirement to visit, but the combo of caffeine and comedy pleased me from the beginning. Coffee shops have become the haven for people needing an office to escape to without the desire to be in the office as it has been set up. Some absorb the energy from those around them, others absorb the energy of bottomless cups of dark roast which cause their fingers to point and shoot like a man trying to meet a 1920's deadline at *The Globe* from behind a noisy typewriter. Then there's the rare gem who just thrives on others seeing them be productive. You can always tell them by where they sit in the room. Though at the end of the day all of you need to be tipping more if you're going to lounge around a four person table by yourself all afternoon. It's still a business, not your loft.

Once the nights show was over I went with a few of the comedians to a back room where they exited through a steel door to a small patio. Following them I came to a table where the majority of them had already sat down to have a cigarette. Soon enough the topic got to Trump, the election, and what we working on related to it. Over the last few months I had been asked my opinion on Trump more times than I would care to put into the narrative of this book. Though it's going to seem like I've put in a lot. With most of the questions hovering around whether or not I had any jokes about him in my act. From my shoes I didn't understand why we had to make jokes, the situation itself was such an obvious joke that I couldn't see what the hell else I was supposed to say. I know as a comedian perhaps I'm supposed to be able to form an opinion about anything, but at the same time aren't I allowed to take the time needed to form that opinion? Then what if I don't think my opinion has anything to add to this particular situation? As I thought about the possibilities I knew if he won it would make for a far more comical presidency than one with Hilary, not that the Clintons didn't open themselves up to plenty, but Trump was a showman like no other. The few times that I had even tried a joke in his name had furthered the suspicion that the crowds liked him more than most people were admitting in mass. Though his fans seemed to have a bit more of a sense of humor about themselves than most people do, they still kinda crossed their arms as you started talking about him. In fairness they still laughed when I first attempted my only good joke on the entire election, *"If the success of Donald Trumps campaign has taught me anything, it's that the hills don't just have eyes, they now have WiFi."*

Though I gained suspicions about the possibility back in Monterrey, it was in Phoenix that I first had the suspicion replaced with the realization that our country was about to elect Donald Trump as our next President. Not the possibility, the certainty. Which was an odd thing to come to terms with to say the least. I had grown up under a series of dichotomies, all of which conflicted with this as a rationale decision, but all of which understood that this was the natural conclusion to the road we had gone down and the fork we had created and the narrative shaped around it. By this time I had listened to people from a majority of the country express their willingness to give any type of different path a chance in the political sphere. Spoken from people even more disillusioned than I had become as a Political Science major and intern my senior year of college. Unfortunately the differences between our disillusionment with the system were about to be broadcasted on a grand scale.

The way Canadians had a weird relationship with Americans, I had a weird relationship with Donald Trump. No, not that type of relationship; we never crossed paths, but I used to hear him in the early 90's on *The Howard Stern Show* which at the time was broadcasts in the middle of the night. Though the very first time was probably in the movie Home Alone 2. As a celebrity he was one of those guys you heard about a lot or saw dropping in for a photo, but what people seemed to love about him was that he would just say whatever was on his mind with no filter in consideration to the outside world. In some ways it was very *American* to like Trump as he represented one of the things we exert almost annoyingly so, that is the desire to say whatever we want. I don't know if you remember politics before him, but there were some people who regularly said how they hated that politicians were like robots and didn't know how to exert themselves or how to play off script. Then comes this guy who was truly against a normalized way of doing things and somehow people were still surprised he was gaining momentum.

He was the one most capable of working the platforms and the situation which had been created given the current media environment. Though truth be told I was most ashamed of what he was making us look like. He made us look like a place where we accepted hating the other. Because we didn't. Nothing I knew about the nation I was from represented the view of us he was creating. It was created, fabricated, and honed in on by the necessities of mass media. Although I also found it odd that we were considering someone like Hilary Clinton who had somehow gone from the Presidents wife, to the head of the State Department, to Presidential Candidate. A hell of a trajectory if you ask me. If that's how I felt, imagine how the rest of the country was feeling?

For those who didn't understand why some people didn't like Hilary, maybe to some it's like hearing a model talk about insecurity, the messenger just doesn't fit the message. But then if one were to kill themselves we would suddenly have sympathy for these people who unknowingly had it *just like the rest of us*. The problem was, nothing like her felt like *the rest of us*. A problem which was fixed in many ways too late when she gave a candid and I dare say amazingly personable interview on the Stern Show somewhere after the election. Even telling

162

a funny story about the day of the inauguration. And if anyone deserved to have a laugh that, it was her.

Walking around asking one person after another I found that people felt as if they needed to be silent about their building conclusion. Which showed me that those asking the questions at the exit polls had no idea what was going on. There was a self-censoring happening in front of the cameras and to reporters that was soon to rip the rug out from everyone. For those that want to cancel him my argument against it would be you never want your crazy hidden, and you certainly never want it to feel like it has to hide and coerce in secret with it's other crazies. I'd support this by giving you an example of what most of his supporters said to me in private corners, usually going a little something like this, *"Well they call me crazy if I say anything, so I'll keep my mouth shut."* The thing I realized was the nobody was listening. They were only judging. Nobody understood. For the first time in my life, it felt like the mainstream media had no idea what was going on.

If the conversations weren't enough I could tell something was up from the crowds reaction to jokes about him as well. Though it may now be hard to recall, at first nobody really took him or his campaign seriously. Hell, at first even his own party didn't take him seriously. Truth was those politicians had never really had to battle a master of both theatre and persuasion. Say what you want about him. Most of it's probably true, but never may someone say that Donald Trump was politically inept on the stage. Even when he wasn't literally on a stage it was hard to touch him up there. The few times I took a stab at joking more and more about the possibility of handing the *keys to the bus* to a man such as Donald Trump I felt the crowd begin to separate from my understanding.

There were plenty of normal things about him as a politician, but it was weird to have a President who reacted to instigations in the manner that he did. Many odd beings have been elected, but a reality t.v. star really seemed like a new low. This coming from someone who was wildly entertained by Trump when he was serving as a guest on *The Howard Stern Show*. That's the definition of the fucking problem with him being President right there. He was great as the character on a morning radio show, not as leader of the free world. In some ways I admire his ability to do what he did. Then the rest of the time I despise him for exercising the power to do so.

The further down the rabbit hole we went the more I worried that my country was beginning to look like it was less aware of itself than it had been in a while. I hated to think my country was appearing not to know itself, especially as that thought made me further realize that it meant we hadn't really been talking to each other because we had no idea the *other* side felt like this. Until this time I don't think we fully realized how differently some of us were living and coming up in the world. We had so many identities evolving at one time that it was inevitable that a moment like this would happen. Each one of us capable of falling victim to the circus of personality.

Overall he was one of the least active Presidents in my life time beyond creating a lot of headlines, but I would argue that as a candidate the thing he did most effectively was to cause people who had never watched the news before to make it their new hobby. Which is ironic because on the whole I would say the press had no idea how to deal with him. He was one of the few people who took canceling and said *fuck it, not listening to you* in a time when enough people were getting tired of the overused playbook of the sideline cancelers. Through this, this motherfucker somehow managed to not only market himself into the presidency, he also did so while going up against one allegation after another. Now from one end of the spectrum this could be viewed as a wildly stupid decision on the part of the American people. However, on another side, it could also be viewed as the type of thing which happens in the absence of a variety of rational options. In my opinion by trying to cancel him they did the opposite and fed him more attention than any one person can probably process, and without him having to pay a dime for it.

His campaign was the only time I could ever recall my grandma taking an interest enough in politics to bring it up with me on the phone. She despised how crude he was. Truth be told I never understand how he got away with making fun of a mentally challenged man on live television. Perhaps that showed just how much Hilary Clinton wasn't landing with the broader audience. I mean if her campaign had half a brain they would've seen his numbers after that public gaffe and maybe started to switch up the strategy instead of ignoring him as some self-destructive ignoramus; unaware how many people were open to the idea because they like the idea of a *businessman* running the country or how he had positioned himself in their minds as that particular solution. For the record I don't say that as a means of making fun of his voters. I totally understand why people voted for him, especially people already in his party, that's how politics goes. I wouldn't expect a life long Republican to vote for any Democratic candidate because of a rogue candidate who still promised to protect what they saw as the most core of values. That just makes sense.

The most unfortunate side of him was the fact that he never understood that at one point he left the role of playing Donald Trump and entered into the role of President of the United States, which is supposed to have the same duty as a judge considering matters of great importance and consequence, and the same hope of separation that would come from ones ego and personality in those moments of decision, as well as a separation from the projection of an ego during the time in which you're meant to embody the position of that of the ultimate diplomat serving under the representation of the people of the United States of America to the world in the era in which the nation finds itself. The thing different about him and a comedian is that when Trump made it into presidency he became somewhat bound to the promise of trying to speak to the entire audience, the only true projector to *the American people* as the term is used. Meanwhile a comedian can hold true to whatever he has been saying all along. A politician is one sided, but a President is supposed to be uniting. That's a step which is to be taken by everyone the moment they get into office.

Despite his popularity one thing continued to give me some sort of hope about the future. Having been abroad so much in my life it was impossible to avoid Trump as a brief conversation piece with the international numbers in my phone. In those conversations I was always somehow probed about Trump and what was going on in our country. In a lot of ways it was ultimately flattering to see how the world was looking down on us for our situation, all ultimately aware that we were missing the mark this go around like someone willingly entering a failed marriage. Which meant deep down they expected better out of us. As I believe many of us inside the country did as well. I don't think I'm the only person who found a reason to ponder how these were the best two candidates among a country of 350 million people.

One of the most American things about Trump was the way he became a getter of attention for the next four years, dominating the news and the conversation of people from all sides of the spectrum on a daily basis, igniting vigor in both for a duality of reasons. As time went on I began to wonder how much of it was the headline creators pulling and pushing us in a certain direction or how much of it was just the perfect mix of history, technology, and our taste for the sensational combining to create the perfect moment of societal division? In my opinion we probably have the media to blame more for Trumps election more than any other factor. With blame being placed on their part in being a willful participant, like the paper pushers in the Nazi regime. They jumped on everything he said like a kid stirring things up between people after a fight was nearly finished. Without first realizing that their job is to inform those who are busy holding this world together and don't have time to keep up with the nitty gritty of each thing in the world, but still live off a summary of the papers finest. Overall I wonder how many clicks they got and how much money in advertising they generated despite their apparent lack of love for him and his politics. Would his campaign not have quickly fizzled out if it weren't for the media making him the biggest story every night? This type of hypes makes it to where in the long run I worry that his success will drive others who are merely famous for being famous into the path of running for office in the near future. A journalist doesn't have to unite us, but they certainly shouldn't be the ones dividing us for ratings.

We've become a people incredibly numb to anything being considered crazy. We did so in such a short amount of time because I can remember a time when it was scandalous to consider a woman's breast popping out on live t.v., and while that still has an element to surprise to it, it by no means draws the same shock as it once did. I don't even know what could really surprise people anymore. Our eyes have seen it all. Though as far as the grand scales of tragedy goes most of us have only seen photos of the worst it can be. Perhaps a few of us have read the words and accounts of those times, but few of us have ever seen true struggle. I know, I know, don't minimize or maximize someone else's struggle, it's all struggle, blah, blah blah. I don't know about that. I got attacked by a Rottweiler once. Teeth in the legs, all that jazz. I've also been attacked, if you can call it that, by a Maltese when I was younger. They're not the same. Not even fucking close. By the way, you ever think about how intertwined dogs are in our lives and in this world we inhabit? So much so that I'm able to draw nearly any sort of comparison between them in order to make a point about this that and the other?

In a nutshell I would say his presidency created a lull in the comedy world after and towards the end of his era. People were just going after what made them mad. Everyone was on the same train. That's what didn't make sense to me. Despite the fact that I totally understand that it is anger which usually invokes some of the best art and discussion. In regards to Hilary it seemed like no one wanted to hear any jokes about this woman for fear that someone might point out something that was fallible and funny about her. Now truth be told it made no sense to me, we've always made fun of our politicians. That's what you do. Pick on both sides. Though I hate that we always say *both* as if there are only two sides when politics are far more multi-sided.

I don't know if the nation is ready to laugh at it yet. I mean, we elected a reality TV star to be the President of the United States. Now if that's not the definition of a whole slew of terms, ironic being one of them, then I don't know what is. For some his election feels so long ago that it's almost impossible to remember what the country was like before it happened. After his election I felt a combination of ways. As stated before, being a student of political science I had long been a fan of the office of the Presidency and what it represents. That being said I remember when he won I had this weird feeling of sadness and annoyance that there was now some lack of respect to the office which I had grown up admiring. Like there would be an esoteric forever where every President after would be a President *after* Trump. Said as an observer of politicians and as a general supporter of the Democratic side of several agendas post college. That being said I tried to understand why it was that people liked Trump. Because his popularity spoke more about our divide than it did our differences.

Enough politics, I mean it. But, it was important to lay a foundation for where we were as a country at that time. Just in case this book turns out to be one of those that last forever you know? What if by then Trump has rewritten all of the history books and just says he was the best President ever. Best to keep stuff like this around to fact check.

After the show and a slew of internal political rambling I met my host at the pool party she had mentioned the night before. There I was introduced to the family hosting it and quickly realized they already had been given the chance to develop some impression of me in advance. I imagine the fault of the very girl sitting across from me. Granted I didn't do myself any other favors when I started talking about my comedy tour. I think the idea of anyone saying they were on tour gave the impression that they were getting paid on the regular, but before I could explain my truths the conversation had gotten far from the possibility, *"Come on man. When can we see you? Are you on YouTube? Bet you got a lot of new material with Trump in the race..."*

Modern society had become so demanding; there was no time to grow, no time to evolve. Anyone coming to see me would watch me for a few moments and make their judgements about my future based on that momentary observation. Still I gave a few of them my info and decided to leave it at that. Letting them know that I could be seen at an open mic the following night. As the pool dwellers slowly left and went inside I followed my new Indian friend back to the house and to our own private pool under the cover of a moonless sky and a poorly lit patio. Finding myself to be right about her deviant ways I was soon wrapped up in a conversation of flirtations and futures that would get us to laughter and eventually in a spot where she was trying to push me into the pool. Bracing myself with all power on my right foot I fought off her attempts and gave myself enough space between to ensure her long ass arms wouldn't make their way around me until I had moved a bit further from the pool.

"Stop it! Not while my phone is in my pocket."

"You have two seconds to get rid of it."

"God damnit. Your friends have some towels I can use then?"

"I'm sure they do."

"Okay great." And with that I dove into the pool and brought myself back to the edge before opening my eyes and and looking up to see her standing above me. *"Oh COME ON! It's not fun if you push YOURSELF in!"* Reaching up and wrapping my hands around her ankles I uttered, *"So you getting in or do I gotta pull ya?"* Before answering I felt the tensing of her Achilles as she went up on her toes and my grip eased to make room for her feet to follow her body as it leaped over my head and dove into the water behind me. Afterwards we got out and she laid next to me as I started to tease her hair. It was the soft and silky type.

"You don't think it's weird you hang out with your ex's mom?"

"It's not weird. We like each other."

"And where is her son exactly?"

"He's off at college."

"Okay."

"Do you have some weird attachment to this room?"

Kissing me, she stared to go through the routines which I'm sure she had performed in this same backyard before. *"No, but how about I show you a few things I like about it..."*

"Nah. We should probably stay outside..."

"Just trust me. We used to do this all of the time. They won't hear a thing."

"Wait, why don't we go out to your little secret shack over there?"

With her face pressed against my neck she uttered, *"If we do that the flood lights will come on and then everyone wakes up."*

"I'm gonna be sure to leave this on the review page."

As I was putting things back in their place after my morning coffee I was interrupted by the man of the house as he approached in a raggedy blue shirt and a pair of red night shorts. *"If you wanna gimme a ride to pick my car before ya leave I'll take ya to breakfast."*

"Uh yeah. Lemme just make some room up front."

Having already arranged my car for departure I shifted some things around and then asked if I could leave a bag at the back end of his driveway and pick it up later. A request to which he unsurprisingly obliged. Sitting at the diner he started to belt out the thoughts commonly expressed by those wrapping up their forties. *"Kid, you don't know how lucky you are."* Uncertain how to respond to *kid* I looked over at him and just continued eating my sandwich. No offense taken, I just found it odd to be considered a child by someone now that I was 30, though I suppose the relativity of age goes in both directions. We chowed down for the next few minutes in relative silence. He had recently gotten back into comedy listening to the slew of podcasts now available at his fingertips. Sitting across from me he slurped on his spoon as he uttered, *"She's a crazy one isn't she?"* Subsequently alarmed I gave pause to my eggs with a, *"Huh?"*

"My wife. She's a wild one I know. Love her though."

"Oh yea. She's something else..."

As I drove out I started to listen to a podcast with some investment solutions guy as a means of putting something new in my brain. He knew what he was doing. He spoke very fast, as someone who would after five or six cups of coffee and a few martinis. By the time 2 A.M. rolled around I was finally starting to feel the need to sleep and so I toughed it out another thirty miles or so until I came upon a rest stop just shy of the California border, making sure to throw out any avocados I had with me before I attempted to cross.

BREAK A LEG

Days: 45
Miles Traveled: Approx. 6,500
Stages: 17

Los Angeles, California
May 2016

*"It is not be your fault,
but it is now your problem..."*

O ne of the most satisfying moments in my life happened when I took a Saturday morning drive with my grandma out to some lake in the West Virginia panhandle. Not a big lake, just a tiny lake on some back road hidden amongst the endless hills. I didn't even know the lake existed until we stumbled upon it. While on that drive we pulled up to the water and sat for a few minutes talking. At one point she shifted her gaze and stared out the window slowly widening the smile on her face. *"Grandma what are you looking at?"* Without looking to me she replied, *"That tree is so beautiful. I've never seen anything like it."* Seeing that someone in their early 90's could still see novelty somewhere out in the world in something as beautifully simplistic as a tree created an impact on me in that moment. Somewhere later in that same day we stopped off in Panera Bread and shared a croissant and a few bags of chips while we sat and talked about whatever I could think to ask. At one point I was showing her something someone had written to me in French on the inside of my notebook and after translating it she took notice of the following page where I had a list of a few quotes jotted down. One of them was the one which has made it to the top of this page. One which caught her eye with the words, *"It is not your fault, but it is now your problem..."* Perhaps it had something to do with her extensive experience as a nurse, but I always saw her as so knowledgeable that I was shocked to be able to teach her anything. She was such a well read woman, well traveled too. She had become a nurse early in her twenties and used the vocation to see the world long before it was safe to do so. She spent nearly 30 years of her life living in Africa working in a small village up in the high dessert of Cameroon. She did all of that, and she had never seen this quote before. I bring this up because my grandma was on my mind a lot when I was making it to California. She had encouraged me to come here years ago and still promoted it as the place where she decided on what she wanted to do with the rest of her life as a young nurse. No surprise as the California dream had long before been the place for adventurers and wishers alike.

I've always wondered if California was the place with the dream because it was the final frontier or because of the weather. If you ask me it has a lot more to do with the weather. It's not just nice, its really nice. It's so close to everything you could possibly want to do. I mean, you're still in your little California bubble, but you can do almost any activity in the world within the seemingly unlimited area of Southern California. All along the coast there is a noticeable influence of the Spanish language and Mexican culture riddling everything from the Street names to the abundance of taco shops dotting the area. And no matter how many taco shops they put up, it's not likely to ever be enough. Although the people in Austin had been happy to tell me they wished for no new people to enter their neighborhoods, Los Angeles seemed to hold no fantasy about getting smaller anytime soon. The state with the Golden Coast had long ago realized it was the Western lighthouse for cultural exchange in the United States and the stadium kept filling.

I drove around my first morning rediscovering the City of Angels. Though it has gone previously unmentioned in my works, I lived here for a while when I was twenty-four, departing normal life for six months to explore the Golden Coast and absorb all I could from the locals and the industry supporting the cities entire existence; dreams. Doing as we usually do, I took a ride back to my old neighborhood on the borders of Santa Monica and Venice Beach, seeing a completely new set of cars and backyard accessories than when I had lived there. The citrus tree was in season and it looked like this time it was lemons. Taking myself another two blocks and then taking a right I made it down to Rose Boulevard and then down a few more blocks until I parked in front of the original Golds Gym at Venice Beach. There I saw a setting much different than the one I had left. The early morning streets were lined with VW vans and other assorted RVs housing the recently homeless and the permanently transient with generators fueling them from the outside. Germany might have created the Volkswagen, but America created the culture around them, their vans in particular.

In a lot of ways culture is what develops any time that a group of people become bound by something beyond the obvious outward expressions of race or appearance and come together with the decision

173

that they are all about this one way of life. At first glance we think of it as a type of people bound by some historical significance strung along through collective stories, but culture can be way more than cultural. A modern example of this would be gym culture. Something that even among itself has many niche categories of practitioners and preferences. With some for cross-fit, some for physical recovery, and others filled with bronzed men absorbing the eyes of the sun and pumping away for something just short of ego. Seems any group of people sitting together eventually start their own culture and form their own language around the nation of interests within they operate, often more specific the deeper the niche tends to be.

As much as they could turn homelessness into a lifestyle, California is the only place that could have turned health food into a culture. Which works out great for me because it's probably my favorite cuisine. Don't get me wrong, I'm not talking seaweed and tofu, I mean shit like smoothies and juices and maybe an açaí bowl once in a while. It's weird to call health food a culture. I mean, why the fuck should eating not be healthy? I never really understood that. Which may have come from my love of Arnold's statement about food or really anything you're putting in your body; it's either food or poison, there is no other category. Be as body positive as you want, those are the facts. The smoothie shops out here are really cool. Granted they can cost up to $14, which is still similar to a lunch in any other city, and at least a lunch in a healthier packaging, but still it feels weird paying that much for something you can gulp down in under a minute. A thought which I'm sure sounds stupid to one of the better health idols this world has to offer. I don't know if there's an immigrant I am more proud to call an American than Arnold Schwarzennegar. Admittedly part of my bias towards badass films and the gym cultures of Venice Beach. Some of its largest proponents were foreign born, but it was Southern California where they all came together to create the Mecca of their making. Like many truly American things, the characters were an assortment of those already here, and those soon to come.

When connecting the dots in reverse, it's often hard to decide whether your memory is being selective or whether it was the universe which selected you. The same can be said about my comedy career as the memories of my younger days point to the above average handful of occasions when I ran into famous people, most of them being comedians. It was only a few blocks away from where I was now in

Venice where I once met one of the greatest minds to ever grace the comedic world in an interaction that went something like this, *"Norm?"*

"Hey man, what's up?"

If you don't know who Norm is then this will mean basically nothing to you, but he sounded exactly like you've always heard him talking. Which should be obvious, but it always seemed like he had some sort of affect to his speech. It would be like meeting Mike Tyson to hear that's how he really sounds and still not believing it. By this time in life it had become oddly normal for me to come across and meet comedians of a variety of fame. Whether it was the one sitting in a back alley on a dark Manhattan night, or the one standing outside a college town pub smoking a cigarette in a place where I was lucky to know the bartender and eventually received a text telling me to come by. It's like I didn't see it back then when the world was smacking me in the face with this world. I lived blocks from a club where Jay Leno performed on a regular basis and never even saw him. I don't know what was wrong with me. Not that I woulda known how to make it work in LA even if I had been on the right path. NYC feels like the place that you get famous by the people, LA feels like the place where you get famous by the machine. California had a separation just wide enough from New York that it was able to separate itself from the East coast identity and establish its own broadcasting ways, soon becoming the place for film over television. Over time we created so many movies that we projected every possible version of life to the world and each other; providing a voice to each individual. However, the number of possibilities to be found in the human experience are endless. Merely for the fact of the saying which states,*"no man enters the same river twice."* Or some shit like that. As the river flows so it constantly melds together, remaining in an every changing state of shift.

Los Angeles was one of my favorite places to walk around, and that's not just because of my joy for taking a stroll. It's also the best place to practice the art of window shopping. With each store advertising something which could only be found there. Usually it also matched everything else around it. Every now and then you come across a store with an old mattress frame set next to seven pink fluffy pillows attached to a 100 year old wooden table. The cars here were so much more colorful too. A sharp contrast to the many white face buildings that you would see doing their best not to absorb too much of that famous California sun.

Long before I was born the culture of the 70's took over as one of the primary images of an American era and still floats in the minds of those far and wide. There was a time when you could get lost in the 70's and it meant something completely different but just as cool. It was the first time that they were able to get out and escape the life which had been assigned to them via the situations of birth. Over time we created Rock and Roll. Well, that's kinda false, the Blues created Rock and Roll. Once that was done we exported the shit out of it after putting every set of bells and whistles on the side before.

My first night in Los Angeles was weird, I made the cardinal mistake of inviting some people to an open mic at a spot I had never been to before, even worse I agreed to sit with them. Added to the fact that the people I was with were not really into comedy, and they had shit to do the next day. So you know, apathy, awkwardness, and an urgency to leave all combined into one lovely four top at the bar in the back. If there was ever a time where I wish I could have someone exercise their rudeness it would have been now because I wanted them there about as much as they actually wanted to be there. Maybe even less. When my set finally happened I found myself once again in a very small spotlight and was forced to stand almost completely still as I glanced up towards the offending brightness.

The next morning I woke up to a text delivering a bit of bad news. Another friend had overdosed. Some type of opioid. The name of which doesn't really matter. They were all the same anyway. Each with a new fancy name and a series of pharmaceutical drug dealers standing behind them with billions of dollars for advertising and enough ink to write prescriptions for as long as they could keep you hooked. By now we all know how the story goes. Sadly this type of thing had happened more and more these days, but this time it was someone who I knew to be a drug user before their death. Last time it was someone who caught me off guard, as much by their death as their use. I should have said something this time around. How many times have I not been able to tell a person what should be said? It would concern me one day if I had a situation in my family where my children couldn't talk to me. I sat there hoping I had never been the person from whom people felt they needed to keep their honest opinions. We're allowed to tell someone that they're overdoing it with drugs, but never with food. We can shame someone who has rings under their eyes from drug use, but ask someone about their double chin because you're concerned with their health and all of a sudden you're a fat-shamer. Apparently the only time it's okay to make anyone feel bad about something they do that is detrimental to their health is when they're an inch from death. Most of the world would tell you not to shame someone for anything. Well, that's ridiculous because sometimes shame is a part of accountability. I looked in my Facebook and hoped to find that I had not ignored some long attempted shot at contact. Truth is I felt worse to see not only had we spoken, but I had completely forgot about it. He sent me a *lol* to a joke he liked and I had never responded. Now I would never get to. Much like the politicians and regulators who have turned their backs on prosecuting the corporate pushers of these drugs for fear of losing their yearly donations allowing their corrupt asses to stay in office. I too had put a friend in need in the back seat hoping someone else was handling the problem.

When I had lived here early in my twenties I was unaware of any buzz surrounding a comedy club at the top of Sunset. My lack of previous awareness aside there was a clear influx of people hoping to get themselves on the stage in front of the likes at *The Comedy Store*. It was only after a few big names started to reappear around 2013 that the masses began to regain interest in this entertainment landmark. Which is cool to know, but makes no difference with regards to my past as I doubt I would have been urged to show up had I heard the doors were open. The one thing I had going for me at the moment was that I knew the inside of the club from a time before. At least as much as one can know a place they've been to once. My first and only time in side was somewhere around 2014 when I helped a friend and a dog move cross country before starting grad school and starting her first business.

When I got to *The Comedy Store* I sent a text to Bobby informing him I had arrived. A few moments later a man in a grey hoodie came up to me with a face worn hard by the previous 29 years. He then took me aside and tried to be casual about our introduction and make us look like old friends as he whispered into my ear, "*Look. Keep your mouth shut and don't tell anyone you know me. Just go write your name down and text me which number you are on the list. I'll do what I can to get you up. Make sure you do your tightest 5.*" I went from there and joined the list of comics waiting to jot down their names and found myself a space next to number 41. There I wrote my name as legibly as possible and sent him a text to which he simply responded, "*Okay*".

As I paced around the parking lot I waited for the next thirty minutes while a series of comics stood in circles smoking cigarettes and jiving with one another. Surrounded by chalkboard walls with the names of famed comedians signed in a chalk font around the entire building made me feel a bit like a fraud and honored at the same time. I looked around and felt a bit out of place. In some ways I didn't belong. But in other ways I was the only one who belonged. I had just driven 3,000 miles. Why not a shot? As the time passed eventually two previously unrecognized comedians came out from the front door with a list in their hands and began to read off the numbers of those chosen. As the numbers started at 2 and worked their way up to 27 I began to feel a bit uneasy at my chances. *"Okay. And lastly we've got number 37 and number 41. Doors open in 10 minutes. Your order will be posted on the door"*. Holy shit. Hearing my number I was suddenly struck with the deep reality that I was about to perform at one of the most famous clubs in the country, albeit an open-mic broadcasting to a room of mainly comics. Nonetheless I prepped my best stuff, only needing 3 minutes from my 5. Honestly, I didn't know for sure what my best stuff was, not to them at least. Even my best stuff had failed more than a time or two when I found a crowd indifferent to the topics I had to offer. I knew what was funny, but how was I supposed to know what was funniest? Isn't it always dependent on who's listening? Though tonight of all nights some of the best could be listening. There was even a chance, though small it was, that Mitzi Shore would be there at her club listening to my set. Just the possibility that one of the greatest cultivators of comedy could see me was all the reason for why I had come to Los Angeles. It was either here or New York at the end of the day.

Whether you're one of the funny or one of the fake, there's a lot of standing around in this game. Though not in the same way that there is in Hollywood in general. When I was younger I got the chance to work on an indie film set for about a week and I quickly saw that a lot of people want to look like CEO. The numbers of those who actually wanted to do the work to deserve the title were far fewer. Still, so many of us just standing there waiting, hoping to be seen by the right person at the right moment. When Aryana arrived I felt a sense of comfort that I didn't know I had been needing. I don't know if there's anything needed more than support when you're out there trying to risk your ass at something you don't have a clue about. I would have hated to admit it to you then, but at the time I felt nervous. Only because of the favor involved. Not that I couldn't do it. Just the first time pressure of having someone watch me from a far who had vouched for me. I wondered all evening about why that guy had decided to stick his neck on the line and let me go up like that. Even that sentence above kinda bothers me. I wasn't risking my ass the way a soldier does, or even someone working on the side of the road in the middle of the night. I was only risking my reputation and my chance at a secure future. Seeing as I was still largely alone in this world, the risk seemed small.

As a performer I didn't have what the generation before me had, I had never seen crowds of seventy-thousand people moved by one person, or one song. I grew up thinking of entertainment happening in small rooms and basements, but *this* was the room of rooms. The red curtains, the dark hallways, it all felt like somewhere worth being. It was such an honor to be introduced by Joey Diaz. I knew deep down in meant nothing beyond a happy coincidence to an already serendipitous day. I hadn't gotten in this spot because I was particularly talented. I wasn't some known guy. I was just lucky enough to know a guy who knew a guy. Nonetheless, I was thrilled to have the opportunity at a time when I knew I had the right material. In staying with the goal of this trip I wanted to perform new stuff, but this was not the place. I needed to do my best regardless of the fact that it was just an open-mic. Though no one coming around that night would know it's an open-mic since the illusion was being created that it was a show filled with qualified individuals showcasing their best.

After introduced by Joey I rambled for a moment and then almost immediately lost the crowd with a poor choice of words. Nothing of the offensive nature, I just mistakenly referred to the place as a basement and then called it shitty; something which the open-mic crowd did not like being thrown at their honored club. I should have used the word creepy instead of shitty. That was my bad. I knew it the moment it came out. Immediately I made the people turn against me. It took a minute before I even had a chance of getting them back. That and the daylight peering through the windows behind me did enough to dampen any of my early attempts at comedy. Still I was where I was and I had the words *The Comedy Store* behind me. And to a guy who started less than a year ago, that meant something to me. After getting off stage I went and sat next to Aryana and watched the next comedians go through their own moments of glory. I don't know if I've ever felt a more natural high than the excitement I felt after leaving *The Comedy Store*. It was a weird feeling to know I was finally doing something which was gaining momentum. I had never really gained that before. At least not from an accomplishment or series of steps. Sure, picking up Spanish had been somewhat of a series of steps, but it just felt like something I was doing as I went along. This drive, this push. It was all with the most deliberate of intentions. I was so hyped. No part of me wanted to leave. The energy in that building was drawing me into every corner. Each time gaining a new perspective on the stage in front of me. Going back into the main room I stood in the back and watched one of the final open mic'ers going up to a room three times as full as the one I had performed for. Not noticing the crowd around me I watched for a minute or two until my attention was interrupted by a guy next to me who leaned in and said, *"Hey man, you were up there earlier weren't you?"*

"Yeah. I was the third one up."

"You got good ideas. Keep writing."

"Thanks. I will."

"Good good. That's all you gotta do. Keep writing." As I went to say a bit more to him the final act finished and Joey Diaz got back on the stage where he uttered the sentence, *"And now tonights headliner, Preacher Lawson!"* At which point the guy next to me shook my hand and said, *"Later bro"* and rushed himself to the front of the room where he got on stage to an applauding crowd.

I had always heard that I needed to be bad for a while, but if I was already funny to some people, didn't I just need to figure out how to capture that side of me? I suppose part of making it was deciding if you were gonna hone towards the masses or zone in on your niche. I've always hated self-defeating language, mine or anyone else's, too often our uncertainties are fed better between our two ears than from the funnels of sound delivering those same messages from the outside world. Which is to say, don't talk shit on yourself if you can avoid it.

Although I wanted to stay at the club for as long as possible I had agreed to drive Aryana and a friend of hers to some house party on the other side of the Valley. Sticking to my word I piled them in my front seat and made the trip while still riding on the internal high from the performance that meant so much to me. Once at the party I found myself wondering around the backyard amongst a group of strangers until I was approached by a dog and a girl attached as an owner. At the moment I was unaware how this dog would come into play at the end of my summer. Long story short, they knew my roommate back in

NYC. I learned this one night while going through some recent clips of a pilot he and his friend had been shooting; one of the many artistic exchanges I noticed Nick take part in during my time living in NYC. I'm still not sure if there was ever anyone who worked harder than that guy. Worked harder or planned better. Guy had it going on. Anyway, this one time we're sitting there going through these videos and I notice this dog jump into the bed in one of the clips. As I looked at it I got this weird feeling of dejavu mixed with like *'Hey, I know that dog,'* which is an odd thought in general, but especially weird when it gives you the rickets of memory, and I suddenly had chills running up my arm as I pieced together the night and turned to Nick asking him, *"Hey man, have you ever been to this house where they filmed this?"* To which he replied, *"Yeah, I was there this summer."* Clamping down on my lip I looked over at him hesitantly, *"Do they have a weird painting of Larry David in their kitchen by chance?"*. His voiceless response and wide eyes confirmed our mutual friend and furthered my belief that the world is not small once you start asking around. This was the night I was at that house.

Luckily the party provided me with a place to stay and I was able to wake up to an early sunrise and a cool breeze. Seeing no one to say bye to I got in my car and headed down to the beach. One of my favorite parts of Californian life is seeing someone just doing their thing on the beach in the morning. Along this coast the locals used the beaches more than most places, but it's not like they use the water. Most people just hang out on the beaches. A few of the brave who ventured into the water did so in a wet-suit. Despite all of my talk yesterday about the wonders of fitness and the California lifestyle I didn't actually end up working out or going to the gym for anything beyond sightseeing. So my morning started by heading to the gym, I wanted to get in a workout and take a shower before meeting with Aryana and her roommates. Although I shouldn't have said anything about my workout plan that morning as I soon found that even when you plan for others they don't always plan for you.

"Hey I'm almost there. You ready?" - Patrick

"Hey not yet! Sorry we're running a little late." - Aryana

"Any chance I can still get inside to use the bathroom?" - Patrick

"Absolutely not! If she sees you on her camera she's gonna ask me who the hell you are." - Aryana

"Are you fucking serious? Whatever. I'm gonna go find a coffee shop or

something. Hit me up when you're done fucking around." - Patrick

I was in such a hurry, I had to pee so bad. I don't think you can understand. I pulled over to the side of the road and quickly googled coffee shops in the area, knowing they were one of the few places where I could probably find a public bathroom. Had I been back in my hometown I would have found some side-back road and just walked into the grass and taken a good long piss. Instead I was forced to drive another 1.4 miles where a *Coffee Bean & Tea Leaf* sat at the corner of Wilshire and something else. Coming from the south side of the street I pulled up til I found an opening between two cars and parallel parked with only two turns of the steering wheel. Scrambling to find my debit card I collected a few dollars and the card before getting out of the car. As I opened the door I got out and then slammed the door, keeping my hand on the top of the car as I looked to either side of the street. After allowing a blue Mercedes to cruise by I looked once more to my right and then sprinted across the street. I was almost at the line of parked cars across the asphalt when I was suddenly hit from behind by something forceful and constant. Then in one seemingly fluid motion I was spun around and planted onto the ground where both my feet laid out in front of me as my hands caught me from behind and lightly blunted the impact from my ass to the ground. In a moment of disbelief I looked forward as the side of a grey Honda Civic moved in front of me. Luckily I was able to pull my left leg more towards my waist, but the left didn't respond as quickly and all I could hear my brain say was *"Oh Fuck. No."* As I watched the front tire of the previously mentioned car roll over my ankle, somehow not squashing the entirety of my leg as one might imagine happening in a cartoon. The car in this moment stopped completely and I found myself rolling on the ground under the perception of pain without the actual feeling. Keeping my eyes closed I continued to tell myself *"It's not broken, it's not broken"* and barely noticed that my aviators had somehow flown off me and were now in the middle of the road where they would soon be hit by the next passing vehicle. I heard the car door open, but I never saw the driver get out, all I heard was the panicked voice of a teenager standing over me as he said, *"Uhh it's probably just sprained"*. To which I replied in a long drawn out, *"NO IT IS NOT"* as I continued to hold onto my leg and rock back and forth, then furthering my seriousness by taking my fist and attempting to slam it against the hood of his car only to miss and land itself furiously on the asphalt, adding to the cuts my skin would receive that day. *"OUCH! FUCK!"*. Over the next minute or so a few people came running to my assistance and one woman in particular made herself more than useful by asking me what she could get me. The only thing I could think of at the moment was ice. Pleading for some ice I watched as she ran off in her high heels and blue pant suit, quickly fading into the blur of existence happening around me. Then, I swear no more than thirty seconds later, she reappeared with a giant bag of ice without any labels on it. Even in my adrenaline blunted pain I remember wondering where the hell had she gotten this ice from and wondering if she paid for it.

"That's fine, bones weren't made for cars..."

No part of me was okay being that guy in the middle of the street.

"Stop moving," said the kind man hovering above me.

"No," I said, scooting myself a few more inches to the left, *"I can't be that dude."*

"What dude?"

"That mother fucker blocking traffic in the middle of Los Angeles at noon on a fucking Friday. Ahh. Fuck."

My hands braced myself, with most of my weight on the thickest part of my palm, the coral like nature to the road now more apparent than before. Continuing to scoot away I picked up my right leg at the calf and perched it on top of the lefty blowing me to drag my legs across the concrete without aggravating the injury and cringed each time my ankle stuttered across the asphalt.

In the ambulance I lost control for a moment as I remembered the series of injuries which had plagued my leg over the last few years, the knee cap hit by the corner of that chair that I must have asked that man to move at least five times before it finally struck me, the dog that bit me, the toe that was stubbed to the point of breaking in the middle of a late night bathroom run. All of those memories spurred up inside of me at once and their fury was let out with one quick swing of my clenched right fist against the side panel shelving of the ambulance. *"It's always my fucking leg. Fuck!"*

"Now that you've got that out of your system....can you.. calm down?"

I know hospitals in the US have a reputation for being slow and lacking this and that and all these complaints, but I gotta be honest, I felt like everything happened pretty quick. I didn't even get the idea they wanted me there particularly long. The guys were all pretty cool too, especially the one who re-wrapped my leg. He laughed at something I said, but it was so situationally funny that I can't translate it here for you. I think I told them something along the lines of how I would be able to use the *"break a leg"* line for some weeks to come.

"You should come see me tonight."

"You're going up tonight?" With a squint in my eyes I responded as he wrapped under my calf, *"Yup."*

"Alright. Where you gonna be?"

"I don't know yet. When you guys finish up I'll start looking for some shows."

"Here man. Just lay still for a moment."

Once I was able to get a few moments to myself I asked the guys if I could finally use the bathroom and then so was able to wobble my ass over to the bathroom. Standing there in the stall I was a little frustrated at the evaluation that I could have waited to bee pee for a very long time. Even as it ran out of me it barely felt like I had to go. I had lost feeling. I had lost contact with the feeling I had so long ago with the need to pee. It was like it had completely gone away.

I quickly started thinking of all of the things I had hoped to do that I would now have to cast to the side. It's amazing how quickly your mind can make a shift when something big happens. It's like a lot of my friends told me when they hear me say that I *don't know how they do it* after seeing them raising kids and making money where they never did before, *"Once it's a problem, you figure it out"*. Never before had I been in such a situation where suddenly the urgency of the moment caused me to cast aside any and all feelings of distraction that didn't have to do with healing my leg. Prior to getting injured I had held such high hopes that I could see a few of the National Parks. I even wanted to visit Wes on this go around, but with my leg what was the point. I realized at this moment that I had to give in to the fact that the next 40 days did not belong to me, at least not in the manner that I was used to. It's funny how quickly your priorities can and must change once a moment like this hits you. There's no denying it and early acceptance is the one thing I attribute to successfully dealing with this during all of the hardships of which you are about to hear. Hardships is perhaps a tough way to put it, but inconvenient for sure. Either way it wasn't easy to deal with without having a lot of money.

In the middle of a text updating a friend on the day I was interrupted by a doctor giving me a debriefing on my situation from hereon out. In this set of instructions and guidelines I was given a prescription for 45 days worth of painkillers. When he went to hand me the piece of paper giving me such permissions I kept my hands to myself and thought for a moment how to phrase my next idea. I was only a day separated from discovering a good friend had died from the results of a long road which had started as a mild addiction to opioids. Knowing myself and my love of anything altering I decided to opt myself out of the possibility. The most logical reason was that I flat out didn't want to try to trust myself for a month. Even though I was more of a fan of uppers than downers as it was, the history of others more so than myself made me hesitant.

Shortly after this I was discharged from the hospital and thrown back out into the world with my new set of accessories. Leaving the hospital I did the best to stand at the corner and squinted down the 4 PM sun; only now realizing I was without my sunglasses which somehow ended up lost in the commotion. Taking a deep breath I started lifting my right crutch and stabbed at the ground about 12 inches in front of me. Then anchoring myself I swung my body forward as my left crutch lifted and then landed shoulders width from where my right one had landed, both times with a force shooting into my armpits, adding pain to a new part of the body while the oxycodone's continued to dull the pain of my lower half. I continued this process over the next stretch of sidewalk until I came to my first street crossing. There I looked to my left, traffic zooming by without concern. There was no crosswalk, there was no light, just a STOP sign for those coming along the street to my right. Seeing no one around I moved myself into the street for what would hopefully be a far better crossing than my most recent attempt. Never losing peripheral track of the cars to my left, I heaved my body one stride after another until I had reached the sidewalk again. The next two blocks were no easy accomplishment and when some kid in a Subaru pulled over to ask me if I needed a ride I wasn't sure whether him or the ice bag woman earlier was the bigger savior.

Later when given the chance it was a combo of pain and annoyance that led me to say a few of the things on my mind when speaking to Aryana. *"I'm not tryin to be rude or unreasonable, but I couldn't even park outside of your place for a moment and come inside to pee?"*

"I'm sorry. It wasn't my place in the first place! What can I do to make up for it? " Starring out my windshield I weighed the moments available to me, *"You mind going with me to the beach?"*

"No of course not. Should you have your cast around sand though?"

"I won't. I just wanna go swing on the monkey bars."

Letting out a giggle she looked back at me, *"Oh you're serious?"*

"Sure am. If I had just gone there this morning I might have avoided all of this. So you coming or not?"

Knowing I was fucked no matter which way I went I decided to just hop on the interstate and avoid the most amount of lights of all the routes available. Relying on all I knew from the past I found a spot a few blocks away near where I used to live and left the car there as Aryana and I battled each others slowness all the way to the playground. I only now know how stupid I was. Apparently there's parking a lot closer to the jungle gym than I realized that night. This of course being written from the perspective of someone who has learned his fucking lesson.

Having not spent much time with her since college, I was really pleased with how well we continued to vibe with each other on our ride to the beach. The whole time I was reminded why we had gotten along so well all those years before. Even if some of those conversations led to brief arguments. *"Why couldn't you just say, he's my friend when he first asked about me?"*

"Why couldn't you have said nothing when you met him? You were the one who started this whole thing!"

She was right. I had made two bad impressions with regards to my friendship with her. One was a friend who was instantly annoyed at my bluntness and the other was a boyfriend who I didn't know how to talk to. So here I was suffering the long term consequences of words that could have been left unsaid. We drove back to her place with a bit more silence than the ride to the beach. I had perhaps said too much, maybe I let the draw down of the pain medication get to me, or maybe I just realized how much I missed my friend. As I dropped her off she gave me a big hug with a tear coming from eye which made me tell her to shut the fuck up and stop feeling bad. The last thing I needed was the guilt of sympathy to add onto my night.

Once at my car I knew I needed to move the car and then get myself situated for the night. Arriving at the loop I pulled the car up on the right and placed her in park, pulling up on the e-brake for added assurance. Sitting there in the back of my car I felt such a mix of emotions. Or maybe it was noticing my lack of emotions. It was one of those moments where we tell ourselves never again. One of those times where we swear there is gonna be a turn around. But it was hard not to be mad at myself for getting in this situation in the first place. Laying there encapsulated by the shell of my car I closed my eyes and began to speak to the air around me, not even necessarily to myself, just to whatever side of existence was listening. *"This is where you wanted to be. This is the experience you wanted. This is part of your story."* I had to remind myself of one thing; I was completely free. I may have been in the worst position possible for my current situation, yet I was still there on my own volition, appreciating the opportunity to close my eyes knowing that no one expected me anywhere tomorrow, and while for some that might have made them feel alone, it made me feel free. I felt conflicted because I could have used the money to make the first part of my existence way more convenient, but something inside of me wouldn't allow myself to do that. I knew if I started using that money I would never figure out a way to make it back as I went along and I would end up being screwed at some point.

Somewhere in the middle of the night I was awakened by a sudden stinging in the center of my foot as the last of the oxycodone was beginning to wear off. I had more or less taken care of my body for my entire life. More so out of obligation to myself than anything else. Though I remember once being accused of something similar to vanity by someone who continued to try to convince me that I didn't like going to the gym and that I only liked the results of going to the gym. An argument to which I still disagree. Laying there I kept thinking how I once saw a documentary called *Misery Loves Comedy* and it asked the question, *"Do you need to be miserable to be funny?"* And though there is some seriousness to the consideration at this moment in my life, I would argue that the answer is not at all. But you MUST be capable of getting frustrated at the smallest of things and turning them into the biggest of things. A power you hopefully confine to that of your stage preparation and not your actual living. I bring this up because it is my opinion that something like stand-up could have only come from a city center where one individual got to see such a collection of things going on that they felt the need to talk bout them. You must be frustrated by the world to wanna go on stage and say, *"You know what the hell I think? Don't worry, I'm about to tell ya."* It takes a certain level of discontent with the world around you to put something on the stage. If there was any truth to that I was sure about to come up with some good stuff to say.

Although the world may have been taking care of my needs from a comedic perspective, I needed to take charge of my physical healing better than I had my first week on cutches. I knew I needed a place to go, somewhere to think, even if only for a few days. There I stood deeply feeling the true pain of being unprepared. I had enough money for this trip, but nothing else. My plan had not allowed any room for hiccups. Perhaps it was arrogant of me to think that things would go so smoothly. Then again I had been the constantly positive person. I couldn't go and start being down on myself. Not after all of this time. I had to figure something out. I had nowhere to go. I had given up my apartment. I couldn't take it back without a series of struggles both financial and situational. Even then, what the fuck would I do limping my way up and down four floors every morning? I hated to admit it, but I had really backed myself into a corner. The fucked nature of that corner wouldn't change much with regards to resources anytime soon, but through the text of a damn good friend I did manage to pull through, *"Fly your ass down here and come stay with me."*

"You're sure man?" Knowing I was fucked is partly what made Florida seem like such a good place to use as a base. With an abundance of retired persons I had to imagine they had plenty of hospital care. *"Yeah dude. Get your ass down here. Lemme know when you're flying in."*

That night I crawled into the trunk and did my best to situate myself amongst my things. I remembered a girl who told me something once about how my life wouldn't go how I wanted just because I acted right or tried to live virtuously. Laying in my car I kept thinking of the first time I saw someone do stand-up my Junior year of college. I was seeing a girl who wanted to go to a show and ended up dragging me to see Dane Cook perform at some big theatre. At the time I didn't know what a monster of a career I was witnessing. I had listened to his albums, but his stage presence was truly something to admire. Maybe it's the fact that he's six foot something with another half-foot of hair. Regardless of what it is, you may be able to ignore him passing on the street, but you could never ignore him with a mic in his hand. The girl I went with was way too hot for me. Oddly enough I don't think she knew that about herself. Though the gap in looks was exceeded by the gap in our age, and I think that gap made up for anything I lacked in her mind. Maybe she really liked me. Maybe I need to stop doubting some sexy blonde could be so interested in me. That's all this is about.

That girl. She changed my life. In more ways than this paragraph can tell you. So instead I'll just sum it up by telling you that she was the catalyst which ultimately led towards me pursuing stand-up comedy as a legitimate career. Not to get her attention or anything. She was actually dead by the time that side of my existence started. And I'm sorry, but I don't have time to go into her death. It was tragic, it broke my heart, and it drastically impacted the way I thought about my time on this earth. So years later I had ditched my job, burnt any bridge back to reality, and dug myself into the trenches of the entertainment world.

Every now and then I would be filled with bursts of adrenaline and rage that would desire a way to be addressed without kicking my foot at the back of the front seat supporting it. I wanted so badly to be at home so I could punch some defenseless pillow masquerading as a living room decoration. I wondered so much if my anger was for my situation, for getting myself in the situation, or for being susceptible to this situation at this stage in my life. Or maybe it was just that the pain meds were starting to wear off and even my body was becoming aware of how fucked I was.

That first morning alone in my car was a combination of things, mostly annoying. Somewhat sad, though only sad because of my natural self-loathing more so than the actual situation. I woke up to a series of texts from friends or family asking me if I was okay. The relative nature of such a question halted me from responding at first while I sat there trying to wrap my head around everything happening, alerted not just by the reality of the situation, but also by the seemingly immediate need to take a piss. I would in this moment learn a series of things. The first of which was just how much preparation was going to be required any time I needed to use the bathroom. Even via the support of text messages from friends all around I found it hard to find any good in my situation.

As a self-proclaimed positive thinker no part of me wanted to come to terms with the reality of how fucked I was. I was without health insurance, and without anyone to call. Such a conflict. When I thought about the debt I wasn't really stressing anything. I mean, as far as I was concerned when I had the money, they would get it, but until then, why stress myself? If this is what I gotta do, it's what I gotta do. It's not like I asked for this. In fact, I don't recall calling you guys to show up. I didn't wanna give up and I didn't wanna stop my trip, but the bottom line was I couldn't be driving around for the next month like this. First of all, it was terrifying anyone who saw me get out and pump gas. If a cop pulled me over I don't really think I could play off the foot as no big deal. Plus it wasn't gonna heal if I had to spend all day driving around. I needed to be able to sit and chill and elevate it. That became my new mission for the next 40 days.

Before departing the next morning I planned on going by the doctor to get my cast redone. Not knowing anywhere else to go I went to an Emergi-care a few miles from where I had spent my night. To my surprise I went in and they wouldn't see me because I didn't have insurance and I wasn't from the area. At this moment I felt only anger for being poor. For being broke and being in such a position that all I would look to ask for help is pathetic. With no luck or prospects of future luck I decided to cut my losses and get my ass back down to the beach where I would wait out my flight.

People in Venice play by their own rules. Walking around you see every type of hippy there is. First of note was the man with speakers taped together as he rollerbladed by, blaring tunes from the year of his high school graduation, *Guns-n-Roses Sweet Child of Mine*. Sitting there with all of my belongings and a set of crutches I didn't even look odd. It woulda probably worked to my advantage if I had just decided to put up a mic and start talking. With sweat dripping down my face I looked on as a giant jeep pulled up next to me, wheels level with my armpits, and a set of handles meant to help the driver hike themselves up inside. Perhaps the oddest accessory to the vehicle that I noticed was a handicapped tag hanging from the window, matching the symbol marked on their license plate. It was red, wrapped in black, if you've seen it you'll know it.

I knew not to make a decision at the moment. First I needed to do some reflection. There was something about this which reminded me of when I had taken that time away from the outside influences of my existence to reset the situation of my mind. Though this time nature and circumstance were leading to an internal revamp more than a direct desire to do so. I needed somewhere to sit and think. The only place I knew I could go was my old street in Santa Monica. With that knowledge I drifted towards 4th street and wedged my car between the appropriate signs under a few palm trees imported from long ago.

LA has the reputation for fake friends and fake tits, but I gotta be honest, during my time there neither one of them ended up in my hands. I was one of the lucky ones to find a few good souls willing to help a fellow East Coaster. The best of which was actually my landlord from when I spent a winter trying to live at the beach and learn what the West Coast was all about. Hitting him up I was happy to find that he was still in the area and in charge of most of the homes I had remembered; most importantly the one I was only a few cars away from at the moment. During my first few weeks in California he had helped me fill some of the days by driving me around his properties and showing me the routine maintenance he had to perform throughout the Hermosa Beach Area. Upon hitting him up about my current situation he agreed to meet up with me to discuss how he could help. *"I wish I could offer you a room but everything is all filled up right now."* He relayed this message to me with a grim helpless look on his face and I did my best to brush off the lack of luck in the situation. *"You can park your car behind your old house if you need to though."*

At this moment my car felt like all I had, leaving it would be surrendering myself to a certain level of incapable that I had not dealt with in many years. I had done anything possible to keep a car within my grasp ever since the years as a teenager when I had to go without the possibility of driving due to some dead tags and the inability to pay the state the required fees to get myself back on the road. During that time I learned to be grateful for rides, I also learned how to drive all the backroads to avoid cops at every chance. There was one time where I had to bite my tongue that I regretted it the most, and that was the one time I dealt with the police in Harrisonburg, Virginia. They pulled me and my sister over and then continuously tried to probe at the possibility she was a prostitute because she didn't have a drivers license at the time and therefore no way to prove who she was or wasn't. I can recall them asking her outside of the car, *"Mam, how do you really know the guy in the car?"* To which she pleasantly responded, *"He's my fucking brother, just like I told you before."* I wanted to tell them what they were doing was harassment, and I wanted to tell them what they were doing was going over board, but I had to keep my fucking mouth shut because at the end of the day I was a 20 year old kid with a gallon of vodka in my trunk and a fake ID hiding in my glovebox. For those that have issues with the police I feel you. Something not often spoken about is that though the thoughts around police often involve racism, there's not enough reality spoken to the matter that in an area where the majority of kids are white, as where I came from, the police will still find people to fuck with.

I quickly learned that the things you get away with that are socially acceptable when you're disabled or with a broken body change dramatically. All formalities about clean clothes or anything other than a disheveled look go out the window. Especially with the presence of a cast. Here at the airport I waited for my Alaska Airlines flight and begged the world to provide me with a place to sit, somewhere elevated. Each time I thought a spot had opened up I would see it immediately taken away. Some seats just flat out didn't work. In reality I needed a seat with a seat open next to it. As this continue persisted I went and planted myself next to a trash can and boosted myself up on top of it. If this didn't send a signal that *"you're all assholes"* then I don't know what would have. Assholes aside I still tried to remember to be grateful for being in this spot during this time of the human existence, because honestly life before the Industrial Age would have been far more difficult to navigate as a man in a state of temporary disablement. By the time I was settled in my seat the first class passengers had started to board and I watched as each one settled into their own little cubby, each with a reclining seat to get them through their flight. I could see it in her eyes as she approached her seat next to me at 29D. As she noticed she was the one who had been seated next to the man on crutches she winced. She was on her way to tell her parents about her girlfriend. Someone she was planning to marry. According to her, her parents were oblivious to the news they were about to receive. Which makes sense since guys usually make it way more obvious that they are gay than girls. I wished her luck along with a congratulations and reminded her that whether they accept it now or accept it later, their acceptance wasn't her problem anymore than it was their choice. Aside from the baggage weighing on her mind, she also brought with her a tiny dog, something like a Weiner-dog with longer hair. I'm sure you've seen one before. It's America, dogs are everywhere.

Another thought this time of my life provoked was that of my new opinion on emotional support dogs in restaurants. I get it makes traveling easier, but let's stop lying and calling them service dogs. I'm as embarrassed as I am angry to have to look at someone when they come into a restaurant with a chihuahua and demand that their dog is a service dog but I'm not at all allowed to question their ailment, signed off by some quack doctor who sees fluff as an emotional necessity in an ever weakening world. If we're going to let this nonsense continue they should at least have to wear those little service dog jackets and act like a working dog and not a pet. Though my overall opinion is that if you don't have the emotional capacity to handle a trip to Starbucks without your dog maybe you shouldn't be adding caffeine to your internal workings.

PORTLAND, OREGON

June 2016

"So are you suing...?"

I f you've never been to the Pacific Northwest then it's going to be very difficult for you to understand why people want to live there based on its reputation. It rains on average, eh, all the fucking time. When it's not wet, but it's usually wet, it's also cold. However, due to such things, it is also one of the best environments for growing certain crops in the entire country. The soil is rich and anything you put in it becomes green seemingly overnight; which is basically why a group of guys I knew moved there right after finishing college to get in early on the weed business. They weren't from my high school, and we never played them in any sports so it was only my own stupidity which led me into inheriting this group of guys in the first place. Guess I should explain that story. Somewhere around my junior year of high school I was at a basketball game where local schools had sent their yearbook squads to grab some photos. Before the game I was bombarded with a series of photos by this girl who had a crush on me at the time and honestly I was a shy fucking kid with no idea what I was doing in the ladies department. I was always good at talking to them, but that's just because it was talking, not because it was them. So when this girl from the yearbook comes up on me sitting at bleachers and starts snapping pictures I handled it poorly and tried to be cool. Once covering my face, and then eventually putting up the middle finger as a seemingly normal thing to do as many others have done in photos. I didn't even know it was a problem until a week later when I was pulled into the principals office and asked to explain my behavior. Apparently, she hand't taken it upon herself to delete those photos from the schools digital camera before handing it back to the yearbook department. I'm so glad the local news didn't pick it up. Can you imagine the outrage? *"Local adult misfit incapable of controlling the urge of a retractable joint now on the loose. Is he at YOUR high school football game!?"* These days I reserve the middle finger for rush hour traffic and keep it away from the camera. Anyways, after this visit in the office it was determined that I wasn't allowed at any more of the high school sporting events or dances for the remainder of the year. Since it was only September this didn't work too well for me as the rest of my year was already set for doom with the promised missing of my junior prom. This all ended up being a blessing in disguise. Technically the expulsion carried to games within the rest of the county, but I soon found that not to be as strictly enforced. At the time I really loved watching football, and due to my age, it was usually high school football. Fortunately, my town hugged the county line of a mountainous region with a high school a short drive away. Attempting to give myself something to do I sent a message to this girl I knew from around that way and was invited to one of their upcoming Friday games. I went to the game and was quickly picked up by a group of guys mingling with the few students I already knew. As luck would have it, the one known for throwing parties was the first one to befriend me and from there the rest was history. Soon after I started meeting everyone from the area and a whole new world opened up.

One of the people in that world was a kid named Mason. We would meet a few times in high school, but it wouldn't be until college and the mutual major of Political Science that we would become good friends. Going all the way from morning hikes in the mountains to running drugs across Central American borders. Although that in itself is another story which this book won't allow me the time to tell. All in all I don't think I've ever been happier to have raised that middle finger, because it led me to where I was this morning, at the PDX airport waiting to be picked up by my friend after his morning run. Oh, and I do mean after. He told me he wasn't cutting his run short to *come get my ass*.

Portland has that same vibe that Austin does, where it's a little weirder than everything around it, though the weirdness of Portland is a bit more expected than the weirdness of Austin. It was that type of environment far enough away from the capital which made for the start of the drug revolution back in the 60's. My buddy saw the next revolution coming a long time ago. Not investing with him after college was the only legitimate mistake I had ever made. That is to say it is the only one I've ever made which has the ability and the voice to remind me annually of the monetary losses of my hesitation. Nonetheless I was glad to see his illegally financed vehicle making it towards the edge of the sidewalk.

"Well look at you Mr. Funny guy."

I shrugged my bag up to the front seat and grabbed the *oh shit* handle at the top by the window, remembering that the last time I braced myself with such a handle it was for the purpose of bracing myself while enjoying the sexual exertions of a slightly older woman. This time I was lucky if I didn't fall down while bringing myself up. Thankfully, Mason had thrown my bag into the back by now so I was able to hurl myself onto the seat and stretch out. Darting both eyes to my left I gave him a look I can only hope you're able to imagine and then replied, *"Fuck yourself sir. Thanks for picking me up."*

Then I was interrupted by a series of quick annoying licks from his tiger striped boxer named Nia, an overall bitch of a dog and a true ride or die in Masons life. *"So lemme hear the story, how did this accident happen."*

After telling him I received the same response I heard from everyone I mentioned the incident to since, *"So are you suing?"*

"Hope I don't have to. I just want my bills covered."

"Are you stupid? The guy broke your foot and you can't work. What do you think insurance is for? Sue the fuck out of that guy."

There was admittedly a part of me which fantasized about this scenario, but I also didn't wanna use the system the way I had seen it used when I was younger. Specifically I'm talking about the weekend after the court case was decided which found McDonalds guilty of serving a woman a cup of coffee deemed dangerously and irresponsibly hot. At the time I was working at Burger King and I'll never forget how the next day we had to throw away close to 5,000 Styrofoam cups and replace them with freshly minted ones with, *"CAUTION. CALIENTE. HOT"* stamped on every side possible. Whew *breathes a sigh of relief* now the people will be safe even though the turtles won't be. That was a terrible moment where our justice system basically said, *"Hey, you know what? Fuck personal responsibility and common sense, no one should have to carry the burden of knowledge that a cup of coffee might be hot."* That being said I hated hearing that attitude of, *"You're gonna win a ton of money off of that."* Or *"Lucky You."* Uh No. Not lucky me. Still makes me kinda sick to see that mentality developing in the society around me. Not just with regards to insurance and entitlement, but of personal responsibility. It's on you to know that a coffee is going to be hot just as much as it's on you to know a comedy club is where people go to hear the realest of the real. Granted, it's not like I didn't want enough money to pay back the ambulance which was demanding somewhere in the realm of $1,500 by the time it was all done. However, the idea that I would or should get rich from this seemed entitled. Though I would soon learn that without suing I was unlikely to ever get any of the debt paid. A weird conundrum in our medical and judicial system.

This obviously brings me to the topic of health care in the United States. I had heard many fallacies and misunderstandings from the international world about my own country, but this was one area where I had always held some conflicting agreements. The idea of having to take out loans to afford a healthy life was absurd. Granted, I was also someone who had a gym membership his entire life and would do just about anything to facilitate eating well at every chance. I was admittedly lucky in the fact that I never had much of a sweet tooth, so the chains of discipline were not so hard to abide by. Nonetheless, I did what I could to keep investing in my health throughout the years. Plus at the end of the day this wasn't a health thing, this was an accident. No human bone is meant to withstand the force of a 2,000 pound car no matter how much calcium they've pumped inside of themselves. Not long before this accident the legislators of my country had tried to institute their own form of universal healthcare with Obamacare and a sweeping promise to have everyone covered. Which I know sounds great, but personally I don't want to pay into a system that says it will take care of people and then not require those people to give more than a few fucks about their body. It was also equally annoying to me how much all of the things I had done for my body over the years amounted to nothing against something as simple as a Michelin tire on a sunny day[5]. Nonetheless, I was operating from a healthier baseline than a majority of those I shared these borders with. Which is why I was mad at the thought of being averaged in with others my age when considerations of health insurance rates came up. That and prohibitive pricing eventually kept me from getting Obamacare no matter what the financial penalty at the end of the year. It would still be cheaper than actually having insurance. They claimed the prices were reasonable for everyone but in a year when you don't even make $35,000 what is reasonable each month? Then, and I promise I'm done after this, why can't I opt out of having health insurance? And why must I pay a penalty for doing so? Furthermore, isn't paying full price for medical care my punishment? Which by the way is exactly what I did during

---

[5] no fault attributed to the specific brand mentioned.

this entire ordeal. I told each doctor I was paying cash and a few of them even gave me discounts for avoiding the inconvenience of having to deal with insurance companies. The whole system is honestly fucked. No one is required or encouraged to live a healthy lifestyle, but everyone is required to pay into a system that avoids preventative treatment. A pill for this, a pill for that, and a pat on the back for swallowing when they tell you to.

After spending the afternoon at the house I soon saw he and his friends had maintained their nature to do as they pleased and all developed the same look of Portland outdoor goers. Each one of them wearing pants, not made of any material any of us grew up walking around in. This was a light winder breaker type stuff. Most of their pants were baggy. Though the ones wearing jeans usually had holes and a tighter fit than one would deem comfortable. No one's hair was trimmed. Not necessarily disheveled, just not in any sort of order. So when you met one of them without this appearance you learn to manage expectations. Any time I found myself talking with a clean-cut individual I found myself asking, *"So you from Oregon?"* Seeing no beard or tattoos and lacking all outdoorsiness if you will, I had little reason to assume a yes would follow my inquiry, even more so when he said, *"Yeah. I grew up far from the city."*

A broken leg would get me more friends this summer than my current strategy had been doing for me and one of those friends was a man relating to me on the issues of injuries that evening named Felix. I met him for the first time when I went outside to take a piss and avoid the difficulties of taking my crutches into the bathroom. Standing there taking care of my business I heard the opening of a door coming from a trailer parked next to Masons truck. From that swinging door, a tall man with long blonde dreadlocks and no shirt came walking out. Despite not having a shirt, he was far from uncovered. His body must have been a good forty-percent ink, thirty percent dreadlocks, and the rest skin. He was a former Olympic skier; two time qualifier, and one time winner. Now he made his life going back and forth between Alaska and Montana; skiing when he could, giving fly fishing lessons when he couldn't.

"Oh. I remember when I had my leg wrapped up."

"What happened to you?"

"Tore it up trying to do this jumper out in Truckee. Shit was gnarly. Tore my ACL all up."

"Sounds painful..."

With a deep laugh he responded, *"Oh it was."*

"You still able to ski?"

"Oh yeah. Just gotta take it easier these days. Not many back flips."

As we sat there he started to explain his life and all of the time he had spent becoming sober over the last year. I had a hard time understanding him on this topic in particular. I understood the plight of a drug addict on opioids, I had seen uppers take more than one friend, but this was the first time I heard someone telling me that they *had* to stop smoking weed. It didn't even compute. Granted he caught me dealing with some of my own demons at the moment as I sat with the uncomfortable fact that I would be on that very substance for the next month or more. Places out West were a good reminder to how archaic some of my thinking was, especially in regards to drugs, or at least that of marijuana. I had some sort of weird aversion to drugs when I was earlier, partly out of self-discipline and partly out of the desire to not be one of the crowd just snorting and smoking everything I could get my hands on. Which probably doesn't even sound as bad a thing to do now as it did back then before the culture shifted in favor of the more nefarious.

That same character would come back around a few nights later when we were picked up in an Uber at the corner of Powell and Duquard Street on our way to some house part hosted by a friend of theirs. Everyone got inside the van and then scooted over to make room for me and my accessories. Once inside we slid the door closed and all took a deep breath to make the herd fit. As it often does in Oregon the conversation got to weed and it became loudly expressed that one of the members of the van could roll a joint one handed in only a few seconds, a fact to which the driver scoffed in disbelief. This lack of faith being met by a question from the back seat, *"How far are we from our destination?"*

"Under a mile."

"Bet you I could roll a joint before we get there from start to finish."

"No you couldn't."

"Bro, I could have the joint rolled and lit before we get to that last light."

From the middle of the van I peered forward and looked at the row of lights ahead of us, 2 of the 3 red and with 2 cars in our way behind those delays.

"$20 tip if I can't. Free ride if I do."

199

"I can't give you a free ride. That's not in my control."

"Well can my friends smoke it if I have it rolled before we get there?"

"Okay sure," and with a dismissive flutter of her hands she looked both ways at our first light before entering the neighborhood.

"Weed me."

Rolling a joint in the most impressive time I'd ever seen he barely held onto his smile long enough to notice it before his cheek was turned into a flesh balloon filling with the first hit of his freshly rolled doobie.

"I thought you said you quit?"

"I'm like Bill Clinton bro, no inhaling."

The driver looked on in an innocent shock as she pressed the button on her windows to immediately start the process of airing out. Once we got to the party I did my best to wobble up the stairs and looked into the open door and down the hallway where small crowds stood every few feet. Looking at the floor and weighing the balances I looked over at Mason and said, *"I'm gonna stay on the porch a bit..."*

I wish I could remember how this next part came to happen. Although we've grown up being told we shouldn't talk about religion or politics, I will make an argument that there is no off limits to the list of topics two strangers can cover with one another. Dare I say that amongst the company of only one other it is much easier to have a fluid conversation and exchange of ideas. Something about egos seem a bit thinner when in the presence of a stranger, someone whom will likely forget you the moment you disappear. Though this kid I doubt I'll ever forget. Him and his girlfriend had come outside for a cigarette and started talking to me when they noticed me sitting alone. One thing led to another and soon enough the kid came to say something interesting to me about how there was so much information out in the world that it sometimes overwhelmed him. I initially shrugged off his comment as another thing said by the stoned on this Portland porch, but he soon pried back a bit more to reveal that he wasn't being philosophical, he was being as literal as could be. Apparently he had grown up the first 18 years of his life in what would be labeled a cult by most, but to him was still just seen as a religious household. Though the word compound would soon be seen as the most accurate way to word the area he grew up in. One which did not let him out in his younger years and dictated the level and type of information his brain was exposed to as a young kid. So when he said that he was overwhelmed by all of the information, he meant just that. He had left when able to and joined the military almost instantly. While there he soon found himself to be one of the only people who didn't really understand the concept of planets or the idea that there might be more to the world than the words taught to him as a child. This all led to his feeling of overwhelm each time he learned of something knew. He didn't even know what to say when I started talking to him about all of the countries I had visited. I don't think he had ever even heard of Colombia before. Listening to him it felt less and less fair to say I or anyone I knew had grown up in a religiously oppressive home, it wasn't even close to it. Though religion undoubtedly played a role in some of the censorship which took place around me and the lack of movies in my house as a child.

Sitting there listening to him I found myself doing something I hadn't really ever done before, which is to say I was wondering how much I really believed in the freedom of religion. How could such a thing justify what had been done to this kid? It was like watching someone learn to speak late in life. He would go and understand an idea and then have no frame of reference for the next thing I brought up. It was like he had nothing inside of him. Showing me that if all that happens inside of us is a result of what has already happened inside of someone else, and we ourselves are simply a mirror of all of those whom we encounter, then there is nothing outside or in, it all just fluidly statics through the ether as one receptor or another chooses to express it's coding, free of ownership. Thankfully the innocence of his soul and the purity which he had maintained was too much for her to ignore. I related to his experience of being enlightened by a woman, and as I understood, so would most men who ever became anything. Her cheerleading for him made you want him to succeed even more. When he got up to go to the bathroom his girlfriend stayed behind and continued talking. *"I wish he would find a way to be more open to the idea of some type of spirituality. I get why he's hesitant, but I don't want him to go completely rogue."*

"Let him live long enough and he'll swing more towards the middle like the rest of us." To my comment she looked away and seemed to relish in her doubt more than my certainty. *"Look, just trust me. Life is a pendulum. One thing is just a reaction to another, and right now he's reacting."*

Not a man of particular religion, I still found some of the foundational messages within it to be worthy of some remembering. Hard to argue against the *thou shall not kill* part of the whole scripture.

201

Curious to know his thoughts when he returned I asked him, *"So did you ever bring any of this up with your family? I mean I was raised in a religious house, but not a literal complex."*

"No. I haven't seen any of them in years. Don't even know what I'll say when I do."

"That's wild. Gonna be an interesting day."

"Yeah. Probably."

"So do you believe in anything anymore?"

"I don't know. Not really looking for that. I just want meaning for myself without someone else trying to tell me what it is."

"That's fair. I mean, we're all looking for some type of meaning, we all seem to want to understand what this is and how it came to be. Truth be told I don't think it matters. The reason for life. None of it. Definitely not the origin. I can't really understand why we spend so much time worrying about that when we should be focused on where we're going next."

"You're not worried about why you're alive?"

"Like me specifically? No."

"Doesn't that matter to you?"

"I mean, I suppose giving it some thought isn't a bad idea, but what can I do other than concern myself with it? I don't know why any of us are here. I'm just here hoping to make people laugh and have some good times."

It was terrible to see the type of stifling which had been done to this kids mind over the years. He was curious as fuck and to hear him speak was like listening to a reawakening. And I do not say he should have been denied that which his parents wanted to tell him, but at some point he should have had the walk through the forest where his parents guide him to a point where the sun shines through, leaving him to come up with his own ideas. To harvest his own wonders. To form his own truths. There are only so many truths to the being of human, but the being of the individual is an infinitely diverse kaleidoscope, seamlessly adapting to the existence of each experiencer, adding to the vastness of the genetic memory of our species and informational database as a whole. Surely he had some advantages to his life. He seemed unconcerned. He seemed more concerned about the fact that there were so many things that could be out there than actually concerned about any of those devilish things for which he had definitions. It was the vast existence of an unknown which kept his mind in terror. Like a kid who just discovered his closet went dark when he closed the doors. With a perception of depth in the dark that was impossible. Adding a fear which is unknown and beyond the understanding of an anyone without such sheltering.

The Northwest was another place I could have lived if life had gone differently after college. Gone differently, as if it went any way, the truth is I took my life every place it went. In many ways I had. My mind had thought about it since coming here years ago. At the time I had the picture of a girl in my head and how I could maybe make a life with her here if I could only convince her to leave her tiny Latin town. Though I knew the change would be far more drastic for her than for myself. The culture here was different. Not in a bad way. But in a way far different from someone who grew up in the Caribbean. All the while considering that if one doesn't possess the desire to relocate to a cooler climate, they're not likely to appreciate the unintended alteration.

Waking up that next morning the only thing I could really feel was a deep lack of independence. There was a clear shift in my mental state and my identity. My mind was filled with so many conflicting desires. I needed to pee, I wanted some coffee, I wanted another blanket. Maybe I just wanted something different than that which the world was giving me. I kept trying to remind myself how much I needed to brace myself for the reality of the moment and how much I needed to get to the point of acceptance. One of the unfortunate sides of my time there was that I had plenty of it to think. Which was oddly one of the reasons this sucked so much. It was one thing to use my time when I'm sitting around doing nothing, it was straight up rude to have my body wake me up to give me more time to think about it. Of course from there one of the things which started to creep even further into my mind was that of doubt. And as we know, doubt eventually leads to the worst of human emotions; hopelessness.

I quickly learned that I would have to figure out how to deal with the reality of being on crutches on the go and all that would entail. Part of me was glad to have my body constantly moving, but I still think I would have wanted my first week to be one more of relaxation than activity. Realizing I was at the whim of others I let go of any fantasies I may have had about how my day was going to be and just went along for the ride. Somewhere stuck in a stoners haze I had lost track of where we were going or why and seemingly out of nowhere my peripheral was filled with a giant span of blue, horizon barely distinguishable from the flat line of ocean sprawling before and below to the cliffs of the Oregon Coast. Along the guardrail gargantuan pine trees shot from steep drop offs moistened by the surrounding bay over a twenty-four hour basis. We hugged the coastal road and slowly snaked our way down to the beach where Mason parked his car amongst a group of friends who had arrived before us.

"I can't get down there man." To that complaint he built a fire for me and then went on his way. Despite being slightly abandoned I found myself enjoying the solitude of a beachside fire while the guys we had joined all surfed in some of the coldest waters a surfer could find. I don't care what time of year you're here or what you've heard from those who are used to it, but the Pacific waters are the fucking coldest thing you'll ever have to deal with as far as the continental coasts go in my country. Those same cold waters were the reason for which I later needed to curl up even closer to that fire as the late night breeze proved too cold to deal with.

The next day I was caught in an admittedly high daze when the realities of time caught up with the perceptions of it and I noticed that we had been driving for a little over three hours since leaving the beach and now found ourselves somewhere in central Oregon. Naturally I had to inquire, though the answer would make no difference, *"Where we going?"*

"Smith rock. Few of the guys are out there climbin'. Views are sick."

Looking down at my crutches I muttered, *"Am I gonna be able to get around..."*

"Gonna let a little injury stop ya? I got extra gear."

Staring back at a set of puppy dog eyes laced with confusion I doubted each of his previous statements.

"You know what? Leave me the keys to the truck and you can take me wherever the fuck you want. Nia you got me?"

"Nah homeboy, she's the only loyal bitch out there. She'll be circling a dustbowl wherever we leave our packs until our feet hit the ground."

Looking over my left shoulder I caught eyes with his droopy faced dog and knew there must be more to the story. There was no way he was taking that dog up the ropes. Though I wouldn't put it past him to make me hobble my ass up a mountain. He's the same guy who didn't bother telling me we would be wading through a river at night in the middle of the jungle the first time I left the country on an excursion to visit him during a summer spent inside a cluster of Central American Islands. Like many times before, my friends didn't tell me shit. They just brought me along. Camilo and I used to always talk about being down for anything and how that quality had led people to invite us along for pretty much anything and everything.

This part of Oregon has a neat blend of looking like a wheat field where there be grass, and a rocky dessert where there be rock, with a fairly even blend covering all the eye sees in either direction. Then almost out of nowhere you come around a turn and what was just a rolling hill suddenly reveals the face of a rock nearly 600 feet high. When we arrived I opened the door and stretched my legs out as I took in the view of Smith Rock off in the distance. As they readied their ropes and clips I starred at his dog who anxiously shook her button of a tale as she watched her owner add on layer upon layer of supplies, darting a panicked glance my way every few moments. I couldn't tell if there was some weird part of her that knew her companion was about to be risking his life, or if she merely had the understanding that he was about to be out of an ears-scratch reach for some extended period of time, remembering the many times he had abandoned her before. I didn't have the same sadness as that dog, but I was really bummed out watching the guys go up and down the rocks, especially once they made it to the top, and it made me feel even worse about the prospect of my future as I realized no part of this summer would qualify me to come out here on my own and explore. There was perhaps nothing more torturous than being surrounded by the best nature had to offer, and the greatest of weather, yet all without the ability to enjoy any of it. It made me think that perhaps virtual reality could have benefits beyond that of what I had thought a few cities before. Sitting by the fire later he began to ask me my least favorite questions about my future, *"So what are you gonna go do?"*

"I don't know. I gotta kill 40 days."

"Back to New York?"

"That's no place to operate on crutches."

"You can stay here if you want."

"Nah. Your place is too far from the doctors. It's awesome, but there's not much in the world of convenience out here for me."

"How many times do you need to go to the doctor? Why not stay and ride into the city when you wanna do stand up?"

"Well, if I'm gonna stay somewhere and do stand-up it's not gonna be Portland. The scene is good, but not that good."

"Where have you seen so far that looks good?"

"I don't know man. I keep hearing about Denver, but I don't have

anywhere to stay there. Not for that long. I could go to Florida. That worked
pretty well last time, and the comedy was good there."

"Fuck that man. I wouldn't wanna be wearing a cast in that humidity.
Just stay here. I'll take you to a few shows."

"Maybe."

"Come on, You gonna do a set while you're here at least?"

"I don't know. I don't have anything new to say. I don't wanna bore you
with my old shit."

"Then just go up there and start riffing. You're not going up there for me.
You're going up there for you dude."

"Yeah."

"If not, maybe it's time you start thinking about finding a real job with
health insurance. I don't know what else to tell ya." In that final sentence I
was freed from obligation. He was only able to come at me from his
understanding of the world and his view on what created the ideal life.
For whatever reason he viewed this as some permanent thing, though I
told myself I would not. Though I wasn't saying it, in those moments I
would have killed to be one of those people who had worked a decade
to have all of this money and suddenly an idea of what to do with it. I
was jealous of people who had gone off after college to make a lot of
money and *then* have their existential *what the fuck do I do with my life*
crisis. Just seems a lot easier to go off on these types of adventures
when you've got a safety net. If I was going to make this summer still
work I had to do whatever I could to save money at every opportunity.

Starring out the window over the next few days watching water
pour from the pull-up bar I accepted I would not be going outside day
after day. Cracking the window I let the cool air rush in as I laid in the
bean bag next to the window. Mason assured me it was an outburst of
rain and that it wasn't something I had to worry about over the next
few months. Despite this promise the next few mornings I woke up
with a little bit of panic and a little bit of calm. Each day imagining a
series of weeks spent inside. The next day I called Camilo and he
ultimately offered me a place to stay with him back in Florida. Having
that be no more difficult than returning to my old home base I gave
him a quick chance to get out of it, *"You sure?"*

"Yeah man, plus, I'm gonna be taking a transfer to California at the end of
the summer."

"When do you have to be in Cali by?"

"I told them I could start August 15th, so far as I'm concerned we can leave

as soon as you get your cast off, thats' like what, mid-July?"

"Yeah give or take. They told me a little more than 40 days, depends how it heals up, we're already 5 days in. So it would basically be a month from now. I mean, that's what they told me. I'm not gonna promise anything."

Hearing him take in a deep inhale of his bong I waited til it was blown out before he said, "Fuck all that hiking while you're laid up like that. Get on a plane and get your ass down here."

It wasn't that I didn't wanna stay here for the next month, but I lacked so many of the things that I knew I could get via one simple flight to Florida. Ultimately I had to make the decision that made the most sense. Spend the next month being dragged around the wilderness or go chill in the tropics? With that thought I got in touch with a friend of mine living near Hermosa beach. Through a series of texts I promised I wouldn't become *that friend* who stays seven days instead of three, resting her nerves a bit more with a photo of my flight confirmation leaving on the day I claimed to be leaving. "Thanks in advance. I should be there by 7 or so."

"I'll send you my address. I won't be home so I'll leave a key with my brother. He lives a few houses down."

Before leaving Mason and I went to a spot near the airport and grabbed a burger and some fries. Once at the airport I was immediately greeted by a man working for a rival airline urging to help me with a motorized ride to my terminal. After seeing my ticket information he used his walkie talkie to call someone else over and I was soon intercepted by someone from Delta. Hopping on a motorized cart I sat and put my bag on my lap as they drove me through the terminal and to my gate about half way down. Once again I took a seat down by the front and waited to be as discrete as possible when getting on. Sitting there I kept trying to go through the best self-talk I had ever had access to. The obstacle is the way, that's the message I had to keep telling myself. In my opinion self-talk had never been more important than it was in those moments.

Back in Cali my friend lived only a few blocks from the beach so I did my best each morning to kill some time down on the shore while her roommate got ready for work. I'll sum up my days. I basically got up early enough to get out of the way in the mornings. Then chilled on the couch with my afternoons. Then went down to the beach in the evenings. I think I listened to three different audiobooks and discovered at least two new podcasts. My flight out of California and off to the Florida coast was set to leave somewhere just before sunset so I spent my final afternoon hanging out at Venice beach people watching while I perched myself on a bike rack that nobody was using. Or maybe nobody was using it because I was. Either way it served its purpose of storage until the moment came and I left one coast for the other.

Ft. Lauderdale, Florida pt. 2

June 2016

"Are those the same jokes you were doing last time...?"

U pon landing I took my phone off airplane mode to get the first in a series of messages. The first of which started like this, *"I gotta find out you broke your leg on a Facebook post??? WTF BRO? WHATS THE TEA?"*

"Sup Jax? Sorry. It's been a hell of a week. I been all fucked up."

"Looks like it. You good?"

"Yeah. I'm getting off this plane tho. Lemme holler at you later."

Following that brief exchange I went through another painstaking process of exiting a plane as the last to leave, doing so with great ease once the twenty minutes or so had gone by. When I made it to the baggage claim Camilo was already there waiting to meet me and help with my luggage. Driving home I looked out again on the flat Florida landscape of trimmed gardens and hidden canals taking a deep breathe at the thought of this is where I was going to be for the next month and some change no matter what. When we got home Camilo led me inside where I once again saw Loki who this time looked at me with his own set of suspicious eyes as his animal brain processed the sight of my cast in the same spot where he had worn his. Surely he worried I was going to steal away his sympathy thunder. As we entered the bedroom Camilo looked down at my cast and said, *"Okay, so I can give you the couch or I can blow up a mattress and put it over here for ya."*

"Dude, whatever is easiest."

"No. Which do you prefer?"

"Uh, the mattress if I could. That way I'm not in the way when you wanna sit down and watch t.v. or something."

"Alright cool. Loki, get out of the way!"

With nothing else to do I sat there and gave myself a sensory tour of the room. First touching the dresser, then the light switch. Still my mind was consumed with the idea of money. The lack of money if we are going to be specific. It was consuming me to know I was bleeding money each day I existed without any possible way to recover. I didn't even know how to make money virtually. Something for which I am kinda embarrassed. I could have somehow logged in and taught English for eight hours a day and made plenty to finance the next few months of my life with ease. Life could have been better, but at that time I was too negative. It was also hard to not sit here and dwell on each memory of a person telling me to find my passion and not to do it for the money and how that was working for me now.

My first night there was a conflict of climates. Laying there feeling just a few degrees too hot for the blanket layered on my cast I struggled through the process of kicking it off as it continued to get caught on the final peak of the big toe and pulled ever so slightly at the fabric. Waiting for the rotating fan to make its way I sighed disappointedly as it halted and then began its' counterrotation back to pointlessly coat the majority of the adjacent wall with freshly circulated oxygen. *"Fuck."* Kicking my leg up and bracing myself on the left arm I balanced and wobbled myself to a final point of stillness. *"Okay. Game plan. Two hops. Move the fan. Two hops back. Don't knock anything over."* Managing to do so without waking up Camilo was one of the biggest accomplishments of my time in Florida.

Next I'm gonna talk with you about one of the most inconvenient sides of being on crutches, the bathroom, not as a location, but as an entire experience. Nothing is great about taking a shower with your one leg half-way out. It also would have helped a great deal had my other leg been broken instead. Not that either of them was preferred, but at least if it had been my left leg I could have kept that leg outside of the shower and wrapped it up easily and had the water hit my chest all the same while being prevented from letting the water run down the side of the tub and onto the ground. But, with my right leg broken I had to turn my back to the shower head and this caused a weird situation where I kept trying to keep my leg dry, but nothing seemed to keep the mist from making its way on top of the hardened fabric. Oh and ALL of this is being done while trying to balance my over worked foot on a wet floor with water and soap streaming non-stop. I hadn't noticed this problem in Oregon because Masons bathtub was so big that you could stand in there and dance with two other people if you wanted to.

It only took a few text messages the next day before I was able to line myself up with another chance on the mic. The guys were meeting at the *Funky Buddha* again and Camilo had the entire evening free. *"You want me to drop you off?"*

"Yeah dude. I just wanna get there early so I can find a place to sit."

When I arrived the guys were quick to notice the change in my situation and made all of the proper inquiries about what happened. Hearing the story they all lightened up about the situation, each happy to know that no one had been hurt other than myself. Getting on stage I made a daring move and jolted myself up by skipping the last step. Then almost as if time had stopped, I heard the people behind me hold their breath as the bottoms of my crutches just barely inched their way beyond the point of clearing the stage, ending in an abrupt stopping sound as one would hear from the pivot of a pair of basketball shoes on a freshly waxed floor. I'm not sure whether it was the situation or their sympathy, but I was told that night I was welcome at any mics over the next few weeks. Many of these were of no particular note, but that one night at the Improv a week later is worth a bit of your time.

By the time I had been there a week I was willing to go along with Camilo for anytime he wanted to get out of the house. This meant trips of struggle to the grocery store or just a ride around the block while he listened to some music; the grocery store being a place for a book full of stories if I wanted to. Each time we went I had to find the closest motorized cart and hope it was charged, with the unfortunate discovery that somewhere close to a third of the time it was not. Each one of those particular moments prompting me to return to the car so it would be charged for whatever overweight person was going to take advantage of it later. Something which discouraged Camilo a few times after he had discovered the level of ease I could create in his grocery story experience by following him around with a motorized basket.

One night we got looped into cooking dinner at this girls house he was talking to from his work. When we got to her house I did my usual thing and did my best to get out of everyones way. Of course there were more new people at the house this time and therefore more people awaiting the explanation as to how my leg became wrapped up. My explanation led to conversation and before I knew it I was sitting there talking to Jazmine's mom, her 11 year old son, and his friend all the while with no idea where Jazmine or Camilo had gone. As her mother went outside and closed the door I perched myself up a bit higher and asked the boys, *"So, you guys got any questions about girls or anything you need to know?"*

As if my question had triggered the opening of some internal filing cabinet the two boys both talked over one another to ultimately deliver the same question banging at the back of their heads.

"So what are you supposed to do if you like a girl, and she doesn't like you back?"

"Easy. Realize there are 7 billion other people out there, a good percentage of them women, and go find another one."

"But what if you reallllly like her?"

"Okay, for that my answer is still largely the same, but if you wanna try anything, ignore her. Go live your life and find another girl. The ironically sad part is, once you've found someone, the girl you originally like is likely to come back around and see you in a different light. Weird, but that's how it goes. You're more desired once you're already desired. It's a fucked up world."

With an unsatisfied look of confusion weighted by a temporary crease on his forehead he kinda looked down and accepted that which he did not yet understand.

"Okay."

"Yeah. Any other questions?"

Then, as if the mind had switched from that which he couldn't ask his mother to that which he feared asking anyone, *"So when you die, is it just like"* *clicks fingers* *"boom, you're done. Lights out?"*

"Uhh..."

Chiming in the other boy echoed the same curiosities, *"Yeah, what happens when you die?"* Shrugging a bit I looked over the granite countertop and saw both of them hanging on my response. For one, this felt like beyond my pay grade, and also a bit outside of my allowed areas of conversations for someone else's kids. Using the situation to let them know that adults didn't always know, I responded with the best I could. *"Look man. I don't actually know. Which is kinda the cool part. None of us do. All I KNOW is that I'm here now and that this life is pretty cool, this place in time is pretty cool, so I'm gonna make the most out of this experience, and if there's something after this, I'll do my best there too. But for now, my suggestion would be to live this experience to its fullest and hope there's an afterparty."*

Standing there uncertain what bounds I had crossed I awaited another line of questioning. Not sure if I should tell them that there's more proof of divinity than there is the afterlife. I started wondering if perhaps they would next ask me where babies came from. Luckily this was avoided by the sound of a sliding glass door which opened from the deck to reveal Camilo coming back in to grab a candle for repealing mosquitos. Of course they did my next favorite thing by asking me what I did or a living. I still found myself with this sinking feeling each time someone asked what I was doing with my life. I wondered at what point I would have enough done to consider myself an artist, or if it would take until I had my big break. Why did I feel so confident telling them about the ways of life with women and dating and even my uncertainties about death, but felt weird telling them I was a comedian?

When the night for my performance at the Improv came I made sure to get myself down there with plenty of time to spare. When I first arrived I found a parking spot about two blocks away. A little better this time, but still not close enough to call to my liking. *Why the fuck did I not push to get a handicapped sticker?* Not being sure if it was going to rain yet or not I waited inside of the car for about an hour before the show started, using the time to look at my material and try to relax a bit before the show. As the appropriate time came I made my way to the club and took brief notice of a small line of people waiting outside. In fact, this was the first time I had seen the club with any type of velvet ropes or indicators of crowds needing separation. Maneuvering through the tables inside I worked my way to the back and found a cluster of comedians sitting at a table next to the DJ booth. Upon seeing me Santos wedged between two guys and tapped me on my shoulder, *"Thanks for dressing up."* As a part of making my life easier I had committed to an existence of gym shorts and a white t-shirt. Though had I known that this was a show for paying guests I may have dolled myself up just a bit more. Stuttering I fumbled through an, *"I'm sorry, I didn't know,"* and moved myself out of the way and over to booth where two other comics sat with their heads face down in their notebooks.

Angry at myself for being so underdressed I limped towards the stage and tried to project myself as quickly as possible down the aisle and towards the stairs. Looking down at a dangling cast and one sturdy foot I re-directed my attention to the three stairs ahead meant to lead me beyond a velvet curtain and onto a hardwood coated stage where a mic stand awaited me to perform to a crowd of nearly 350 people all situating themselves after a brief intermission from the evenings events. I couldn't believe it. Then at the same time, why not? What should be any different about making 350 people laugh if you can make 20 laugh?

As I awaited the mentioning of the next act my mind took me back to staring at my breath float away outside of the club on that cold January night just before I would go inside to sign up for the open mic and tell jokes for the first time in my life. My mind was no less cluttered with angst this time as I worried less about my act and more about getting myself across the stage without a mishap of sorts from the borrowed set of crutches I found myself needing. Though I do suppose the point of a performer is to perform, I could always keep falling down in my back pocket if things go south, nothing better than a sympathy laugh to propel them back in my favor. When my name was called I took a deep breath and focused all of my attention on making it up the stairs. Limping onto stage I was jolted by some sort of magical confidence. This here is the part I can't seem to latch an explanation to. My confidence isn't undeserved, but it's also not completely earned. Here I was going on stage in front of 350 people wearing fucking gym shorts. My largest audience ever. It was a bit unreal to think I was projecting to a group of people that was as large as the number of students I went to high school with. I could bomb all I wanted, but I could not fall off this stage or off these fucking steps. I was staring at a room full of people. A cluster of 45 people laughing is a lot of people laughing even amongst 350. If grouped together it wells up. It made me think of that video game where the board lights up in random places and you must tap on it during that moment. Each time you're looking for the largest possible square, often times getting the sporadic lucky strikes of a *Battleship* board. After announced I went to the mic and immediately called out everyone in the crowd for ignoring me when I was asking for money earlier. *"Yeah, you didn't think you'd see me again did you!?"* That got a chuckle. Half-way through someone from the crowd commented on an object sitting on the stool behind me. Somewhere in going to the bathroom I had missed a few minutes of the act before me and was caught very off guard when I turned around and saw the packaging of a very large dildo sitting behind me. Not loving the task of bantering with the crowd I was lucky to find the right words and told them I had been through enough talk of prosthetics over the last few weeks and we needed to move on. A few minutes later I saw Santos coming up on the right side of the stage. He had a leaning antsy motion to his movements and I got the feeling that I was starting to go over my time, despite not having seen any warning lights. Feeling the situation I decided to just use the advantage of possessing a mic to look his way and ask if my act needed to come to an end.

"Ladies and Gentlemen, I am only here tonight by the grace of this nice man to my right. Santos Garcia. Santos. It looks like you need something from *me. Did I over my time?"*

He lightened up the look on his face and threw a smile my way along with a confirmation and a finger which pointed at his watch.

"My bad bro. Alright guys. Thank you for listening and stay strong. Don't forget how much you like me when I try to wipe down your windshield tomorrow."

When I got off the stage I gave a few polite smiles to some people hoping to move a few chords out of my way and made my way down the aisle and back to my camera. After that I sat around the table with the rest of the comedians half listening to the rest of the show and looking around at the crowd. My life had clearly changed, but I would only be able to do this type of material for the next 40 days. Then it would be about what my life WAS like.

As I started to leave I was suddenly stopped by the usual occurrence of a 20-minute tropical storm comprised of bucket like streams dumping all around me. Muttering a quick *fuck* I hobbled my way back under an awning and found a tall cocktail table with two seats open and plopped myself down. Those around me split their actions between running hurriedly to their cars while the other half found refuge in the surroundings awnings as I had. Sitting there I was approached by a girl with a Florida tan and a red sundress to compliment her green eyes. *"Do you mind if we steal this chair?"*

Lifting my cast from the bottom rung of the chair I started to remove myself and lean back as the woman began to notice what I was doing.

"Oh My God. I'm so sorry. I didn't realize you were using it."

"No it's cool. I can get up and lean on the crutches. It's all the same."

"No really. I don't want your cast to get wet. Here. I can just put my butt on the side of the seat."

Scooting herself up on the edge of the seat she carefully placed her feet to the other side and gave me a satisfied smile, *"See. All good."*

I gave her a nod and turned my head back towards the street and watched as the rain continued to batter the world around me.

"Didn't I see you on stage earlier?"

I looked around as if slightly stupid and asked her, *"You mean me? Yeah. I was up at the improv. You went to the show?"*

"Yeah we always go! You were so funny. That bit about your girlfriends dog was so great."

With a hesitation in my voice I looked beyond her, *"Thanks."*

"What's wrong? You don't think so?"

"I gotta stop calling her my girlfriend, but if I call her my ex I sound mean."

"Oh you're single?"

"They keep making me that way."

"So you coming home with me then?"

Caught off by her abruptness and somewhat unsure if she was serious I sat there a moment looking at her and I must say I saw a sparkle in her eye which concerned me. Some sort of intention hiding behind a glimmer. Not in a manner which implied she would kill me, but I wasn't certain that the next two months tied to her bed frame was how I wanted to recover from injury. Plus, I just wasn't feeling it given my situation at the moment.

"No, I don't think so. I can't."

"Oh come on," she urged as her right hand reached in and landed itself on my knee with the tips of her fingers grazing the middle of my thigh. *"You won't have to do any of the hard work."*

"NO seriously. I can't. I uh. Look. This is weird to explain, but showering isn't the easiest right now and I just don't feel good about myself being naked with anybody. Please. Do yourself the favor."

With a confused twitch on her face she moved her hand back slightly, *"Are you serious?"*

"I'm afraid I am. I'm not letting my current state be your first impression. Why not give me your number and I'll call you when this cast is off."

"You can always shower at my place..."

"I appreciate it. Really I do. Maybe we can get coffee later this week though..."

From there our conversation slowly trickled and despite her last second instance that I go home with her, I managed to make it to my car and get on home without any distractions. It did feel weird though. Good and weird. Rejecting someone so outright. That's a privilege that women have that they never talk about like it matters; it's like being super tall, you just forget you've got it like that, but they have the certainty of sex. Granted, standards are often to be argued, and there is almost always an aspect of settling. That being said, she couldn't take a hint when I was trying to brush her off. In some ways I was interested, in some ways I wasn't interested at all. It's hard to recall a day when I would have been so reluctant to accept the invitation to a good time.

Though there's plenty of times I would have and plenty of times I did. Then again it could have been the lessons from those times which caused my hesitation.

One of the coolest parts of a college town is the variety of characters you meet. You're never in a place so much surrounded by clusters of people each with a certain level of intention in their existence. However, you also meet people who are smart and cunning, which when you're young and horny can be dangerous. Which brings me to this one time I met a girl at a party on the outskirts of town. See, I didn't know most of the group attending that night, just a few of them. Her boyfriend being one people I knew. Well that's not entirely true, I knew his cousin from having gone to a high school not far from me though he graduated a year or two before. So yeah. I meet this couple and we started talking, and then later I drive them home because Uber didn't exist yet and otherwise people were just out driving drunk like it was no problem. The next day I get a text from some number that I don't know, and turns out this girl had gotten my number from her boyfriends cousins phone. That didn't bother me much, her text was nice to start. She said *Thank You* and all of that and a few days later she tried to spark up the conversation again. So speed through a lot of shady conversations and a few late night meet ups and next thing I know we're laying there in bed one day and she starts to tell me about this history paper she had due. Being in college myself I was familiar with the statement and for the sake of conversation asked her what class it was for, hoping for some more specificity and perhaps the opportunity to bore her with my knowledge of whatever era she was studying. At which time she replied, *"Mrs. Shepards."* Immediately noticing the oddity of not hearing something like *"History 103"* or *"Ancient Civ"*, I perked up a bit and continued through a few utterances to clarify, all leading to a final question. *"So uh. What school do you go to again?"* At first her speech stammered as she tried to reframe her sentence. Then she gave up. When she replied with a string of words ending in High School I took my right canine to my bottom lip and breathed in deeply, *"Wonderful, so how old does that make you?"* My heart only thumped out of beat once when she responded, *"17"*, and tried to brush it off like it was no big deal. Don't worry, I didn't suddenly switch up my morals there and get all self-righteous. I mean, we had already done all we could do, and this conversation happened in her bed, so I don't think I've gotta explain this any further. Nonetheless, I did refrain from seeing her again in such a manner afterwards. She kept calling me a bitch for it and I couldn't really argue against her complaints, but I couldn't knowingly drive to a 17 year olds house in the middle of the night anymore as a guy who was closer to 21 than to 20. Especially not now that I understood it was her mom and not her *roommates* who she was trying to keep me from by assuring I always came over after midnight. Oh yeah, I forgot to tell you that fuckin' part. She told me her one roommate was really good friends with that dude so I had to come over late at night the first two times we hung out together so I wouldn't be seen, and it's not like I was browsing the living room mantel for photos, I just walked right up the stairs and went about my way. Though even now it boggles my mind to think how uninhibited she was in such close proximity to her moms room.

"So do I have to worry about running into your parents? Is that why I'm sneaking around like this?"

"No. My moms not here tonight. She's working. If she's not here, her boyfriend's not gonna be here either."

"Jesus fucking christ."

Upon concluding that evening I put this story on a short list of things I shouldn't ever talk about. Mainly because at the time what we were doing was technically illegal. I say technically because if we had been a few months closer in age on either side of the board there would have been no issue. Still, this created a weird power dynamic, because a few times afterwards she would half-jokingly tell me that if I didn't fuck her again she was gonna go tell people I did anyways. I didn't give in, but the thought still made me paranoid once in a while. What if I pissed her off? What if her boyfriend found out? All valid concerns since what *WE* were doing was only illegal for *ME*. Though, the weirder part the older I get is that if she were just a few months older it wouldn't matter one bit how much older I was. In fact, the moment she turned 18 it suddenly became okay for me to sleep with her, or for anyone over the age of 18 to sleep with her no matter how far from that age they may be. I don't know that my brain can fully understand that because the version of me at 20 related with the version of her at 17 far more than the version of me in my 30s ever could, though technically speaking the law would see us as equals. She wouldn't be the last of women to lie to me about their age as a means of getting me to fuck them, but was happily the only one to do so while under the age of 18. The rest just used fake ID's on me as a bartender to play as a 21 year old and then ultimately have to shy away from a bar entrance when they realized that certain places scanned your ID for certainty. Each time leading to an interesting conversation and a haphazard explanation on their part.

Being on crutches really was a great way to teach a series of things; chief among them patience. I often tried to sit and consider the fact that there would be a day in the future where in some moment of annoyance I will miss the moment here, where though I am unable to do or be all which I normally am, at least I'm not being annoyed by another soul. It was a neat time to just observe the world and see what was going on. There is a certain freedom to knowing that you are where you are. Unlike life where momentum tends to get you going, this particular set of motions required a person to be able to bounce from one tired exertion to the next. I remember feeling a certain privilege in my life, that I could just sit down. No one was going to fuck with me. Still it took everything in me not to live in a negative mindset at this time in my life. When I reflected on decisions better made I was always reminded of something better I could be doing with my time. I could be in New York making money, performing, and doing everything I was doing, but in a place where it made sense, with all of my limbs in a proper state of function. Ultimately the only thing I could do to improve my situation was to put focus into its improvement. Which is why I started writing to myself more than I ever had before. The situation called for it. I was in desperate need of someone to talk to and it was important to see my thoughts written out. At times there needed to be a written account of all going on around me; and to say, *all going on,* I literally mean that. I kept track of pretty much anything happening. It's like in a dream I knew what was going to happen if I didn't. I realized how easily I would lose track of the days. Here I was a week in and I already watched the minutes crawl by. One day sporadically enjoying three movies. The next having nothing to do. It's annoying to have to *wait* for anything to happen. I was never good at waiting. A type-A personality and an internal ball of energy kept my feet moving forward every other day of my life. It was an act of discipline not to wallow in my own regret and self-pity during the next few weeks. Sitting outside I felt bored. I felt useless. I had nothing but infinite drive and yet, here I was, unable to move. Unable to go anywhere. Sure I could write, I could always write, but writing was nothing more than reflecting; and reflecting took something on which one can reflect upon.

Ultimately I hated who the broken foot situation made me in moments of anger. Moments which came sometimes rather violently despite all of my previously positive self-talk. It created an environment which allowed for the cultivation of a much more frustrated person. It's one thing to be frustrated when a few inconveniences and speed bumps come your way each day, it's a whole new thing when putting your socks on feels like a fucking task. It also went and just made me think more negatively about life. I was glad that for some reason I was able to sit and make myself slip into a mode of remembering that I needed gratitude and appreciation in my life. Try getting up from the toilet with your leg wrapped up, try taking a shower, even the most minute of tasks are worlds more difficult than you could ever imagine. *Keep the positive self talk going. Keep it going. Keep speaking healthily to yourself.* Those are the types of sentences I would write and read aloud to myself each day. Sometimes I would forget how much I needed it, other times I would recite the lines a few times a day like a priest trying to repent for his sins from years past.

Through this time I gained a new found respect for an individual in from my childhood who I saw growing up with the consequences of cerebral palsy. His movements had taught me how to monitor my distance and make sure I was never being reckless around him, but this experience soon ingrained just how difficult his day to day was. Not that I hadn't been filled with respect for him and his life as I grew up, but as my time in this situation went on I began to feel as if I was now overflowing with an empathy that I had never felt before. Although my personal experience with crutches was only going to scratch the surface of what a lifetime would be like, for a second I was able to grasp the difficulty in even the simplest of tasks. Not that this needs to be an essay of sympathy. The last thing anyone needs is your sympathy if it in turn does not lead to some great action. Thoughts are nice and vibes are great, but change is the only thing truly useful.

I preferred the days when everyone didn't work from home. Not for any lack of love, it was just the added pressure of another person I had to be invisible to throughout the day. Which wasn't easy to do because even the slip of my crutches was enough to alert the next room that I had arrived for my morning coffee. Or even worse, startle the dog and start a barking fit that would ring into the next yard. In fairness his bark was more of a yap, but its consistency was one which sprouted annoyance in no time. Though I had never been the type to bury myself in a show not to my liking my friend was catching up on *Game of Thrones* and finishing up season 6. So as a means of finding something to do I sat there and watched each episode with him. By episode 3 he had stopped trying to fill me in on who characters were, whose sister they had slept with, and from which family they came. It was a bit much to keep up with. If he had told me from the beginning it was about something historical then I would have followed along a bit differently. Though I'm still confused about the white walkers and why they were so angry. Speaking of that, why is it that in every possible instance of some creature being invincible are they so damn angry and discontent? Those who die in a century are always more pleasant than those allowed to live forever.

During this time I was also reminded of the importance of habit and routine. Routine saves you. I remembered reading Viktor Frankle's Book, *"Man's Search For Meaning"* and taking away that a man needs a routine. I've also read that during wars it's often said that those who survive POW camps are those who keep shaving each morning. *(They give them razors?)* Keeping routine in mind when Camilo was gone during the day I would do my best to use the time to get a workout in and take the time to flex my feet any chance I got. Hoping that muscle memory was real and that I would benefit from this practice two months from now. I was happy to have the time and the capacity to help myself heal faster. I kept wishing I had the same ability in speeding up my comedy by getting on stage more.

I spent most of my afternoons playing with Loki tossing a tangled up piece of rope time and time again to the end of the backyard and then waiting for it to be returned, each time slightly more wet. Gonna admit something here that you may find more throughout my literature but won't really understand until you're around me, but I don't really like dogs. I love animals. Big fan of wildlife, and to say I don't like dogs even eliminates some of the truth, but what I don't like is pets. I've never really enjoyed the idea of having an animal whose entire existence is dependent on my ability and desire to come back to the house every few hours to feed and or walk them. Which should show just how much I loved the girls who I ended up dating with pets. That's why at best you might be able to convince me that a cat is worthwhile venture, given that it can fend for itself and generally doesn't care if you ever come back or not. While conversations about not loving dogs didn't tend to take me anywhere good, neither did those surrounded by the question of how I was doing at this time.

"What's good. How's the trip treating ya?" - Jax

"It's good." - Patrick

"Glad to hear. Hadn't seen you post in a few days..." - Jax

"I've been laying low. Not really feelin' myself right now." - Patrick

"Wanna talk?" - Jax

"Nah, just in a rut. This humidity and this cast are getting to me. Everything itches." - Patrick

"Sounds shitty. Well holler at me if you need anything." - Jax

"Will do. I'll be leaving here in a few days. Hit you up when I'm on the road." - Patrick

The next morning I attended my last trip to the doctors. As he took off my cast I starred down at my foot with utter amazement and disappointment. I couldn't believe how it looked. It was swollen, still slightly discolored, and the shin seemed to blend into top of the ankle with a bloating of the skin that hadn't settled down. Attempting to stretch my toes I watched as the rest of my foot responded in concurrence with the rest of the muscle involved. There the doctor told me it would be a few days before I felt normal. Even then I was to expect another two to three weeks of irregularity in the overall feeling of my legs and my ability to move long distances without the use of crutches. Adding to that knowledge I was advised to keep my crutches with me til mid August just in case I felt the need.

EAST TO WEST
July 2016

"I'm going...going...back...back..to Cali...Cali...."
Notorious B.I.G

L ooking around at a set of guys standing next to a moving
container I lifted my body just enough to show some effort,
knowing in the end I couldn't really help, *"Need a hand
grabbing a few bags?"*

"Don't worry about it man," directing his look to my legs he uttered,
"Do we still need to bring your crutches?" Not even trying to hide the
look on my face I starred across the top of the car and gave a quick,
"Yeah." I wanted to give them up, but I still didn't feel confident in the
limited stability I had regained since starting to wobble around. I still
needed to use my crutches for efficient movement. According to the
doctors my foot was supposed to be healed by now, and perhaps it was,
but no part of my foot felt 100%. The bone was probably the only part
of the foot that was good to go. The rest of it was in definite need of
rehabilitation. The allowed stagnation of being in the car a few days
would give me a little extra time in the healing department, but I was
going to make getting my feet in the sand one of my first priorities. The
doctor had given me the suggestion of imagining flexing my foot along
the way as a means of keeping the nerves strong. The true test would
be in a few days when that very foot would be expected to once again
respond to the woes of Los Angeles traffic and respond properly on a
stiff clutch and new set of brakes.

It's supposed to be easier to travel cross country with someone else
than it is alone, but I'm not sure that's true. There's a natural benefit to
driving such a long distance with another person, but the perfect
number of people if you're not doing it alone is three. I've driven cross
country in all combos from alone to 3 people and a Rottweiler, and once
across Central America with 3 first time travelers and a girl who had no
idea what she was getting into. So trust me when I say three is ideal.
Which sucks because the best number of people to travel with is one.
Yourself. That's it. Nobody else. That all being said, if you gotta travel
with anyone, Camilo's the one you wanna do it with. Regardless it's
awkward having to ask someone else to pull over to use the bathroom.

It keeps me from drinking whenever I'm thirsty. At least out here in the middle of nowhere I can pull over and pee if the moment becomes an emergency. It was funny because part of the selling point was that I was going to be able to drive, and yet as we got in the car together I didn't really feel like he wanted me there. I went from being a friend he was proud of to a friend who was kind of a burden. I felt like I had begun to overstay my welcome, but maybe this was just a stage in our friendship, another test used later as a marker to make the decision to double down once again or to fade back. A fading which never happened because you just don't give up friends like this in life. By now I was entering the 9th day of my life spent crossing Texas. Camilo had been going most of the driving so I figured I would ask his status before volunteering my hand behind the wheel.

"Do you wanna stop and sleep?" - Patrick

"Nah, I'm cool. You good to take over in a few hours?" - Camilo

"Yeah I got you. Might take a nap. How long you good for?" - Patrick

"I can go til at least 3 or so. Who knows. I'm gonna light up and just cruise until I can't no more. I'll wake ya up." - Camilo

As I sunk down into my seat I listened as Camilo began to sing to himself, gazing off into the distance as his head began to shake with the music.

"So what you think's gonna happen if Trump wins?" - Patrick

"All I know is that mother fucker better legalize weed. I'm tired of having to figure out where to get this shit each time I decide to hop out of town. It's fucking annoying. And it's stupid." - Camilo

"I don't disagree. Stupid law. So you wanna get some?" - Patrick

"Always. You know anyone around here?" - Camilo

"Yeah." Fast forward another hour or so and there I was again, in the middle of Texas, going out of the way to break the law to find strangers and travel with drugs. Which by now I know seems normal, but it doesn't mean I'm ever any more comfortable with it than any time before. It only means I should be. As we started to smoke het let his guard down and the anxiety of his new adventure began to surface.

"What are you worried about man? You seem really stressed." - Patrick

"I am." - Camilo

"Someone who loves you is trying to help you. Take that. They wouldn't offer it if they could't help you." - Patrick

"I barely know this lady." - Camilo

"What do you mean? It's your fuckin aunt." -Patrick

"Yeah. I mean we're related, but it's not like I know this bitch." - Camilo
"You're family. I'm sure it'll be cool." - Patrick
"I need to do this on another level. I can't keep fuckin' around." - Camilo

Sitting there listening to him I couldn't quite understand why he was so hesitant about his future capabilities to make a change in his life work. He had done a career change much like myself, though his was somewhat more reasonable. His wasn't even a change as much as it was a transfer of existence to another coast to be closer to the surfers who would eventually ride his surfboards. Mine wasn't even a career change as much as it was an attempt at something completely out of left field. A constant reminder that I was lucky to live in a place where this was possible. Another reason I tell myself this country is amazing. Everyone is more open to everything than you may have been previously led to believe. For starters, you can go to Texas and own a fucking tiger. I mean, I don't actually think that's a good idea, but still, you can go own a fucking tiger. There's actually very few things you can't do in the United States, and currently I'm at a loss to think of what. Well, okay here's a few things, you can't get a free heart surgery. Not even an affordable one. All this is to say I didn't realize until that moment how similar my struggle was to that of Camilo's, with both of us making a shift on hyperdrive at the hopes of making up for lost time.

When we got to El Paso area the two of us were plenty hungry and by now had been on the road in eight hours of sunlight without a bit of food ingested. I had driven since the last gas up and with twenty miles left on the tank I was met with no questions when I pulled off the third El Paso off-ramp and asked Camilo where he wanted to eat. The options were plentiful and if your choice was a chain restaurant of sorts I would argue this city had more than another other I had ever seen. Before going in we lit up a spliff and parked towards the back of the parking lot to put the cherry on top of our appetite in peace. Which turned out not to be the best of decisions because the moment we got inside the restaurant they sat us next to a table of Border Patrol and Customs Agents.

"God damnit. I'm too brown for this shit right now. Let's ask to move to another table." - Camilo
"Bro. They're just on a break. No one is looking for us." - Patrick
"Still don't wanna be sitting next to them while I'm high." - Camilo
"Just enjoy your food. Looks way weirder if we get up." - Patrick

"Where are we gonna stay tonight?" - Camilo

"We have a few options in Phoenix. Not sure they had another bed, but I can take the couch." - Patrick

"Yeah, anything we could do to save some money would be great." - Camilo

Upon leaving we drove, and drove, and drove. At one point we crossed over into New Mexico, and at another passed by Albuquerque. The scenery changed, the sun-set, and when we pulled up to the crash pad in Phoenix I saw a look of uncertainty land on Camilo's face, *"Are you sure about this spot?"* - Camilo

"Yeah. These people are cool." - Patrick

Our host did her best later to disprove me of this certainty by later telling us a story which left her as the prime suspect in a ton of money missing from a family member back in Minnesota. I say this with no disrespect to her now, but based on the humble means of the house, it seems unlikely that she was the receiver of such gifts. If she were, she did not spend them well or had a level of patience like no other.

The next day we had the unfortunate situation of creeping into the greater Los Angeles area just as rush hour traffic was starting. All two-million cars and their drivers were slowly making their way out of the city and into the spiderweb of towns surrounding the many desert valleys. Camilo seemed annoyed. Not by me, but with the reality that we were in California, but nowhere near where he needed to be.

"Do you mind if I take you to your car in the morning?" - Camilo

"Yeah, I can wait. Your buddy won't mind if I crash?" - Patrick

"I'm paying him $1,000 for three weeks, I don't care if he minds." - Camilo

Walking back to my car with a handful of bags I struggled balancing the shoulder straps as I wobbled into the backyard. I hadn't seen a car of mine this dirty in my entire life. The type of dirty you see when a car has been parked outside after a long drive through the mud only to be bombarded with pollen and sand particles for the next month, the type of dirty that draws attention. The outside was caked with a combination of sand and salt as a layer of bird shit covered the right side which had been left only slightly within the reach of the highest branches of a tree dangling over the fence. Popping the trunk I fought against two months of rubber sealing and suction and placed my crutches inside, glancing through my things to check for everything as if the lack of a broken window wasn't enough to tell me all of my

226

shit was still there. The moment I got back to my car I was filled with the same surge of urgency which had filled my body when I first decided to take this trip. Finally having a sense of autonomy back I sat in my front seat with my hands clenched in excitement as I tried not to let the outside world see my internal celebrations. The lack of independence without a car had been almost as debilitating as the temporary lack of use in my legs, slowing me down from a speed I once readily kept. After having spent so much time on the road in such a series of uncomfortable positions when I finally got a moment to myself I felt a thud of exhaustion come over my body. Although I was no further ahead than I was months before, arguably doing worse, I still felt a sense of relief. I was finally on my own again. I was finally able to live for me again. The first thing I did for myself was take myself down to the Santa Monica area and park along Ocean Park Blvd between 3rd and 4th street. I wanted to leave one of the crutches in the car, but truth be told there's nothing easier about walking with one crutch than there is two. At least not once you had a general sense of movement back about. At least with the crutches I could use the power of propulsion to project myself forward and save my overall energy. Departing from Camilo I was back out on my own again, determined more than ever to get my shit together. I wanted to be able to prove to him the next time I saw him that his time spent helping me was not done so in vain, that his small amount of resources had not been wasted.

Days: 31
Miles Traveled: 1,714
Stages: 7

SAN DIEGO, CALIFORNIA
July 2016

"Will that broken foot fit in your mouth?"

E nough was enough, I needed to get walking again. I had done all of the toe stretching and foot work I could over the last two months, the only thing I hadn't been able to work on was re-stabilizing and that was only going to happen one way. The fortunate part about the neighborhood I found to stay in was that the entire sidewalk was in one way or another lined with a series of things to hold onto, most of the time that being part of some stone wall which lined the property or a railing atop some gate. With that advantage in mind I left my crutches in the car and hopped over towards the sidewalk and leaned up against one of the previously mentioned stone walls and started to plant my foot down and move forward one step at a time. Walking down the sidewalk I began to stumble as my right foot started to give way. No amount of confidence was available to make up for the fact that my muscles had fallen out of practice. By now I was a block away and committed to the distance I had covered, more so than I gave consideration to the distance still yet to be surmounted. I had heard this same sort of learning to walk again can happen to entertainers who spend too much time off of the stage. Too much time away they say.

It was really cool to be staying across from the Top Gun house. My first day there I wobbled my way over and took a look around through the gates which had been erected as a way to shut it off to the public while it goes through the hands of judicial argument over whether or not to tear it down and build another hotel; a decision which would undoubtedly displease the fine people at the hotel I found myself, serving as an obstruction to an otherwise perfect view of the Pacific Ocean. As I was leaning against the fence taking in the view I was interrupted by a voice from my side. *"You know they made that movie for 15$ million? Made 20 times that."*

"Oh yeah?"

"Yeah. Tom loved it."

"Tom? Like Cruise?"

"The one and only. You an actor?"

"No."

"Military?"

"Nope. Comedian."

"Writer?"

"Stand-up."

"Oh. Well you're an actor too. Even if you don't know it. Lots of work available. You ever audition for anything?"

"Nah man. Got to be an extra once on some indie film that never got picked up. But that was just a cold call, no audition, no photo. Literally responded to a Craigslist ad."

"You should consider getting an agent. Why don't you come and talk with me about what to do with your career."

"My career?"

"I think I could find you something. When are you free to talk about your future?"

Excited as could be I perked up a bit and straightened out my legs the best I could.

"I'll give you my number and we can meet whenever you've got the time."

"What area in town are you staying in?"

"Literally around the corner."

"So is my office. Why don't you meet me there say 2 o'clock?"

"Perfect. I'll be there. What's the address?"

Relaying the address to confirm once more I thanked him for his time and then politely moved away from the table to give the man the privacy from which I had stolen him from. When the hour came I worked my way to the address on Fountain street as I had previously agreed.

"I see on your twitter here it says, former stripper, I would take that down, you want people to take you a bit more seriously."

Considering the confusion of the fact that I was a comedian and this guy wanted me to appear more serious continued to go through my mind. "UH, it doesn't seem to have hurt me so far."

"So you were a stripper, why don't you tell me about that time. Must be some good jokes in there."

"It was just something I did a few times. One of those things I fell into."

"Oh. Well I'm sure a guy like yourself didn't find it hard finding work in the industry."

"I don't know. Each time was a word of mouth kind of reference. Fun times though, definitely glad I didn't back down the first time I got invited."

"It's that do what your heart tells you type of spirit. That's great. That's exactly what this town needs. Still important to watch your Twitter feed though. You never know what someone might think."

Given the ever-changing state of the world I found myself getting annoyed every time I had to watch someone dance their way out of words previously said. Though I didn't tell him I've deleted more than a few tweets. None because of this book. But any that I did delete were based on the fact that two hours later I thought to myself, *well that wasn't nice,* or *that was fucking stupid.* Not because of any sense of need to please a PR firm, I just happened to realize that what I said wasn't well thought out and probably hurt someone without making any type of humor as a means of blunting the blow. To me deleting a tweet is just like wishing you could take something back after an argument, except actually being able to take it back. I just pressed delete. Thankfully at the time I only had 45 followers, and none of them were so-called journalist wanting to ruin my day and my livelihood. This is an important time for me to say something about journalist. We need to stop pretending like everyone who writes an article is a journalist or a reporter of the news. We also need to directly separate someone who actually gives us informative news based around the world that we need to know about, and someone who gives us something with a sensationalist spin. It used to be really easy. Now it's so easy to make a website that looks legitimate, not everybody knows when something is news or not. To members of my generation it probably seems crazy to think any of our parents would ever click on those fake e-mails from online platforms telling them they know how to pay for their services when they were once free, but to that older generation there is no easy way to distinguish between the realities and falsehoods of the web, each side looking more convincing each day.

I can't say exactly how one thing led to another, but I do recall a moment about thirty minutes into being at this guys place where things got weird. *"Would you mind if we put on a movie?"*

"It's your place."

When the t.v. turned on the screen went to a menu of movies, many in foreign languages. As he scrolled down the list and made a selection the screen then went black and slowly brought up a series of credits attached to a weird set of tunes getting louder. At first I was polite and tried to keep my mind on the screen, but the further it went along the more it appeared like some sort of noir porn. Upon noticing this I decided I had the right to interject and try to figure out what was going on, *"So is there someone in this movie you wanted me to see or...?"*

"No no, I just thought this was something you might like. Being a stripper and all..."

In my mind I kept thinking how this wasn't supposed to be happening to me, this was the type of thing that happened to girls from the MidWest unaware of the ways of the world and how the city can be for those not keeping watch. I had always wondered how anyone got themselves into some of those situations, and here I was in my own. As I darted my eyes around and leaned forward I saw his hand start to go and unbutton his pants, at which point I perched my crutches up and shot to attention.

"I'm sorry. I uh. This just isn't the type of job I was looking for."

"I didn't know you were one of those up tight type of guys."

"I'm not. And I'm not judging you, but I'm pretty certain this isn't normal no matter what circles you're hanging out in. Thank you for lunch, but I gotta run."

With that I hobbled my ass to the elevator and went on my way, never to respond to any of his messages again, of which there were many. It was odd, they said *MY* Twitter wasn't professional, and then those same hypocrites tried to whip out their dicks in their apartment. As I wish to continue to be honest this wasn't the first time I had been hit on by a man. Having been a bartender I can't really count the amount of times it has happened actually. Though I do remember a few of the highlights because each one was a situation where had it been a man hitting on a woman instead of a man hitting on me, they would have all been subject to charges or jail time. This one time I was in a sauna, and no, not like a bathhouse, it was at my local gym, and I go in there and there's this guy sitting inside with a red USC hat on. Weird yes, but not a detail that I found startling enough to turn around and leave. Doing as one does I made room between us and sat down at the opposite end of the room. I suppose it's important to tell you this was a room which could have fit about 8 people in it, so its' not like we needed to be crowded. Anyway, there I am listening to my music, headphones on and all that good stuff, and kinda out of nowhere I start to notice this hand in my peripheral vision that wasn't there before. Not thinking too much of it I kept my head down and continued to stare at the discolored puddle that kept mounting on the wooden panels beneath me. Then I saw that hand getting closer. Then closer. Then, as if to impress me with the flexibility of his pinky finger he started to widen the spaces between his hands, resulting in the pinky finger making its way to the outside of my right thigh, which at the time was uncovered and exposing my increasingly sweaty leg. New to such a situation I wasn't sure how to act as his pinky then stroked up against my leg. It was in that moment that I was faced with a series of conflicts, do I get up and leave, do I hurriedly brush his hand away, do I turn to him and say, *"What the fuck are you doing?"* Or do I give him no warning and just take a swing at him? Well, being in touch with two realities at that moment; one, that I was only a towel shy of naked in a sauna at midnight, and two, not wanting to be that guy who got kicked out of the gym for punching some gay dude in the sauna (and let's be honest, that's the only way it would be seen by anyone working at the gym who had heard the story). That being realized I decided to be the bigger man (and from what I remember I was) and just slid away to the furthest possible reach. In scooting over I relieved myself from his touch as well as any future touch and decided to go about my sweat. After all, I was in there to sweat it out and that's what I was going to do. I figured this late at night in such an environment might have been one of those places where those things happen and maybe in the days when homophobia still existed this was the way in which he was choosing to test the waters. I had flirted with plenty of women in my life who never gave me a moments worth of attention after my attempt and I figured maybe this was just one of those instances but from the other sex. Well, actually from the same sex. I held onto that thought until the next part happened. I'd say by then about a minute and a half had gone by, and what do you know, there's that same fucking hand again, creeping steadily into my vision. At this point I realized my refusal had to speak a bit louder than before, but at the same time I was thinking, *"Okay, there's no way this dude is trying again…."* But what do you know, he was. So for what reason I'll never know, probably stubbornness and an inexplicable love for the sauna, I continued to sit there, hoping to drip off as much water weight as I could before the moment came to some sort of conclusion. Then just like the time before, his finger stretched away from his palm and he attempted to touch me. Only this time I decided I was going to be a bit vocal. So without looking over, without turning down my music, and without hesitation I said, *"Okay, I'm outta here"* then stood up, tightened the towel around me, kept my head forward, and walked towards the door, only uttering one more sentence before I opened the door and left, *"I wasn't fucking playing hard to get you fucking creep."* That sauna would be the cause of my hauntings only twice more, once when a guy cat called me, not like hollering, more like a legitimate sound like the one you would make trying to get a cats attention or someones attention from across a counter with a *psst* followed by the question, *"Can I just suck on it?"* A question so bold that I only wish he had taught a few of my ex-girlfriends how to approach me after a fight and one to which I responded with a shocked look and a quick departure, easily more creeped out than the time before. The last time I walked in that sauna was a few months later when I interrupted two men as one was actually sucking on it. Seriously, I still don't fucking get it. I mean, the first time it was after midnight, I guess those are the types of hours one can expect some weird shit to go down, but the dick sucking that I interrupted was literally at around 9 PM when the gym is far from short on people. I never even told the front desk about any of this because I was worried about being called a homophobe or even worse, having them close the sauna entirely. When the reality is I just wanna be able sit in the sauna without someone touching me, hell, I imagine that's the majority of the reason why women would want the male and female saunas separated in the first place, so no one has to deal with that type of bullshit. I know I said I'm open; but I don't even like all women, I definitely don't have time for men. Plus I find the thought gross. I'll be honest with you, I'm amazed I'm able to get women to fuck me and I think I've got a decent figure on me. Mens bodies are just gross by the comparison of that of the female figure.

Getting back to the hotel I went digging through my bag and started to leave. Finding Camilo out in the lobby I took a seat next to him and motioned for the bartender to come over.

"I don't say this a lot, but I need a drink."

"You wanna smoke a joint and go for a walk?"

"That works too."

As I got back to his room Camilo turned in and asked, *"How the meeting with that executive guy go?*

"Huh? Oh. Uh. He didn't show up. Said we'll have to reschedule."

"That's fuckin lame."

"I know. It's whatever. How bout you? How was your day? Getting shit

together?"

"Yeah. I gotta get some fucking darker shades. That morning light is coming in too hot."

"A.C.?"

"No, I mean that shit is intense, I'm not trying to have that shit come in my room and wake me up on Saturday's. It's whatever, I'm gonna go to Target here in a bit if you wanna ride."

"I'm down. Just lemme know when."

"When do you gotta get outta here?"

"I don't know. I gotta hit a few people up and see who along the way can meet me when and see what makes the most sense. Fuckin Southern California ain't cheap. So I gotta get going sooner than later."

Eyes widening as he took a hit of his bowl Camilo responded, *"I fuckin' know. I went to the grocery store earlier, that shit ain't Southern Florida prices that's for sure."*

"Oh I bet. You're two layers of bureaucracy from anything you need now. Fucking California."

Waking up the next morning I stumbled around the room for a bit and did my usual morning maintenance. At one point I saw my reflection hobbling in the mirror and through the haze of warped glass I noticed the shape of my head in a way I never had before. At this point my face was so tan that the sun kissed follicles on my head were not easily distinguished from a distance, a feature even more so noticed when you calculate the sheer lack of volume to my hair. Looking in the mirror I started to trim my neck and then my checks. Lightly brushing my sideburns with the clippers as I leaned in at the mirror. For whatever reason I took the clippers and started to run them along the sides of my head, removing a row of hair above my ears. Closing my eyes and looking down I started to the run the clippers over my entire head. Stepping back more I took a moment and gave my legs a look in the mirror, developing a grim awareness about the difference in muscular structure between the two legs. Looking in the mirror it made me laugh to remember a man at the Vitamin Shoppe who had once tried to tell me, *"There's just as many women who like bald men as there are men with hair."* (Which is to say there's just as many women who like dudes under 6 foot compared to the ungrateful bitches who don't.) As if that was my biggest issue. It was more of the paleness factor which I found hindering me. Then again maybe he was just trying to tell himself that. All I knew is that I was on my way to looking like I was either in the military, or a white supremacist. Of course there was always the option of growing a beard to counter the look. Though the combination of colors in my beard were just as varied as the shade of my freckles and I had always preferred to keep myself at no more than a five o'clock shadow, something easily done as long as I brought the trimmer out once every few days. Large parts of me hated that I looked like a cop or military man as it hadn't helped in a positive manner when I was trying to slip about throughout the world. A lot of the time I had to stay high just to maintain the more than certain image that I wasn't an undercover cop, all a consequence of an unfortunate pattern of hair growth which led me to having a horseshoe shaped scalp on the front end of my forehead which progressed aggressively in my late twenties and then made a thankful stop. By the time I was done trimming and shaving I felt more different than I looked, with an identity that was unlike one I had hoped for at any time before. Yet I wondered if this same change would be more traumatic or altering for someone who had a head of hair like Thor as opposed to one that looked like Jason Statham.

I wanted to *hit the ground running* sort of speak, but I was soon humbled by the fact that I would be doing no running anytime soon and for that matter it would be much longer than expected before I would be doing what I considered normal walking. It's a weird feeling to know you're ready and willing and yet unable. Anyone who had ever walked on a roof or tried to navigate the shaky deck of a boat speeding across the waves knew exactly what I was talking about. My legs just didn't feel right. Though it was a relief being able to look at them both again and see the twitch in my foot each time I tried to wiggle my toes, and holy-fuck was it nice being able to scratch them again without having to use a clothes hanger. Along with all of the other changes in my life I quickly became comfortable with my new look, even loving the consistency of my head. Only downside was how pale I was, but I had to imagine that would change soon enough, especially roaming around the part of the country at this time of the year.

After I left the hotel I hobbled my way to the left and started down a very steeply inclined street and was lucky not to eat shit a few times when the bottom of my crutches slipped up on clumps of sand left on the sidewalk. The beach looked busier than the day before, busy in an organized way. There were flags waving every twenty yards or so and it appeared like one of the lifeguard stands had been converted into an announcers booth. This happened to be the annual Oceanside Surf competition. Today were only the trials, but all of the competition was out and the waves had shown up accordingly. Though the place was crowded there was still plenty of room at the jungle gym so I hobbled my ass over and placed myself under a pull-up bar. While doing a few pull-ups I was approached by your typical Cali-surfer looking dude with shaggy brown hair and a skateboarders hat on who already had my attention before he said, *"My man. Look at you go."* I struggled through my last pull up and then went limp as my body continued to latch onto the bars by a few sweaty finger tips. Releasing myself I landed my good foot on the ground and allowed myself to collapse to the sand in-order to not put any impact on my healing leg. Pushing myself up I was greeted by the surfers hand as he helped pull me up.

When I got back to the hotel I saw that my friends truck was gone from the parking lot and a realization that my phone was on silent let me know that I was going to be fucked for the evening. Apparently I had missed a few calls and *"Back in 3 hours"* was the last of his messages to be received behind the *"Where are you?"* ones that came trickling in before. With no key to the room I found my way to the terrace by the pool and sat down near a large family of Mexicans grilling an assortment of meats to be wrapped in tortillas at any moment. I was on a couch built of several sectionals with a table-top fireplace sitting in the middle of them. At one point a guy in his twenties with a muscle shirt and a few tattoos starting from the shoulder down to his wrists came towards one of the couches with a cooler being dragged at his side. Leaning in at one point I asked, *"Any of that birria?"* This led to one answer of *no,* and then to an offer of what they did have once it was cooked; an obvious advantage of traveling alone and only being one mouth to feed. As their numbers grew the family welcomed me in and soon enough I was sitting at the center listening to them all joke with each other. Once again the curses of being the one to just sit there put me in a position to listen a bit longer than I would have preferred, and as would be the case, the only one wanting to talk was the one who had already worn out the ears of everyone else with them.

"I'm ready to go home. We've been seeing too much of each other."

"Do you all not take trips together that often?"

"Honey this isn't a vacation. We're staying here because our basement

flooded and the insurance company is having us relocate while they fix
everything. It's taking so long."

"How long you been here?"

"Almost a MONTH."

"Ouch. I can't imagine living in a hotel room with my family for that
long."

As it went on to be explained I came to hear, as did much of the
surrounding crowd, about how the family, specifically the matriarch
and patriarch of the family, had been going through a split since the
new year and only via the scenario of a flooded basement and no other
choice were they now all under he same roof once more. More
accurately under the same roof and two rooms where previously they
had maintained their situation by sequestering one or the other to the
basement. Under normal circumstances I believe I would have done
what I could to slowly walk us away from the circle, or used even the
slightest of opportunity to usher myself slowly to the side and block
her voice from those around us. Soon there was a weird set of motions
being made between the eyes of the guys standing around me. I could't
quite tell what was going on, but I quickly felt things turning away
from my favor. *"Mom. Would you shut the fuck up? You don't need to tell*
every stranger our business like that." Followed by a, *"Don't talk to mom*
like that." And then a, *"Well she's over here telling some guy our family*
business and dad's right there."

Something they don't tell you about being on crutches is how
awkward moments can get. Not moments that you create, but moments
you end up being a part of that you would normally take as an
opportunity to walk away, but that's the thing, you can't just walk
away. Luckily one of the more logical members of the family came over
to the angry brother and took over. *"Look man it's cool. You didn't know.*
My mom should have kept that shit to herself." A comment soon
interrupted by the reassurance, *"No one is mad at you."* After which it
was clear my absence would be more appreciated than my presence so I
did my best to get going after awkwardly maneuvering myself from the
group around me. I had created this awkward moment, or created the
environment which allowed for it, and now I was stuck inside of it. No
easy coming and no easy going.

After the day I had yesterday I decided it was time to get my ass
back on the stage. Before that show I met with a friend of mine from
college and walked around the park. In our walk I couldn't help but

notice that she looked drastically different than the time I saw her before. Though no one would tell her at the time, she was once in an obvious battle with an eating disorder that she once looked to be losing. In noticing this I hesitated for the first hour or so through conversation with the cloud of wanting to address the past. To my surprise I saw that she had her own view of it which was much different than mine. *"Did you know what was going on or were you blind like I was?" - Sarah*

"No, I wanted to say something to you or ask if you were okay, but I was worried about offending you and I didn't wanna make the issue worse."

The show that night was in a restaurant attached to a mall. At every other location I had been the unique one waiting to go on stage without the ability to cruise on to stage easily standing out as the guy on crutches. Yet when someone in a wheel-chair was waiting, I almost looked like the asshole. He had figured out how to deal with the situation of his existence. He even had a few one liners ready for those he met on crutches who might live under the false impression that they know what his life is like, *"You have that look of hope in your eyes like you know you'll walk again."*

With no clever response I nervously nodded, unable to scoot away as I pleased, and proceeded to float there awkwardly for the next few minutes. Going on stage that night I felt like I couldn't use my typical jokes. Something which my friend decided to call me out on later.

"You go up there for ten minutes and don't say anything about it are you serious? Look at those things, you can't not say something."

"Well I don't have much I can say that's still going to apply two months from now."

"Who cares? It's about the laughs tonight."

I woke up the next morning and found the left-overs of someone leaving the room in a hurry laid scattered throughout the floor with some clothing dangling from a door handle only a quarter-inch and a small breeze from falling off. Upon exiting the room I went downstairs and wobbled my way around the breakfast buffet. As I ate my eggs the seats across from me were suddenly filled with 4 guys fitting your typical SoCal look; blonde hair, bright blue eyes, and skin that always seemed to hold a bit of the sea salted air in its pores. Each one looked tired, and each one devoured the plate in front of them in a matter of moments. Truth be told I can't quite recall what it was that got us talking to one another, but I came to find out that none of them were actually staying inside of the hotel. After which the leader of the group told me about the bus they had out front and that they were on a road trip from Southern Florida.

"What are you guys doing? Just chillin?"

"Kinda. My brother and I started a clothing company last year, that's him over there."

"What kinda clothes?"

"Surfing apparel. KOWASA Clothing Co. We started selling shirts around campus and after we graduated we rebuilt the inside of this bus to turn it into a store."

"So you're living on it and crashing hotel buffets when you can?"

"Basically."

Laughing to myself I lit up with a smile and looked up from my eggs, *"Good for you all."*

Going further into our stories I was eventually invited onto the bus and given one of their phone numbers in order to meet up later. Pulling myself up the stairs I found myself greeted by the inside of a tiny display shop for clothes. *"Yo this is sick...You all made these?"*

"Yeah bruh. What size you wear? Medium?"

Sifting through a roundabout rack he pulled a light blue t-shirt off a hanger and tossed it my way, landing it on top of my left shoulder. Tightening the crutch under my right side in between my lat and my pit I put my hand across and pulled it off my shoulder, then unfolding it in the middle to read the logo embedded inside. *"KO.WA.SA."*

"So who makes the clothes? Like do you guys do them or have it done elsewhere and then get em?"

"Check it out. We got all of the equipment on the bus."

To the best of my knowledge I was looking at a sewing machine and a paper cutter next to a laptop all spread across a designers board...I fantasized about how awesome it would be to be in their situation and traveling the country in a bus. At times becoming painfully aware of the bad sides that would accompany the good; the gas, the parking.

At the end of the weekend I decided I was going to leave and sleep in my car for a few days taking my time up the coast. I needed to float around for a few more days before I could move onto to a new place and a new group of people where my inconvenience would be freshly felt and no longer burden the foundations of my youth. That was the worst part about this whole thing, being in the way. The feeling of being in the way. This time made me think of so much, is this how old

241

age would be? Is this what would become of all of us in some down the road eventuality? If so how could someone commit themselves to anything less than a life that pursues the most longevity possible. I also didn't need any one else to see me wallow in my own indecision any longer. Sitting there with Camilo I dragged on my evening aware that when I left this time I would not be turning around. I had gotten so used to his presence and help as a friend that I was genuinely going to miss him and his company for the next leg of my trip. Even worse, I had no idea when I would get a chance to hang with him again. I didn't know how to tell him how much I appreciated his help. Even in his moments of frustration he had never done anything to try and shame me for my decision to try this crazy pass at life. I wished him well, hoping that I could return one day to see him thriving in whatever new position of life he had chosen.

On my way out I decided to get an oil change and decided to do a complete coolant switch at the urging of the mechanics, probably the first in this cars history. As I approached the never-ending set of exits gearing me towards Los Angeles I started to think of something that was still in the back of mind. All of this shit over a cup of coffee and a childlike bladder? Here it was July and I was just now getting out of California, thought my ass would be gone form here by mid-June. I had just had enough of Los Angeles for one summer. Before leaving entirely I decided to finally go back to that coffee shop and to take that piss I never got to take. The coffee was average. The gummy bears were brilliant, but the bathroom was something else. I hesitated for a moment, somewhat embarrassed that I was about to buy another bag of the same gummy bears I had just bought only a few minutes before, but if I didn't I knew I would just end up searching for the next closest shop which had them and for reasons recently embedded in me I had no desire to make a new coffee shop my last stop before trying to leave Los Angeles. Satisfied with my bravest sides I walked outside and looked to my left where I saw a red glow in the sky with the silhouette of a shirtless man running my way. Looking at the pink and orange tinged sky I felt no certainty about how much of the color was fire and how much was the sun, not caring much either way as the view was unlike any other. As the silhouette got closer the mans black skin contrasted ever more with his orange shorts and soon enough his face became visible and shockingly recognizable. It was Preacher Lawson. As he got closer I put my hand up and he began to add a stutter to his

step and stopped before me. Well, not really stopped. He kept his feet moving the entire time, but the jump in his step had slowed down. He stood there and took a photo with me. I showed him my notebook.
"This is all of the writing I did since I last saw you."

"Good for you man. Keep it up."

Watching the rising star jog away I was filled with a bit of hope and joy over the serendipitous nature of the moment, no matter how random or divinely planned it may have been.

SAN FRANCISCO, CALIFORNIA
July 2016

"You think they could make that movie today?"

S*till half-way to go.* A thought which struck me as I pulled out of sight from the greater Los Angeles area and finally made it north up the PCH where I had intended on being nearly two months ago. Using my satellite radio I tuned into the *RAW DOG COMEDY* station and caught myself listening to a clip of Chris Tucker performing for *DEF JAM* comedy somewhere in the late 1990's. I was laughing my ass off before I realized how I hadn't listened to comedy for pleasure in longer that I could remember. Maybe that's a natural tragedy to all arts, you eventually separate from them the more involved you get. Especially as we hear of stories non-stop and further embed them in our mind on a regular basis. Chris Tucker was one of those who was outrageously funny and was scooped up by the film industry before he got to let the world know that his talent was in front of the mic; same thing with Jim Carrey. Go watch some of his stuff, the one where he's wearing this crazy colored shirt that kinda looks like a Picasso painting. By the end of it his physical involvement has got him sweating and the crowd is dying. Same thing with the early days of DEF Comedy JAM. You'll see a fair amount of people you recognize but didn't know were comedians.

Driving through the center of California you come across a lot more farmland than anyone outside of the state would assume to see before getting a chance to witness it themselves. At one point you drive through an area near Bakersfield where you're surrounded by cattle on either side for a stretch of a few miles. Driving up the coast of California is like going from one country to another with a completely different brain controlling each. I recall growing up with the knowledge that California had been and was somewhere around the 9th largest economy in the world. Except for the taxes it's hard to understand why everyone hasn't moved here yet, and even then I can't understand how so many people live there and they still can't seem to keep their state at a level budget year to year. I mean I can, but I won't bore you with a history of their economic fuck-ups. I didn't like math at 8 A.M. and I don't expect you to like it 200 pages in.

Somewhere still south of San Francisco I found myself on an incline which was surrounded on either side by what can only be described as the plains after being torched. Perhaps a recent occurrence since my cars external thermometer was indicating temperatures of almost 112 degrees. Only dipping below hot as fuck a few times when I managed to get in the shade of one of the hills. I needed to give my engine a break if possible and more importantly I needed to use the bathroom. According to the powers of the internet a man I knew from Guatemala was now living just outside of the city and suggested I stop by to catch up. Eager to jump at the opportunity to see an old friend I responded with a quick yes and entered his address into my phone. Getting to his house only took me a few miles off course and brought me off of the main road about twenty miles ahead of schedule. When I got to his house he ran outside and went through the motions of greeting. I trusted his choice in foods and went to a Spanish joint in the middle of some shopping center. Sitting there we were catching up as some loud noise came from the parking lot, perhaps two cars running into one another, I can't really be all certain, all I know is that for some reason I internally freaked out. In light of some sort of memory of a movie scene where a shooting took place in such a similar setting, perhaps a brief touch with the reality that I was still quite vulnerable, not just slow, but slower than anyone else around me. That and the lack of places to hide suddenly brought a rush of urgency to get us out of there. Which we did soon after, but not because of my paranoia, but because my buddy had to go to work. Either way I was glad to get the hell out of there.

After dropping him off I turned around and left the city just as the morning started and the city bridges began to fill with hoards of traffic from the AM rush hour. Being that it was on my way and I had nothing else specific to do I had to go to one of my favorite places along the California coast, and home to one of the prettiest universities in the state. Stanford had held a place of prestige in my mind for a long time now. Whatever it was, I respected it before I even stepped foot on the campus. The Spaniard style and the red roof all around made the whole place feel academic and aesthetically pleasing.

In venturing off to explore the campus I decided it could be done so fastest and with the most safety if I took my crutches with me. I had been doing my best to stay off of them, but a weird part of me had gotten used to the propulsion aspect of these particular crutches. Plus, the crutches had proven a good way to lead to new conversations and being forgiven for sitting wherever I wanted. As they proved to my advantage once more I don't even remember how we started talking or what it was that made this woman want to help me, but we went from *"Hello"* to *"So do you wanna come with us into this tennis match?"* really quickly. Which was good because as quickly as I saw her getting to the point I saw her husband look down at his watch and begin to urge his wife to wrap it up with their new found friend. A lovely couple somewhere in their late 60's wearing windbreakers and lanyards allowing them access to the days events being hosted by Stanford that day. Moving along with them I stood in line and went with them to the gate where they did their best to coerce the doorman to let me in, even trying to play on my disabled situation. Sadly they were met with resistance and I was denied entry. Though not before being able to look in and see Serena Williams heave her racket at a ball falling from the apex of her toss as she served what would become the matches first point.

Walking through Palo Alto that night I kept thinking of Steve Jobs and how he had died only one day after my last time in town. Which is a complete coincidence and I am in no way implicating myself in regards to his death. That disclaimer aside, it's hard to argue that many people had as large of an impact on my life as he did. A statement which could probably go for a lot more of us on many more levels than we would care to admit. When some type of new technology emerges it takes a matter of finesse to push it forward, but more importantly it takes a smoothness to the operations to keep it in our hands. Were it not for Steve Jobs and his game changing devices, there's no way a trip like this would have even been possible for me. I also find myself often wondering what he would think of the world that has been created as a result of his creation.

In a small town there's usually one exciting thing to do that week. Or the thing everyone is doing. I miss that type of excitement. This place looked like the place you had always heard about from somewhere in the 1950's. Downtown had a few perfectly placed blocks, each containing just what every intellectual family could hope to find. A store to fill your living room with trinkets. A bookshop to stock your shelves with. Even a place to buy your tea, and a separate store for your coffee. Of course you could also stop by *Pluto's* if you just wanted a nice healthy salad. On this particular afternoon the courtyard near Main Street was occupied by a group of Krishna followers who wanted to spread their love of meditative culture and far eastern cuisine. Something which looked more than normal to the locals. Noticing the seamless acceptability the community had with that which was going on it's probably no coincidence that the majority of counter-cultures seem to gain a stronghold somewhere beyond the usual realms of the government; finding their homes in the minds of Californians exploring other worlds while walking around what the rest of us already saw as a dream.

As a result of all of this connectivity we have gotten to a stage likely never before seen in history where the most average of people can have their own avenue for broadcast. It's a decision to or not to more so than it is a struggle to figure out how. Which is why it's odd we often ask the question of whether or not we could make that today. We're all trying to find a side of the story that brings us to some point of laughter. The world is more liberal than any other time before. With that question the example I hear the most is *Tropic Thunder*. What you might not be able to do is get the funding or the time needed by outside sources in order to produce it on your own without much personal financial risk, but the ability to make something artistic is never gone. I would argue that if society doesn't want you to make something that it's become even more important that you do so because society clearly has something they're not ready to deal with and face, so why not put it in their face? At the end of the day, as long as your fans don't abandon you then you're not really *cancelled*. At the end of the day so what if some whiny bitch doesn't like my stuff, who cares? I can see it hitting a few markers in the focus groups, but did it have to be made and laughed at before we could get to the point where we were beyond such humor? Isn't that what the evolution of a thing is? It's like the evolution of everything, it couldn't have been made nor would it be conceived now. I can't find any part of me that doesn't find it funny. Jack Black tied to that tree was one of the funniest scenes I've ever watched. I mean in a lot of ways you couldn't make *The Iliad* or *The Odyssey* these days. Sure you could write it, but who the hell would read it?

We're never going to live in a time when criticism doesn't happen. A reason for which I would never wanna be the member of some publicly traded company subject to the lofty whims of disapproving crowds and the toxic wielding of their big tech buddies. They try to paint themselves as better, but they're not different than the former

Robber-barons of the early 1900's, the only difference is the Vanderbilts and Rockefeller's actually produced things that people needed, as opposed to our tech elites who often don't make much of anything concrete. Facebook isn't a product, it's your social life, but online. It's just a network, *you're* the product. They're the ones driving up the prices of our cities, they're the ones making existence seemingly unaffordable just as much as anyone else in the chain of corruption is. High priced tech salaries and the increasingly ability of those people to work remotely have created the illusion among owners everywhere that they can charge whatever rent they want because someone from somewhere is going to come pay it. A game which is no doubt aided by jumping from one tax break state to the next as any proper corporation or incorporated person does.

The ironic part was the same people who've probably never seen the Grand Canyon spend their days trying to figure out how to get to Mars and those who don't know what it is to be social gave us social networks. People who would prefer to live in a virtual world want us to go explore another? Doesn't make much sense to me. Don't worry Elon, I support you on everything else, gimme batteries that last as long as my life and I'll be thrilled, so will the Earth. It's interesting how much of who is on the front of the tabloids has changed. When I was younger you would never imagine a scientist being on the cover of the gossip rags. Then we took the tabloids and put them on our tablets. Back in the days you had to actually spend $5 to see whatever crazy story was put in there about whatever celebrity was under scrutiny that particular week. I can recall looking on with confusion as I watched people buy the rags as we called them at whatever gas station I was working at back in high school.

Parking on Seneca Drive I hugged my car up against a set of hedges outlining a rare victorian style mansion and turned off the ignition after sitting there with the heat blasting for a few moments. Just based on the beauty of the sight there was never anything surprising about he fact that San Francisco became the most expensive place to live in the United States, seemed kind of inevitable. It has a beautiful bay surrounded by foothills which become mountains and a daily fog which creates perfect kaleidoscope of changes to the sunsets one can see when one moves themself only a few feet in a different direction, forever changing how that particular moment of fog is impacting the array of facades around them.

   With absolutely no attachment to timezones at the moment my
body woke me up at approximately 5:43 A.M. and before I knew it I
was driving with the windows down and cruising through the suburbs
of the San Francisco Bay Area. More specifically the suburbs hugging
the coast near a bunch of old windmills. I'm not kidding. Bet you didn't
know they had any windmills there. I wonder if I'm the first person to
notice how many Chinatowns there are in the United States. Los
Angeles has one. New York City has one. That being stated, Chinese
culture represents a length of history of culture that I can't even begin
to comprehend. The only thing even remotely relatable came to me
when I was stepping inside of a church on the outskirts of Brugge,
Belgium where I noticed the cornerstone with a date that said
something close to 1,010 A.D. indicating a thousand year gap in time
from when it was built to the moment I was in. In an instant I was
flooded with the thought of all of the bodies which had passed through
these doors during that time. It almost made me laugh at the idea of
American history, but then I started to think, well, history is a reflection
and a collection. At the same time I thought of the Egyptians. A group
of people will a history going back and standing firmly from thousands
of years ago. Though I don't know how closely connected the people
there now feel to the history of the Egyptians before then.
   I soon received a response from a fellow couchsurfer telling me I
had a place to stay the following night. Some girl working for the
National Parks who claimed to have a place near the bridge. That being
taken care of I wondered around the city and did what I could to kill
time until my future caretaker was able to meet up. I found one of my
favorite parks in all the United States to this day in the San Francisco
Botanical gardens. Well, for parks that are in the middle of a
metropolis. Surrounded on all sides by redwoods the noises of the city
are drowned out and the cool air stays trapped, adding a level of that
California freshness that I had thought not possible. It wasn't really
easy trying to make my way around the park, and the few ups and
downs on the trails reminded me of the realities I would have faced
had I not decided to reschedule my desires at visiting a few parks along
the way far before my summer was compromised. Not to mention I
didn't need to be limping around a park filled with actual predators. I
had nearly sent someone to the same fate once before when I was
dropping off a friend back in high school. He had recently blown a hole
in his calf in a motorcycle accident and when I got to his driveway he

urged me to let him and go on my way. Not that he didn't want me to drive him, but at the time I had this lowered Honda Civic and his driveway was nearly a mile of harsh gravel and steep hills. Deciding that this wasn't the worse thing to put my already beaten up car through I kept it in first and crept down the driveway, cresting the first hill just as my lights shined onto a trio of coyotes who were sniffing their way across our path.

I started to notice something when walking around the city, homeless people had stopped asking me for money, despite the fact that I was now moving at less than half my normal speed and far more open to the attack. I can only assume they saw my obviously desperate situation and figured why bother. I remember once seeing an episode of *Bizarre Foods* with Andrew Zimmerman where he stated that there was a time when you couldn't feed the homeless in San Francisco. Seriously, we've gotta figure something out about this as a people, not just as a nation, but as members of humanity. For starters I don't know what to do to make sure that solving this situation doesn't somehow incentivize others to fall into a loop of socialistic babysitting. But if I were to guess, the majority of people would rather not have that become their daily situation forever. I would even argue that once that individuals situation has been enhanced they are likely to wish for further enhancing as our hierarchy of needs would dictate, ultimately instilling the fuels of ambition which any self-respecting human being eventually feels once brought from such a low unfavorable position. Then again the same part of me that says they would want independence also says how do I know they won't just fall into a loop of comfort no matter what the world provides for them or any of us? I kept thinking this whole time how I was only sparred of such a destination by the grace of friends scattered throughout the country. Only via a network of people who gave a damn about me was I able to make such a terrible situation so fruitful, only now fully aware of how fruitful and preferred it had been to what could have become of a man suddenly thrown into medical debt in his twenties with no outside resources from which to grasp help. I knew I was blessed to have contacts, but I only now realize how much I relied on them. Inside the country we had some of our own failures to deal with. Homelessness I would say being the biggest of them. It's weird how homelessness just felt *normal* in NYC. I was used to seeing it, but still not used to the idea of it. I get how it happens. I've run out of money before, I've slept in my car plenty, though admittedly most of those times was on my own accord and without the lack of a possible bed at the home of a loved one. Granted, none of those loved ones have to worry about me stealing any of their belongings when they're not looking in-order to afford my drug habit. For that I am as grateful as they are and or should be. How we look at homeless people in a manner of we all wish we could say what can be done about them? No one wants to see encampments in their neighborhood. So why not change that which seems to be creating the situation. Can anything be done about those that don't want to participate in society? I gotta think about that one.

I wouldn't be homeless tonight thanks to a newly employed National Parks worker who was somehow fortunate enough to be assigned the San Francisco Bay Bridge as her first post. Receiving her information I set my GPS and followed along as it guided me over the San Francisco Bay Bridge and into the cove across the bay. Taking a left into a tunnel through the mountain I came out and headed due left until the road led me to a driveway with what looked like a series of rental cabins lining the road. Peering intensely at the doors for numbers I received a text which seemed to have been sent a while ago, *I'm the last house at the end of the road, lemme know when you cross the bridge.* Far beyond the majority of the driveway, I continued on and parked next to a light grey Subaru Outback covered in National Park stickers and various animal outlines picked up from the information centers along the way. When I got to the door a girl only a few inches from the door frame with ginger red hair and a set of piercing green eyes opened the door. Though faintly spotted below the eyes on the peeks of her cheeks, the rest of her arms glowed a florescent milky white with no freckles running down either of her arms, both of which were exposed by her dark black tank top.

"Hey I'm Leyla. I'm hoping you're Patrick...?"

"That would be me. Nice to meet ya."

"Same to you. Now before I forget, don't tell anyone where you're staying or post anything about staying on the park property. I'm not supposed to have people here."

"I passed someone coming in, should that be a problem?"

"Big truck?"

"Yeah I think."

"No. That's Jill. She's fine."

As we sat there and talked she heated up some tea and showed me around the apartment which was surprisingly spacious and clearly meant for a few people to be sharing the space. Told to take my choice of the open rooms, I picked the first one I walked into without any concern and because it already had three pillows on the bed. *"So your profile says you do stand up?"*

"Yeah. But please don't ask me to tell you a joke."

"Will I get to hear them if I come to a show?"

"It's the one place I'll promise it."

"You performing tonight?"

"I'm supposed to tomorrow. There's a show in Oakland tonight if I wanna go, but I'm kinda tired."

"That's perfect! I have a date tomorrow night. I'll get him to take me there."

"Who's the guy?"

"Online. He seems cool. Works for Google."

Putting her phone in my face she showed me the profile of a tall techie and his golden doodle. *"Looks lovely. Hope he likes my jokes."* I would soon find out as she wasted no time to introduce me when we all met out front of the show. *"This is my friend Patrick, the one I was telling you about."* At this point a confused guy hovering just about six foot tall with skinny legs to match his skinny jeans and a set of matte black rims making up for his lack in nearsighted capabilities. With not much time between hello's he asked me, *"So you nervous?"*

"Huh? Oh. No. I'm over that point in the process. I hope you like it, but I also kinda don't care."

"But you're funny right?"

"Enough to keep doing it."

With that he opened up his phone and posed the question, *"Can I see your stuff on YouTube...?"*

"No. I rather you come see me. I assure you I wouldn't continue to do this for my own torture."

Dipping out in the morning I took her and the Google guy back to his car downtown, telling her goodbye and then going back to her apartment to fit all of my things into the back of the car. Before leaving the house I ran back in and sat on the bed once more, laying back and taking in the comforts of a down comforter and trying not to think of how long it would be before I would find a spot of such accommodations again. After locking the door behind me I sat in the car and fed off of her WiFi for a moment to map out a few stops in the city before heading out. Starting the GPS I crossed the Golden Gate Bridge once more and drove to a park in the middle of the city. After parking I closed the door and caught a glimpse of the shattered glass upon the pavement left over from the previous nights break-in and the evidence of a smashed window from either this time or another covered up by a trash bag reinforced with a freshly sealed series of duct-tape strips. Only two cars down a Nissan Altima had its back window smashed out, with a few pieces of clothing scattered about on the back seat. That's what it says, they don't care. When I parked my car I found myself just down the street from Mission Dolores Park.

As I struggled up the hill I perched myself periodically on whatever small leveled patch of green I could find. This was genuinely the hardest my body had been able to work in nearly 3 months. After sitting there for a few minutes enjoying the view I noticed a couple next to me pulling out a giant bong from one of their backpacks, beacon to which I called out, *"It's that kinda day?"* Lifting his head up from the bong the bearer of goods shook his head and motioned for me to come over as his cheeks filled with smoke. Within a few moments the bong was in my hand and a set of new ice cubes were being placed in the chamber. The higher I got the more I started to realize how young this couple next to me looked. They were clearly high schoolers. Though as I stood there with a deep feeling of paranoia I looked around and realized that no one was judging me. For that matter it didn't even look like anyone was noticing. No one was even looking my way disapprovingly. Not one fucking person. Maybe they had some sympathy for the man on crutches and had just chalked me up to another drug doing bum walking around their city. Exterior judgements aside I still decided it was time to distance myself from the crowds and get somewhere a bit more secluded.

One of the weird parts about driving through a city like this with so many hills while also battling the fog is that you soon realize you could never get yourself back to the neighborhood nooks you found while wandering throughout. Not for the impossibility of memory or the inability to drive around aimlessly until finding it again. This view would never exist again no matter how long you drove. This fog, this exact density of moisture in the air, at this time of day as the sun hits ever so faintly, withdrawing beyond the ridge, over the dark silhouette of the largest hillside mansion peaking over the horizon. The smell in the air. The sanded faded green VW parked to my left. It would all be

different next time. Which is why I say San Francisco wins for
originality in views. A gift from its advantageous position nestled
tightly in the truly central part of the state known for the best weather
in the continental US.

Once I finally felt like I had put enough space between me and all
of the open spaces I was able to sit down and burry myself into a
completely different stage. Starring down I scrolled along and found
myself lost in a feed catered just for me on a stage created only an hour
north of where I was I became lost myself in the screen. The modern
stage, developed by those hoping to broadcast into our palms. This was
the first time in history that you could look down at a mirror and then
see the projections of many others continuously displayed and changed
over time in front of you. In thinking about the phone I often think
about how America was the place where the idea of the modern stage
developed and became whole. Pretty sure I can confidently say that as I
don't think there's much dispute over where YouTube and the screens
of today came about. It was all from Silicon Valley. It used to be a fan
base was limited to the reaches of a the largest accessible stadium,
nowadays even the most meager of productions can have their interest
shared with billions of people all at once. People are afraid at
ACTUALLY getting in front of people, but filming themselves for a
stage you can broadcast onto without ever having to arrive; one with
the ability to travel in a pocket, that type of exposure most people seem
fine to submit to without the same fear. A decent personality and a
perfect camera angle is all it takes. One of the bad sides to fame is how
because someone decided to get in the spotlight we assume they're
worth listening to. Sometimes we're fooled by charisma, as I believe
history shows. That's the real issue with celebrity.

SEATTLE, WASHINGTON
July 2016

"Does a raincheck exist here?"

D espite not having a place to stay I decided to venture up towards Seattle and make my way through the final parts of the Pacific Northwest knowing I could always turn around and be back to Portland before the last of the Mount Hood roommates has fallen asleep. I also planned on going to Vancouver no matter what so if I ended up shooting straight through then so be it. I didn't know Seattle to have any type of big comedy scene, this city was known more for its rain than anything, and even that was the result of a slightly false statistic which ranks it as the rainiest place in the US despite it not being in the top ten cities of any rain related statistics. This area of the country had made a pretty large contribution in the early 90's as it provided a home to the grunge movement which would ultimately produce figures like *Nirvana, Alice In Chains,* and *Pearl Jam.*

After looking around the web I found my way onto the *Couchsurfing* website and looked at the local group meet-ups posted in hopes of gathering others for the evening. Downtown I met up with a group of who had convened as some sort of group meeting of international couch surfers. First I met a couple from Boise, making their way around the Pacific North West. An interesting duo, one a tiny asian, the other an average All-American boy from the MidWest with a neatly trimmed beard that was almost hipsterish. Next was a charming German girl, only 20, but very womanly in her manners. Seemed like the type to know how to take care of you and a house. She was the goofy type of funny. At the meeting I made the mistake of mentioning I had a car of my own and within a few moments I was being volunteered for cross city excursions. *"Let's go to the needle!"*

Approaching the building I eased off the gas and popped the clutch into neutral as I drifted to a stop. We were fortunate to be there on the same day as the Blue Angels. At the entrance we learned we were set to see the group do a flyover of Seattle on their way to the airshow in Tacoma. Riding the elevator around 76 floors, our propulsion took only a moment as our ears popped up and released us to a view of the city and surrounding water. Looking to my right I saw a set of four jet fighters getting into formation as they darted towards the city.

"We're staying with this guy downtown. He might let you stay. Here's his number, just send him a text. He's really cool."

The text led to meeting a divorced man in his 50's with a 4-story townhouse and a lakeside view who told me he had space for me if I was willing to sleep on a cot in the basement. Given no better alternative I agreed and followed the address he provided. He was a very nice guy, recently divorced, and only slightly more recently out of the closet. Though he had seemed to waste no time in his step outside. I had seen plenty of friends at different stages of life grapple with the willingness to come out of the closet. Whether or not they wrestled more with the struggle because of a conflict within themselves or the one they expected to have with the world once they spoke their truth I cannot know. It always bothered me to see a friend of mine having to operate in a life false to the one which they hoped to live in their head, both in identity and in practice. I could say it here and now if you only knew some of the guys I knew growing up. One kid in particular was gay from the day I met him in kindergarten. Though I didn't understand what gay really was then. Then in the 5th grade he told me the thought of kissing a girl grossed him out and for the first time I started to get what he was saying. To this day I still love him for admitting those things at such an early age and in such unaccepting times. Then it was memories of guys like him who made me pain for friends of mine that were still lying to the world in their thirties. Though I am no one to speak to such things. I was lying to the world about my own little things during most of my twenties. I would dare to argue that all of us are lying in one way or another to the world around us about who we really are, or who we wish to be. If I had only been more honest from the beginning none of these books would be necessary. I was honestly somewhat skiddish after my most recent experience with men who like men. Though at least this time I would be in one of many guests and it's not like this guy had propositioned me to come to his place.

Sitting there with an Israeli, three blonde Germans, an openly gay man, and myself, all playing cards, all talking and comparing the times we had experienced around the world. With stories of boyfriends, girlfriends, and past loves coming from all sides of the table. I'm sure at the half-way point of the 1940's it seemed impossible to think a diner setting such as this would ever take place, in the minds of the parties from either side I'm sure. Sure plenty of sides of rivalries filled with histories of hate, but how many have such recent histories of such epic proportions? These people were the descendants of such vicious history and yet they were choosing not to continue the feelings of bitterness often passed down from one generation to the next. Instead they embodied the better sides of their culture which had made it through the fabrics of time. Though I make no claim to say these people were saints, I only knew them from that night alone, and a few tattoos I've seen have tried to remind me that each saint has a past as sure as each sinner has a future. I had so much I wanted to ask them about their upbringing, about the things they had heard and how they felt about them. Likely they had the same neutrality of guilt with recognition of evil and sadness in the reality of the things which took place before their time. The only thing they could have really given me any insight on is what it was to talk to their grandparents about the experiences of their youth, with consideration as to what it could mean if those people had grandparents left to talk to. Here these German kids were sitting here without hate and without any baggage from the history of their countries previous generations or their sins against the world and societies as a whole. Even being welcomed inside the home of a man who would have been hauled off by Hitler at first sight of his limp wrist and golden necklace.

We are all a living product of a previous situation, as was each set of people in every line of humanity since the beginning of time. That might be the most uncomfortable thing to live with as humans. Though I found comfort in the fact that I had nothing to do with it. None of us had anything to do with it. So why are we continuing to argue about the past? I say this as an avid consumer of history from all over the place, it's among my favorite topics, but its' not doing any of us any good to dwell on it. Is there anyone out there denying the injustice? There are no slavery deniers in my country. We haven't had to institute laws enforcing a recognition of the past as those in Europe have because we have so many reminders around us already. To those up in arms over the sins of generations past, if you want to give up your land and return it to the rightful owners head-dress and all, by all means. If not. Stop talking. Go sign over your belongings to whatever tribe is documented as having lived there in the past, or, stop talking about it like you're doing anything to help anyone. If you don't own land, devote the rest of your income towards correcting these evils, otherwise, and equally so, shut the fuck up as far as playing the historical blame game. Because the truth is that if a camera had followed me and everyone else I know around for my entire life thus far (*a scary possibility in the years to come*) and monitored my every motion, and used a supercomputer to analyze all of the data, there would still be NOTHING in my existence to place blame on anything that happened before the day before my birth. That's how consequences work. A cause must exist to be considered a cause. To be completely accurate, I am only void of any type of blame or guilt in life until the day before the knowledge of my conception. For even a fetus can cause some problems to the world from inside of its temporary home. I have to imagine my existence disrupted a few weekends here and there before I officially entered the world. Though I'm pretty certain that worldly and cultural genocide are slightly outside of a fetus's realm of capabilities. So talk to me all you want about original sin and how evil man can be from the start, but we do not inherit the evils of our past anymore than we hope to hand them to our children. Should I apologize to the people my father wronged in his life as well? Perhaps the individuals my grandmother snubbed in her earlier days? I don't see a chance for us changing as a society or as groups of people set against one another by historical prejudices. Especially if we continue to think that those historical offenses somehow entitle us to benefits from someones ancestors. On some sides it's done from a sense of justified bitterness. I really wish those people who look like me had never done that, but the reality is, they did. So now what? Should we be set against each other from hereon out as a result? How many of us are holding onto feuds from sides we feel we belong but regarding issues for which were never around to be a part of? I tried to bring this topic up with our friends via a brief mention of a Family Guy episode I had seen before depicting Brian and Stewie on a bus tour of Germany. On the tour Brian notices the historical timeline is missing any information from the 1930's and 40's and when questioned the tour guide abruptly yells, *"Everyone was on vacation!"*

That episode didn't exactly answer all of my questions about what it must be like to be a German today so I took a chance to ask the group about their sense of cultural guilt if any existed.

"You all must be aware of your place in the world right? Like I know it's weird to ask, but no one in Germany talks about Nazi's in a positive manner,

but each one of you walks with that attached to your German reputation. Right?It's a cultural reference for every culture. You have a former leader who is seen as the example for the worst example one can give when trying to label someone evil. There are entire seasons of History Channel shows dedicated to him and what your country did."

"No. Not our country. The Nazi's."

The one German didn't have the English capabilities to truly get what I was asking, but the other two had their opinions on the matter. A summary of which can be made by the statement that they didn't feel any personal guilt, but that they felt it was necessary for their country to be especially tolerant in the world. This then sparked the Israeli to jump in and confirm that they understood he felt no animosity towards them. Though I don't know how much weight his forgiveness carried since he looked as much Arab as he did Israeli.

The next morning when I went for a walk I ran into Anna on her way back from a grocery store with a small plastic bag hanging from her right hand. Inquiring as to what she was doing with her day she threw the question back and I responded that I would eventually be heading downtown.

"Could you give us a ride and leave us downtown?"

"Yeah I can do that. Where you trying to go?"

"Anywhere near the needle is fine."

"You guys really wanna see that needle don't you?"

"Anything else you wanna see?"

"I know this might sound lame, but you wanna go to Starbucks?"

"Yeah of course. If you wanna stop for coffee just tell me where to go."

"No I mean THE Starbucks. The original is somewhere downtown."

"No kidding. I had no idea. Just gimme directions and I'm down."

"Okay, lemme check..."

With a giddy tapping to her fingers she deciphered between the over 15 options available and started directing me towards the streets with an increasing view of the water. Just as I would hear American music abroad and suddenly feel at home by the knowledge of how far my culture had traveled, the random love of American brands by this German girl and her friends gave me a similar warmth. Whether it was coffee beans or a swoosh on the bottom of your shoes, it was all part of a story linking together the American identity as seen from abroad.

"Okay, turn left here, yeah, right down this brick road."

"Cobblestone."

"What?"

"That's what we call this style. We must be close. This area is packed."

"I'm so excited! Let's grab some coffee and then see if there's a place close by where we can grab some wine. This is a great day for a picnic."

Though this was the original Starbucks it had a very different feel than the other coffee dispensaries the company is known for placing at every corner in every city of the country. This was an old school style shop with canvas sacks of beans sitting opened all around with their fine grains scattered and falling to down to the ground around them, all mixing together to give a smell of coffee that is neither definable nor resistible. I give them credit, if this was their pilot store it must have been easy to sell investors on their potential. Though the strategy of becoming the most recognized option soon won out and eventually coffee drinkers started to hear rumors about Starbucks popping up across the street from one another. I do believe they've helped spark the revamping of cool coffee shops. Plenty of places have opened almost in rebellion for the cookie cutter nature of their current cafe monopoly. Something which brings me back to the early days of coffee shops and how that spread of ideas eventually led to the creation of the stock exchange. The general pull to coffee shops is most recently in charge of the revival of the coffee shop scene, despite how much we would like to believe it. I would call it a promotion of a counter-culture via its very existence as a self-proclaimed cool coffee shop.

Finding a spot in the park I sat there and stretched my legs while they unpacked their belongings. In that unpacking the one who spoke very little pulled out a pre-rolled joint and started shamelessly puffing it with huge clouds of deep grey beginning to collect above him. Noticing the concern on my face Anne shared her feelings on the matter as she reached her hand in to take her share. *"If it's legal..."* Shrugging her shoulders as she drew in a few puffs and then used the end to light her cigarette and pass the joint along to the tiny blonde on her left. From her bag she brought out a bag of grapes, a roll of Stilton cheese, and an assortment of crackers which were all placed onto a blanket laid out by their friend.

"You sure you guys don't wanna come to the show?"

"No, we can't. Our flight leaves tonight."

"Back to Germany?"

"Not yet. We're going to Hawaii. So excited!"

After leaving them downtown I went down and circled my car

around the lake for an hour or so while I listened to some clips from my last time on stage. After a combination of cringe worthy grins and noteworthy silences I decided to press pause and try to divert my shame for a few moments. From that moment of shame I found my way to an address set to have my next mic. Shocking as it was to find out this place probably had the coolest group of comedians I had come across since Florida. When I got inside I realized I was about to be doing comedy in one of the more uncomfortable situations you can choose to do so, when people are eating. From the side of the room I peered around trying to figure out if the people dining there that night had known when they entered that comedy was going to be performed in the middle of their appetizers. It would't be the first time I had seen people unaware until the lights had been dimmed and the opener was 20 seconds into his act. From the middle of the crowd the smell of Thai food was thick in the air, and the spice got into my throat just a bit before going on stage. I reached around for a glass of water and chugged it down. The lights were all encompassing, not just of me and the stage, but of everyone. In a spot like this you need to be more interesting than everyones meals, and only slightly more interesting than the person they're sitting across. Then again, that's true on far more stages than this one.

VANCOUVER, CANADA
July 2016

"So you understand the rules right?"

T hough I never did take notice to the numbers slowly flipping on my odometer I would say the line of cars awaiting entrance to Canada stretched nearly half-a-mile away from a beautifully landscaped entrance to a country doing its best to make a good impression from the beginning. Drifting along at 2 and 3 MPH I eased between neutral and first gear with the windows down and some melodic nonsense playing in the background. When it was my turn to face examination I pulled up to the window and awaited the acknowledgement of a face currently scanning the screen in front of him as he went over the details of his last approval. As the questions started I handed him my passport and recited the details as he requested. When he finally got to the part about what I did for a living I took it upon myself to continue my *Fake it til you make it* mentality and replied with strength in my voice as I said *"Stand Up Comedian"* in response to his inquiry about my occupation. Redirecting his attention more deliberately the border agent looked at me with a sarcastically raised brow and said, *"You actually make money with that?"* adding a quick bite to *money* as he turned in my direction. Attempting to live by my new standard of only speaking towards that which I wanted, I looked his way, smiled, and said, *"Yes sir."* Upon asking me where I was staying, I gave him some address I had memorized from a map of downtown Vancouver and was granted entry to Canada. There aren't a lot of things about this trip that I can call truly new, situationally perhaps, but not actually new. Yet, here I was about to cross the Canadian border for my first time. Like most Americans I had a few preconceived notions about the nation north of me my entire life. First and foremost, I would imagine in any conversation that when the moment of dispute comes up, in regards to hockey facts or history, they are deemed automatically correct. I won't even question it. Similar to discussing soccer with a Brit, it's just a different piece inside of them than it is with those raised in the states. I'm sure these days more do than in days past, but my school didn't even have a soccer team until somewhere around my first year in high school.

The southern part of British Vancouver just north of the American border reminded me of my hometown. Everywhere I looked I saw a series of red barns with white framed doors and single rolls of hay out front, tractors of all colors, but all the same make. With a perfectly squared-off piece of property to contain the family and the long exported American dream. The number of analogies one could make here about the neighbor-like relationship between Canada and the United States are endless. More than a time or two we've wondered if they would give us the whole bag when we asked for some sugar, and I'm sure they're just glad we're asking for sugar and not cocaine like we do from our southern brothers.

Taking my first steps around the city I was struck with a feeling of familiarity that I couldn't shake. The place felt very American, only not. It seemed like what people meant when they referred to alternate universes. Almost like I was home, except strangely different. Sitting at a cafe I ate some blueberries while a Japanese girl with pink hair sat across from me maintaining a firm foot on her dogs leash. Attached to the chain on that leash sat an unmotivated French bulldog with a face full of wrinkles and a mouth full of drool. Not that this type of thing usually happens at home.

I don't quite know what part of town I was in, but at some point I heard a distinctly familiar and wildly out of place Mexican accent. Initiating a conversation I soon found myself in the middle of a conversation with some kids from Oaxaca who were nice enough to go inside of the store for me and pick up a few items to help me out. While I waited for them my mind kept going back to the reality of how absurd and annoying this whole thing was. Had I just decided to take the prescription from the doctors in the first place I would have had access to pain killers any time I wanted. Now was the time when one small broken piece would be all I needed. Instead I would have to buy an entire joint and hope that they had given me something to help kill the pain that was continuing to shoot throughout my legs, probably as a result of driving so much since healing. I knew after the show I would be by myself, along the water, in a nice place to light up. I had nothing to do for the day and it was still only 2 P.M.; not enough time in the day to go hiking in the woods or venturing through some grand parks. Having a few hours to do not much of anything I decided to go take a look at where the club was and explore the surrounding area for the day.

My favorite Hockey player had been a Czech, but I gotta admit two of my favorite comedians were actually Canadian; Jim Carry and Norm McDonald. Neither of which I would call similar to the other. From where I was watching Canadians were lucky because they got to be exposed to comedy from the United States as well as that of the British, which gave them a neat blend like Chicano's in SoCal who would get a little bit of Cali and a bit of Mexico. I never thought of Canadians as different people. Probably because they mainly spoke English, though my younger version wouldn't know that for sure since the first Canadians I met were Quebec dwellers visiting a tiny mountain town in Virginia.

Once it was located I parked a block away from the bars entrance and leaned back for a thirty minute nap with an alarm set to keep me honest. With the sensation that my eyes had just closed I opened my eyes thirty minutes later to the buzzing of my alarm between my legs. Quickly splashing some water in my face I pulled myself out of the drivers seat and made my way around the corner. Coming through the bar doors a tinted facade opened up to reveal a ranch style setting with a stage to my right and a set of tables in front. On the sign-up sheet was a large paragraph telling you that you had to keep it clean and non-offensive. A lot of times the rule of keep it clean is meant as a way to avoid offending, as well as a safe-guard against those unable to get their point across in a humorous manner, but if you don't allow someone to try, will they ever get there? If not in front of the crowd, then where? The crowd is what keeps us honest, but that's the deal we make with the crowd when they sit down. We are going to expose ourselves, our ideals, our experiences, and all too often, our faults. As a member of the audience it is hoped and expected that we are there to listen to them. One specific rule said nothing homophobic. So does that mean I can't tell a story about how a gay guy tried to fuck me in the sauna one night after work? I mean what if I make it funny? Does that count as gay? What if I secretly wanted it? I didn't, but still. My experience is my experience, right? When I asked what he meant specifically the show runner asked me if I was gay. When I responded in the negative he said, *"Okay, then don't bring up anything about being gay."*

Sitting there waiting for the show to start after it had gone ten minutes beyond the starting time I asked a comedian next to me, *"Does it normally take this long for them to get started?"*

"Only since they started dating." Motioning to my side she pointed out the host for the night talking with what appeared to be one of the servers from the bar, a short flirty girl with silver streaks purposely placed in her hair. Assessing the situation we were still a good twenty minutes away from the show starting so I got up and went to find the bathroom again.

Being around a girl comedian there is something intimidating about knowing she is not just quicker than you, as there are many, but one who is also prone and apt to turn her observations of you into decisive blows to your ego. Which perhaps makes me understand for a moment why my ex-girlfriend was always so hesitant to come see me perform.

Right before this particular open mic something happened which had never happened before, which was someone announcing not to mention the election before the show started. *"Anything else?"*

"Uh, no jokes about Caitlyn Jenner, things like that."

"Things like that? The guy came out of nowhere and just became a woman, I can't comment on that?"

It should be no surprise by now that the internal interruptor in me did not agree with these parameters. Though I was for once in a country where I couldn't say for certain that I had the right to say what I wanted to say if I said it anyways. It had felt so familiar til now that I had almost forgotten I was in a different country. The fact that you could get de-platformed for mentioning that he/she used to be a man is utter nonsense. Like how is that something you expect people to just move on from? I don't wanna be one of those people who claims that everything is in dire straights. In fact I think it's stupid to perpetuate the whole *"don't have kids cuz the world is going to shit"* narrative. I have and will continue to argue that the world now is better than it's ever been and it continues to move in a similar trajectory.

"You all better be careful. Gonna have to close you borders if Trump wins."

On that note I've always thought it would be great to see what happened if we had a mass exodus to Canada. What would they do about it? How many would it take before they were like. *"Why dontcha go back to where ye came from?"* I know I know, a terrible Canadian impression, and it's rude considering I'm leaving out the French speakers of the Quebec regions. It had me wondering, *"What's French for turn around!?"* (For your information it's *Retournez d'oU vous venez!*)

265

Try that one for a mouthful.

After getting off stage I approached a taller table to the left side of the stage and joined the likes of three teachers enjoying a drink after a round of summer classes. The first was a blonde with that sort of wild eighties hair look. In the middle a man of mixed Asian decent stood with a short mohawk and a shiny barbell going through his eyebrow and a form fitted outfit of leather and denim. All of the locals sounded like everyone else when they would bring up Trump ultimately saying how they thought *"Well yeah, but this must be great for your stand up."* Truth was I didn't think it was. I felt like what Trump was doing to comedy was not on the side of beneficial.

Up here I wondered what people thought of us Americans. I had often wondered this when I was abroad and specifically throughout Latin America, but it seemed easier to provide justification for militaries adventuring around the world in times of global terrorism than it did justifying how we were electing a bumbling idiot as our President. I remember not being shocked when it happened because I had seen the emotions of the crowd change. As our love for the stage was evolving it seemed only inevitable that a celebrity would eventually capture the minds of the politically inclined and sway them into a vote of faith based on the promises of a different way free from the protective shadows of government. I also think the poling happening was generating lies because no one wanted to risk the ridicule of truth in a climate where improper alignments could cost you peace of mind as much friendships curated over a lifetime.

We also opened ourselves up to criticism simply by being the city on the top of the hill and putting a camera into each part of our lives for freelance judgement to be cast by the masses. I hated to say it but in a lot of ways it was like my country was bombing on the main stage of the world, and worst of all, we were broadcasting it live to anyone who would follow. That's one of the many ways in which it was really different being an American compared to growing up in somewhere like Canada. I grew up in the culture capital of the world, but I knew almost nothing of Canada growing up as a child. The country didn't really start hitting my radar until the creators of *South Park* found it upon themselves to use Canada as a comical punching bag for a series of episodes, forever concreting the idea of the polite Canadian in my mind.

Before this next part it's important to understand the thoughts my mind once harbored about government and all of the annoyances that come with having anyone tell me what to do. Something which hasn't sat well with me any of my life if you can't tell by now. So I've been a reader of history and enjoyed all types of back and forth regarding the future of this country, the possibility of one world, and the similarities between the United States and the Roman Empire. That all being said, I've never understood anyone who latches on too long to talk of the inevitability of the downfall of our nation based purely off of the fates of others with seemingly similar histories.

When I think of Americans stating they want to leave I think about how there seems to be some narrative in the United States that there is an eventuality to our downfall. I don't even understand that as a frame of thought to have. Why would you wanna be within your country and not think great of its future? Sure we opened ourselves up to criticisms of stupid leaders prone to mishaps several times throughout my lifetime with the blue dress incident and that time with the guy choking on a pretzel his first few months in office. All that being true this was the first time that people spoke about the United States in a joking manner, as if we didn't see what was going on inside our own country with total awareness to its ridiculousness. I guess from a journalistic standpoint the downfall of empires is a nice story. It's got a lot of teeth, and you can pretty much point to anything changing as evidence of its taking place. For those that want to talk trash I feel you, I think I've made it clear that I haven't always vibed well with some of the enforcement sides of our government. Nonetheless, as far as I'm concerned anyone who ever wants to really leave America is welcomed to leave if they're not a fan. The last thing I would want in America is people who aren't willing to defend it and especially not those who would hope to abandon it when they think it's going through some tough times.

I think Phillip S. Hoffman said it best in the move almost famous when his character gave advice to a kid attempting to become a music writer, *"If you're gonna be a true journalist, you can't be friends with the rockstars."* Delivering the message that a journalists job is not to gain followers or to make friends. Which is hard because journalism has become a part of the same revolving door that they used to hate politicians for walking through. We now live in a world where the pundits and the entertainers are eventually both seated at the same pristine dinner tables as the other.

I worry that it's not just a matter of lazy journalists in our country, in fact I would argue that the majority of them aren't actually journalists, they are just people who have learned that a profit can be made from outrage driven clicks. More so masters of psychology than any other subject. Click bait is what our society decided to call it, as if it were only a lure meant to pull you through the hyperlink and onto another page. Are you here to inform or are you here to entertain? I mean, does anyone wait for Jerry Springers opinion on something happening in the Middle East? Unless they're trying to find out who fathered all of these virgins I doubt it. The bottom line is that outrage journalism *IS* lazy journalism. It's a click-bate society created by lazy journalists and perhaps that's the natural progression of a people in constant need of newer stimuli. As a solution I think it wise to consider eliminating the profitability of the news. Until such a thing is done my biggest concern is the thought of journalistic integrity, as they are the eyes of society and most often the funnels from which people drink their opinions.

Despite my previous paragraph I still think it's important not to completely blame the institution or the media for failing us as much as it is to understand how it fell victim to the circumstances and just kinda wound up that way. In the same way that journalism has become victim to the necessity of click bait. Lazy journalism is first and foremost our fault as readers of the news. A large majority of the friends I've made in media would be more than happy to explore long form stories with passionate insight and detailed work. Readership doesn't seem to be cultivated in that manner anymore. Instead we've been trained to only like the quick bites of information. Bites and Bytes actually. I'm sure a large portion of the blame belongs to the attention span which has been dwindling ten fold since the technological revolution took over. Speaking of short inflammatory articles, if you're finding this book via a short snippet you saw in some inflammatory article, well, I appreciate the blogger taking the time to mention me, and thanks for making it this far. In the end it's on us to actually read the article. It's on us to actually look into what is being said. Sometimes art is meant to speak to you and other times it's meant to make you speak to others. That combo is forever in a cycle. I hate the reminder to be angry that I see every morning on the news, usually starting with some sort of confirmation of blame on this side or the other. It's on us as people for form a bit more self-awareness about how we are reacting to that which we are seeing and perhaps even self-regulating some of our projection of those reactions until we're sure we feel how we feel.

After leaving the club I wandered around the city and did all I could to gain a night view available on a wet evening such as this one. At some point I needed a place to sleep so I did my best to blend in amongst the hedges of a neatly gated neighborhood somewhere along a hill.

I woke up before the sun rose and saw a thin sheet of raindrops resting on my windshield. The passing figures of a few early morning joggers had subconsciously shaken me into a state of alertness and soon enough I too was awake. With that growing alertness I soon found myself wanting to get in a workout. My body needed it. Not knowing quite where to go for such a thing I went to one of the only places I could think of that would be open at that hour, a coffee shop of course. There in the morning darkness I chugged a bottle of water and made a call to a friend out East who I knew to be an early riser. Chatting with him as I drove along the coastline until I found a pull off with an area for docking boats. Seeing no one else around I parked and got myself into a pair of shorts, pacing back and forth in the sand once I had done so. In an instant I decided to go in without dipping my toes and just walked straight into the water where I was met with a rush of cold that shot up and down my limbs before resting itself around my waistline. With my new found energy all of me wanted to swim across that bay, but none of me could muster up the courage to put myself out there and in the middle of the bay only the end up nervously turning around to swim back the whole time pretending that I'm not thinking about the possibility of a shark appearing from the dark at any moment.

Sitting in front of the University of Vancouver I stared at the Neurology department watching the people go in and out. Although I have no real academic reason to believe this about myself, I always assumed I would have done well in sciences such as this which blend the chemical with the social. The brain itself and its self-created consciousness seems like the only true frontier left on this planet. Though exploring our own is task enough before we hope to branch into others. It's neat to think how the brain builds your world and you build your brain. The brain is the coolest of all the organs, it's the only one with a series of physical and social studies built behind it, we all need to breathe but no one is looking to your lungs for the reason you're making bad decisions.

269

For whatever reason I don't think I found one great cup of coffee in this entire city. Granted I didn't try them all. I just expected flavorful coffee to be as abundant as the pines. I mean, it's perfect coffee weather. If coffee didn't grow in tropical lands you wouldn't ask for it there. Sitting in my car outside of the coffee shop I got on the phone and gave my buddy a call on the East Coast, uncertain if he would be awake, at work, busy, or what. Obviously I'm telling you about it so the point to that is that he picked up and we got to catch up for a while. The only reason for doing so is to tell you that for the first time in a while I tried to just listen to a friend tell me about what they were up to. For too long I had been telling people the same story over and over. By now I was tired of hearing myself and I was tired of hearing what I was up to. In a lot of ways I was having start-up fatigue. I was working my ass off, but I was still going through the occasional bouts of imposture syndrome. Each time feeling like a liar when I claimed to be a comedian to some new potential fan. I didn't even know if I could claim to feel like myself. What was the self once I had exposed it all to the world as most I could? In search of more that others had to say I sat there and opened my phone to find a list of bookstores in the area and see which one was closest to me.

Somewhere in the city there's a spot where the tracks split and there's a small exterior resembling an old diner, with books stacked in each window at least half-way. It was early in the morning and for whatever reason I had the instinct to go inside. Upon walking in I noticed that it held books of the exclusive and rare nature. Scanning the shelves I came across a name, Jack Kerouac, followed by a series of at least twenty books all by him or him and another writer. Each title sounded strange as the last, and in the end there were maybe two titles I had heard of before. Seeing that most of them were of surprisingly low cost I texted the only person I knew who might as interested in this as me and found that she was always in the mood to get her hands on a rare edition from the author of *"On The Road"*. Taking a photo of the shelf ahead I tried my best to fit in all of the Kerouac books into one shot. *"Ansley, take a look at what I found."* Strolling through the isles I looked around and tried to understand the categorization chosen to organize this haphazard collection of literature. If I had my way at designing the world bookshelves everywhere would start at eye-level for children and work their way up; allowing for each curiosity to be explored in ascending order of understanding.

With nothing else to do until the mic, I went around the city exploring the outskirts to the north, somehow stumbling across a local baseball game. I couldn't tell you the last time I had sat down and watched a baseball game. I barely had any memories even set on a baseball field. Though one of my earliest does replay in my head often as I imagine a set of teenage lovers who got their braces stuck together one summer in the cul-de-sac near my neighborhood growing up. This is only relevant because he was the same kid who used to smash homers out of the circle and into the main road. It's also one of the first places I can ever remember crying. Something which only happened after I was denied a position at bat more than a few rotations in a row, at the time unaware that while unfair, their assessment of my baseball abilities were pretty on point. I always wondered how that scene would have faired in a revised version of the Sandlot where benny realizes there's no help for Smalls and they chase him out of town. It's probably necessary to say I was somewhere around six years old, and only a few inches taller than the bat. After leaving the park I went to a shady side of town where few rooftop bars lit up the skyline and the underdeveloped townhouses surrounding this gentrified oasis.

Later at the *Eight and 1/2 Club* I met a comedian named Sam. He used clever twists of tongue and hopped around a variety of topics, never slowing down. He was similar to George Carlin in his ability to talk around things and somehow make you laugh while doing so. It was that clever banter about a topic and the absurdities of it which kept me in my seat despite having to pee the entire time. That and the mistake of placing myself in the second row, where an escape was impossible. In his explanation I saw hope through the shred of a goal finally somewhere in the distance. It was now just a matter of numbers.

"Do the math. How many people do you know?" - Sam

"In my life?" - Patrick

"Yeah sure." - Sam

"I don't know. A couple hundred." - Patrick

"How many do you think would come see you do stand up? You just need to fill enough seats in every city to make it worth your time. Anything you make after is just a bit extra quid in your pocket." - Sam

"Sounds good. Just, it's hard enough trying to get my shit out there. I'm already a one man show. Any other advice?" - Patrick

"Record yourself. All of the time. You never know when you're going to have a killer set. When the magic hits, you're gonna want it on film. Will

271

make a great addition to the reel too. Reels aren't just for actors. Comedians need them too. Get a camera. And just keep writing." - Sam

This guy showed me crowds existed everywhere. I am not sure if there is going to be a viable solution to our problems from herein out and from there its are hard to see what's going to happen next and from there I mean then what it's like we won't be able to see eye to eyelet.

Are you supposed to always stay in your lane and is that a lane that you've created or does the audience create the lane and you fill it? Perhaps it's the natural blending of the two which leads to success. I wanted to write to the people who would like my stuff, but I also didn't want to ONLY write to the people who already like me. I wanted nothing to do with creating an echo chamber of affirmers to continue my existence.

I spent a final night in my car in Vancouver parked somewhere along another side street far away from the eyes of concerned Canadians. Laying there I began to think how glad I was to be retuning the next morning to my home. Being a seasoned traveler I've been gone enough to know there's nowhere else I would rather be a citizen than my own country. Even with all of the so called drawbacks, where else would have allowed for me? Since it all began, we know of nowhere that has facilitated more individuals than the hub of individuality which I call my home. A place where people can be themselves to an extent that is sometimes shocking. I support this to an extreme extent despite know that we've yet to figure out what kind of national identity is created when you live in an individualistic society. I suppose the idea of the rebel, the wild child is more representative of the American image than anything else. Though I wonder when everyone is an individual can anyone truly be a rebel anymore? As time goes on the ability to have ultimate freedom of expression creates and environment where the populations eventually evolve into fragmented regions each influenced by their own set of myths and characters to idolize, with few holding grand space in the zeitgeist while others remain more obscure, nonetheless in existence. Over time our identity has been defined more by our variety than any one individual. As history shows us, a nation is first a consolidation of tribes via geography and language, then culture develops and eventually those people evolve long enough to develop a history; a homogeneous blend of time and necessity. Oh, and lingo. Which essentially comes from that combo of culture and language infused over time.

The Pacific Northwest

August 2016

"You think you're gonna keep doing this?"

T he day started visiting our friends food truck once more we grabbed a coffee and wasted a few minutes at the corner, doing nothing in particular the entire time. Nobody just comes to you. Not unless you're doing a residency somewhere like Las Vegas, but that's somehow frowned upon.

All I wanted was my body to be back in the right place. Since I had a place to stay, I figured why not. Will was more than happy to take me along any day I wanted, while I was also welcomed to just hang around the house and take walks in the woods. This type of relaxation went on for the next few days. I even ventured out one day with Will to the farm. There I hung around trimming his plants for a few hours while he worked on some sort of irrigation system. Up here I felt very far away from the noise.

"I need to make some money."

"You could help me at the farm."

"Doing what?"

"Trimming."

The next few days I spent walking up and down the neatly separated isles of freshly matured marijuana plants, taking off a few pounds a day and falling asleep by fireside in a hammock instead of taking the ride back down the road into Portland. Each morning I woke up and completed a set of sprints, doing anything I could to waken my body up. While trimming I would listen to a series of old comedy skits, trying to bring back the memories of an art I had loved so much when I was just an observer. I didn't wanna work there but while in San Fran I had a few bills of annuity hit and boom, I was suddenly broke. This was all on my mind because I was currently working on a farm that I could have once been a part owner if I had not hesitated. It was one of the only investments I had ever passed up on in my life where I knew I was wrong at the time of passing it up. He had wanted me to come away when I was 23, fresh into my post college adventures. A path which would have led me to a small fortune by 26. Now I stood there in a full circle of disappointment being offered a chance to make a few hundred bucks doing errands for a future which could have been mine to share. I can't tell you how odd or off that felt. I had never been more certain of an opportunity missed or a regret to be had and for what reason? But as my leg had taught me, be grateful when the world extends the helping hand you've been needing.

I stayed there for a few days and kept telling myself that I was gonna take myself back into Portland but for some reason I never did. Each time I told myself I was about to I would get caught up trying to reorganize the trunk of my car or some other task around the house to keep myself useful and by the time I knew it I had started smoking with one of the roommates and I suddenly realized I had no reason other than to meander. I couldn't figure out why I was delaying. I wasn't tired. I've never really felt worn down by the road, or tired of the journey, but the non-stop nature of my life was making it hard to leave one of the few places I would walk around without my shirt on. Even the idea of tiding up a friends home while he was gone was more appealing than driving another 120 mile round trip in order to possibly spew some words for 3-5 minutes more. Knowing all too well I could practice all that from the comfort of a recliner while I yelled ideas at his half-baked roommate.

I'll never take for granted how close I came to becoming homeless this summer. I guess if we wanna be technical it wouldn't have been the first time in so far as the definition implies one is without a place to legally register himself as permanently sleeping. I had been evicted from places twice under the circumstances of a landlord not using my money to pay the bank. With a third time happening more voluntarily when I was able to find the logic within myself to justify living in my car for a few weeks as a way to save money as opposed to continuing to double down on an even worse position of paying a rent too high to leave me anything but in debt had I stayed even one month longer. Even so I lived under these conditions each time without much regret or despair. I walked around a lot these last few months thinking how unfortunate it was that I was one injury away from being homeless or one injury away from losing it all if the incident had been of a higher severity. Walking around the city I wondered how many of these men were possibly the results of artistic endeavors gone wrong. How many were perhaps a result of the overindulgence in drugs? What if what had happened to me happened to me but in a time when I had isolated myself from the world and the people I love? Driving around there were noticeably less homeless women than there were men. This was purely an observation, I don't know if there are actually any statistics on such things. Regardless, one can't help but notice the men-centric nature of the homeless world. Had our government abandoned these people or had society? Perhaps it was a combination of both.

I suppose being homeless here wasn't as bad if you had a car. Being in the Pacific Northwest makes it easy to find places to stop and sleep. Though I don't know if care ownership would then disqualify them from being homeless. They don't really care who camps where and it's raining so much and so often that anyone passing by would be unlikely to notice you resting in the front seat even if your windows weren't tinted. In fact here homelessness is so easy it's borderline encouraged on the basis of ease compared to any other type of life. The only catch, here you definitely need a tent, and even if you have one, you're still going to get wet.

Following an address sent to me minutes earlier I turned the necessary corners and avoided the occasional biker to make my way to what I have come to refer to as the hippy house. Though I'm sure it's not even the most hippy of places I've ever seen. The entire place was only one story with an open backyard surrounded by trees on all sides, each one at least twenty feet tall, providing a constant area of shade no matter what time of day, illuminating only fully in the middle of the yard around high noon during the summers. Talking with them I came to find that their backyard was somewhat famous for out of town traffic. *"We let a few people sleep in the backyard every night."* The owner told me as he pointed to the hammocks clustered in the back part of the perimeter. He pointed off in the distance and directed my sight towards what was the top half of a brand new apartment complex. *"Soon enough they'll come for our spot too. I wish we had the money to buy the place..."*

"How long you think you all got?"

"Maybe another year or two. I wish the city would do something to stop it, but you know how it is. Build, build, build."

"What about keep Portland weird?"

"That's what they used to say, but who you gonna get to turn down the type of money they're offering?"

"Let's get away from all of this. Come camping with us. You can stay another night right?"

"Nah I can't."

"Thought you're on a road trip. What the else do you have to do?"

"I wish I could, but I'm not getting any work done here."

"Take out your notebook. Nobody's stopping you."

"There's nowhere to practice."

"Go up to Seattle."

"I'm not driving to Seattle every time I wanna do a show, that makes no sense."

"You just drove across the country to do open-mics and that doesn't make sense to you?"

He was right so I shut up. Not changing my plan of course, but not arguing with his point. Two days later I was waking up in a hammock somewhere in the middle of Oregon. That second morning I looked to my right at the fire still smoldering with the smell of charred wood wafting through the air. An alertness not normally experienced before 6 AM overcame me and I was soon on a footpath nearly half a mile from our campsite. Killing time between the pines I meandered for the next two hours, circling back to my campsite and going out on other legs trails connected to my area. Each time I would wander back I would notice another member of our group momentarily awake and up doing his morning business.

Leaving the campsite I hit a bump and suddenly heard a bursting of some sort, immediately followed by a fountain of steam projecting from my hood. Somewhere near the Deschutes river, I sat with my car steaming, my friends now miles ahead. Sitting there with steam bellowing from my engine I tried to rationalize with myself for a moment to be happy that this had happened here and now as compared to somewhere in Wyoming, which is where I would be if I had just gone on my way and continued driving. Fuck, who knows if I even would have made it out of Oregon. I was fortunately stuck as the part was going to take a few days to get to the shop. Odd to have finally left one crippling situation only to find myself inside of another.

This little ordeal would delay my leaving by another 3 days, all spent sitting around the house and riding along whenever someone had to leave, hoping to soak up every last bit of the mountain I could. Will had to run off to climb some mountain that was getting an odd amount of sun for this time of year so these days were spent alone. On my last morning I remember doing my final pull ups on that porch, soaking up the sun, and an occasional stare from the property dog. I decided to leave my bike, sleeping in the car was still tight and I would need all of the room I could get. Especially if I hoped the hide a bit better when crossing the MidWest and a few of the less vagabond friendly jurisdictions of the nation.

As problems do in life, another came shortly after my car problems. Well, not really a new problem, but the reminder of one recently obtained. This came in the form of disguised numbers with probes from those in the medical and insurance community wondering when I would be paying the rest of my unsettled debts. I could only imagine somewhere there was an old mailbox of mine filled up with bills that would never be retrieved. See, they didn't know my philosophy, though I would soon relay it to every collector who would listen. Which is to say, when I got the money they'll get it, until then, they could politely fuck off. No amount of calls or talks of payment plans would be considered. I would pay in full once I had it, until then, I had more urgent priorities of finance. Luckily I still had a place to stay at the end of the summer and I would be able to continue my life of lease hopping without ever being checked by any creditors as to my ability to pay or not. As if rent and my car payment wouldn't remain a priority over all else.

When I was finally able to leave a few days later I went this time to the left and followed the dotted lines around the base of the mountain and through the twisted growth of Mt. Hood National Park. With ponderosa pines towering all around me I caught only momentary glances from the sun as it peaked through the tree-line. With somewhere around 30 miles of separation between me and the base of Hood I found a small pull-off and decided to take a moment and catch a glimpse of the mountain from a view never before seen. Compare looking at Mount Hood from any angle. I sat there staring off at the moment, knowing I would soon drive beyond it's view and had no idea when I would be back. It almost broke my heart. I was leaving the little snowboard town my friends had created in my mind. That is what my life in America would have been, it was the version I most desired. If I had been given an avatar, and given the chance, I would have sent him down that path. The path of a life I would forever want, but for some reason never experience.

Days: 14
Miles Travled: 2,243
Stages: Only 5

Boise, Idaho
August 2016

"They tell jokes there...?"

Normally I would refrain from talking about some of my favorite places for fear they'll be overrun by the temporarily over-excited, but I feel the secret is already out in enough circles about *Boise* for me to tell you how cool it is. Luckily it's too far away from any oceans or civilization for most people to consider it as a viable option for permanent settlement. My first time approaching this modestly sized marvel I had no preconceived notions about what to expect or what I thought I would see. I only had the idea the bright blue football stadium that Boise State was so famous for in the early days of color television when I thought it was only a rumor that the field so resembled a lake that the school had an ongoing problem with birds nose diving into the turf looking for a place to land. When I was younger I started watching college football and eventually became a big fan of the PAC 10, mainly due to the late nature of their games. Whether it was work or friends I never seemed to be around a t.v. during the day and the only games on later in the evening were those taking place on the west coast. I'm suddenly aware that such things as *"only on at this time"* are just outdated as fuck. Now we can watch whatever, whenever. Though we seem to have an affinity for live sports and if I had to guess we always will. As far as the teams I choose to prefer, well that I can't really explain. I think I just enjoyed their colors at first. Then saw them hand it to Oklahoma during the Fiesta Bowl in 2007 and knew they were the real deal. A game during which they validated themselves with one special moment by showing up when they needed to show up. Chris Peterson was perhaps the best coach college football had to offer that year, and for many years after, with less championships than deserved.

I had been a big fan of college football growing up, enjoying it far better than the NFL. It just seemed more competitive to me with a playing field that was much more even, with everyone between 18 and 22. Albeit at times a very overdeveloped 22. Though those guys tended to go to the NFL earlier than not. For whatever reason I respected how each region of the country had found their own ways to play. The

NorthWest highly based on speed, with tall receivers and plays meant to go the end of the field. Then there was the south with running backs likely to get seven yards[6] on each try and lines that could defend a quarterback forever. Though they rarely chose to use them. It was never common to have a quarter back in the south known for his run or his crazy passing. When one came around he was respected by all.

Arriving at an address sent by Ethan I pulled into the driveway and parked next to an old faded blue chevy truck and a jacked-up red jeep. The same couple from Seattle greeted me at the door joined by another individual of similar facial features to the man I already knew in the doorway. The new guy turning out to be Ethans brother. After giving me a short tour around the house I was shown a room in the walk-out basement to place my things. Afterwards we went outback where I found a group of three guys, one of them turning out to be his other brother, all of whom were slack-lining amongst the trees which dotted the backyard generously. Invited to join I stood there for a moment stretching out my legs and doing my best to get a good grip on the ground with my toes. My weird stretches led to their own conversation and pretty soon I was being told I should try getting on the slack-line to test out my balance. Doing so I did my best to brace all of my weight on the left foot, confirming it had taken charge over the last few months. We got to know each other as people always do and then settled into each others comfortable conversations as Ethans brother set up a slack-line between two trees in his backyard. There I inquired as to what the city had to offer.

"So what should I do tomorrow?" - Patrick

"Have you been to the Basque market?" - Ethan

"Uh no." - Patrick

"Oh, go there! They have some great food." - Ethan

"What the hell is it?" - Patrick

"It's a museum for the Basque people. Just what it sounds like." - Ethan

"The people from Spain?" - Patrick

"Yeah! You got a show tonight?" - Ethan

"No. There's not one here til Thursday." - Patrick

"You wanna go to some hot springs then?" - Ethan

"Hell yeah. When we leaving?" - Patrick

"Well, I'm not actually going, but my brother is gonna go if you want to tag along." - Ethan

---

[6] For the record, 7 yards per carry is a pipe dream. I'm just exaggerating.

Responding in the affirmative I went about my evening and had some dinner with the group as the sun went down. Afterwards Ethans brother Turner and I drove from the city north towards a set of mountains. The same ones with the fire glowing from them earlier. Those this time I did not see any glow nor smoke. To this day I still can't explain to you what it was or where it went. It was as if it never happened. We arrived at the hot springs and I followed Trevor as he made his way along a thin trail which led away from the parking lot. About twenty yards away we were met by the slight glow of a cell phone belonging to a set of two couples using one of the hot springs to harbor their late night mimosas and constantly burning joints. The temperature inside was perfect and the depth was just that needed to sink your whole body down without any issue using the surrounding rocks to latch on and let yourself float. I don't know for how long we were there for until what hour we stayed. I just know I got lost in the dots available in that sky. Even on the drive down I couldn't help but see the approaching city and its scattered specs of brilliance in a different light compared to the dark sea of stars I had just been witness to.

Most unfortunate was the reality that my future would not be able to have any such isolation for quite some time if I wanted to reach the levels of my dreams in comedy. The reality is I gotta be in a city; some cultural hub with enough traffic to justify the need for constant entertainment. Not that this place did't have culture, but it didn't import people to see it. The truth is that middle America embraces new culture a lot more than anyone from the outside of this country would be led to believe. This is something I had come to see as a child growing up in what would typically be labeled a more ignorant backwoods part of the country. Though even I can argue that it's not always the same to be interested in other cultures as it is to be cultured, though I would suggest that the one often leads to the other. I remember when I would talk with country people about my travels outside the world they were usually ultra curious and always happy to hear about them. Though not always with the same excited taste for adventure as myself. Areas like this are often defined as *red with a bit of blue*. Which is funny because it's usually a bunch of rednecks who didn't care about you wanting to marry dudes or growing weed. I been around a good bit of country folk and most of them got no real problem with gay people. Which shows just how much the ideas of liberal and conservative had been twisted in my country. Neither of the two were that which they were once portrayed as.

The next morning I started my day taking myself downtown to visit the Basque museum described to me before. The awesome part about a small town is noted in the experience of getting so much one on one interaction. Same as a village in Europe, it's the eye contact and the unique responses, as opposed to cities were there are more outbursts in communication. Going through their museum I felt some nostalgia for my time abroad as I discovered bits and pieces of a language I had never before seen. Finding one of the curators and Basque natives I posed the question, *"Excuse me, but what the hell brought them here?"*

Without a beat the woman looked up at me and responded, *"Sheep."*
"Sheep?"

"Yup. Herding sheep. The Basque people were great sheep herders. That's why so many of them came here in the late 1800's. You can't see it right now, but this whole area here is surrounded by farmland."

"I kinda figured as much. Neat. I'll definitely check that out. I love Spanish things."

"I wouldn't call it Spanish. It's pretty different."

"I know, I was just saying. I'll check it out for sure."

I'll make the argument that understanding America is impossible for those who stay in just one portion of the country. Anyone who comes to the United States and only deals with populations of our larger cities will walk away with an incomplete picture of our people. The varieties of culture in the United States are larger than anyone outside could know. I suppose part of the argument is that there is nothing that is considered quintessentially American that is not consumer based. If stand-up comedy and jazz are the only things we can truly claim to own, I'm fine with that. Humans consume jokes and generate laughter just as a tree turns our carbon to oxygen, you can't have one without the other. Like trying to have the market without the trinket.

At the direction of my hosts I was led to meet a guy named Shane who worked with one of them downtown. He was a former marine and current stoner with little about him that said *'I'm the guy who follows orders'*. Within only an hour of hanging out with him we were sitting there with a few homeless dudes, with his arms wrapped around one of them, their bare-feet only separated by a few inches. Here he told me how he used to inject between his toes, doing anything to conceal his issue from those in even his tightest of inner circles. Struck with curiosity about his own struggle about the possible mindset of my own once addicted friends I decided to take a moment and poke an inquiry at the man so willing to speak. While talking I kept an eye on his toes looking for the marks of mistakes past. All of the dope heads I had known were nowhere close to looking as sober as this guy. His answer somewhat surprised me. *"I had a ton of money when I got out of the military. I got in when the signing bonuses were great and I never spent my money. My sister was good with numbers and when I got out I had almost 50K sitting in my account. I didn't work for a few months, kept going out, drinking, buying other peoples bar tabs. And one night I fell climbing over this fence and I kinda brought back this injury from basic. Started taking a few pills at night just to fall asleep and like fuckin everything else I do, I over did it. Sure am glad this guys dad took a chance giving me a job"* motioning to Ethan in the next seat.

"So what made you stop then? You're not dead and you're not injecting. I don't know that story to usually go any other way."

"You're so right man. I lost so many guys from that."

"Alright. Soo…what did you do?"

"Drugs. Lots of drugs."

Noticing a brief moment of apprehension the man interjected, *"I mean it. Enough hits of acid and you'll see your life like you've never seen it before."*

Noticing my continued reluctance he responded, *"You're not hearing me. That shit opened my eyes. You should try it. I can get you some if you want."*

"Uh. I'm good. I appreciate it though."

"Alright. Lemme know if you change your mind. Tell ya what, you said you know how to snowboard right?"

"Yeah."

"Alright. We're gonna take you sand boarding out to Bruneau."

"What's that?"

"Sand dunes."

"I don't have a board with me…"

"Doesn't matter. We got a few at the house that are already torn up."

It was great driving out there. Walking through the sand my feet burnt at first, oddly acclimating over time. Noticing a sled abandoned at the end of the trail we dragged it on top of hers and as far us as we deemed necessary in-order to gain some momentum sledding.

On the drive back home I got onto *Couchsurfing* and found the local population to be a bit bare. Then I went and did something I'd not done in forever and logged onto my college alumni thing and found a girl I had graduated with who now lived in the area. I think I remember keeping up with her because I saw her wearing a Boise State jersey in one of her profile updates over the years. This led to a hello which led to her inviting me to meet up the next day with a, *"Do you wanna go floating down the river? Could be a great way to unwind."*

"Absolutely! What time do you wanna meet up?"

"I still need to pick up the rafts. I'll pick you up and we can ride together?"

When I arrived to her house she realized we actually needed two cars in-order to have a way back to where we took off so both of us would need to drive. *"Follow me to my friends. He's just down the road. So glad you said yes. I never get to do anything here, I just hear people talk to me about it all the time. I'll be in Charlotte and some random ass girl who visited here for college has done more things than I have and I live here."*

When we got to the house the garage was already open and a small German Shepard was sitting half-way in and half-way out. As we pulled up, his ears perked up a bit and he soon alerted the house of our presence with a deep bark. After which a side door opened and a tall guy with spiked blonde hair and an orange Oregon State jersey walked outside. *"Come in this way guys. What's up Maria? After all this time inviting you for a day on river and you pick my softball tourney weekend to ask me?"*

"No one is making you play ball. Go swing your bat if it makes you happy."

"I'll take that bat and deflate these inner tubes."

Arriving at the Snake river I parked my car near a dam serving as the indicator the end of our float. From there we got in the same car and took a short drive across town and got ourselves situated along the entrance. Standing around I looked and took some notice to the fact that we were the only ones sitting in inner-tubes. The majority of the groups around us were situated with a six-person raft and at least one oar for steering. Causing me to ask, *"Hey are you sure we can float down this?"*

"Yeah. John said he does it all the time."

Once I had let some of my worries subside I was able to really appreciate what a magical place the snake river really was. It still hangs in my mind as one of the most peaceful places I experienced my entire summer. The quietness of the dessert and the vastness of Texas still hadn't given me this feeling of involvement in nature. As the river slowed I saw a pair of deer grabbing a drink only thirty yards or so from where I saw a river otter dive in the water to grab a bright yellow sunfish. From my tube I saw the world around me in a different speed. It was like time on stage. Somewhere about 2 miles down the river a family of 5 caught up to me as I was in the middle of passing out. Hearing the approaching voices I opened my eyes and glared up river to see a giant raft with two inter tubes following behind with the help of a rope which was attached to a handle of each device. I can recall looking at this kid as he caught a pack of gummy bears and thinking, *damn, he's doing it right.*

At some point I had been by myself for at least a half an hour and I think I had even gone through another set of river branching which kept me in the middle lane and by the best I could tell the river had reconnected to one again. Assuming she would be with me the whole time I hadn't been concurred to ask how long this float was supposed to be or where to look for our drop off point. This worry soon left me as I was given a more legitimate one to think of with a view down river. Somewhere about 50 yards ahead I saw a raft with two people on it being dragged by the current towards a set of trees that were bent over from the shore and dangling into the water. As I observed this raft get drawn closer I saw as the man did all he could to paddle away. Watching them I saw my future happening before my eyes. First their raft shot towards the tree limbs and then the man used the oar to try and push his fate away from reality. With no luck to his efforts I watched as the oar shot up into the air and the raft flipped over throwing both of its riders into the water. Ever more aware of my fucked situation I started to use both hands hoping to keep myself from getting caught by that same current. To no avail I doggie paddled best I could until I had wound up within that same current and began spinning around in circles as I got closer. About 20 feet before the branches I realized I had to accept my fate and adapt to the best possible plan B of non-escape. When I first made impact I tried as the man did to deflect himself off of the trees and soon realized what a feeble effort that was as the strength of the river shoved me aggressively into them and started to flip me over. Losing the inter tube I clenched my keys as I used my right hand to reach out and grab any branch I could. At first I could only hold onto one for a moment. Then I would be pulled by the river towards another. Each time being struck by a limb on my shoulders, then once on my jaw. For a moment I had a clear grip on one of the thicker limbs and tried to regain my breath for a moment. I hadn't taken in any water, but the cold and the commotion had already taken a bit out of me. Inevitably the bark began to wear and my hand slipped away. This time being smacked in the face by a few branches and losing my sunglasses. Watching my black Ray-Ban's fall to the bottom of the river I tried once to capture them with my hand as I let go and gave myself to the river. But as my squinting eyes would later regret, I missed the mark. I forgot in the moment the difference in perception of objects underwater and the angles to consider. In floating down the river I could see my raft drifting off to my left. Knowing it was my only chance to make a steady journey to my destination I swam vigorously and tracked my tube down the river about two-hundred yards before catching up with it and throwing my arm over to pull it closer to me. Once firmly in the embrace of my struggling hug I swung my feet over and positioned myself back in place. The first thing I did once I felt situated was to place my keys on top of my stomach with the lanyard tucked into my shorts. If I had thought about it before perhaps I could have tied them to my belt strings and saved both my keys and my glasses *Sighs deeply in a moment of regrettable remembrance*. As they sat on my stomach I flopped both hands to my side and was finally able to release the tension in my body, letting my fingertips graze across the top of the water as the current spun me around. I kept my eyes open a moment to peer ahead and make sure it would be smooth sailing for the foreseeable future. As my view confirmed I was in the clear I leaned back and tried to bask in any of the suns remaining warmth before the clouds and the dusk took it all away. My body was freezing. The water was freezing. I don't know why I had thought a river in the northern hemisphere would be warm regardless of the time of the year. Sure, the people here probably thought it was warm, but that's the problem with relativity, it's all relative and in this instance I couldn't relate. With the breath finally beginning to fill my lungs I felt like a fucking moron. I hadn't been off of crutches for more than two weeks. What was I thinking sand boarding earlier? Why the fuck was I here in this river? Even more concerning, where the fuck was Maria? I would only get my answer to that one about an hour later when I would pull myself to shore to see her attached to a group of college-aged kids floating together in a long link of rafts and coolers attached to inter-tubes. Upon our reunion I discovered her tube had ripped in half hours ago as she took the wrong lane down an earlier separation in the river and was luckily helped by her new friends, a group of grad students working in Sun Valley for the summer. Still shivering I was thrilled to get back to my car and say goodbye 20 minutes later when we finally got our shit together, driving with the heat on the entire way. Departing she leaned out here window, *"You said you're going on around 8:30 tonight?"*

"Yeah. I'll text you."

Wanting a nap, but having time for not even a coffee I headed downtown where I found a parking spot and made my way to the comedy club. I sat outside for the next hour drying off, changing, and writing in my notebook, trying to remember any of the lighter thoughts I had had run through my mind before the day took a violent turn. Sitting there I received a text from a friend in D.C., one who had always been more supportive than most. Despite his desire to help me find my way in other avenues in life, he was still the most supportive of any of my professional friends. That and a mutual love of fast cars, watches, and inappropriate jokes had kept us linked from the beginning.

"I have some friends who can meet up with you while you're there."

"How do you know them."

"I met them on a tinder a long time ago. They're cool. Trust me."

"THEM? When were you in Boise?"

"Don't worry about the details. So you wanna meet them or not?"

"I fuckin' love you. Link us up, would love to have some extra guests."

"Don't worry if you bomb. I can assure you that they're both used to being let down."

"Lmao. Awesome. Send me their numbers."

"I already gave them yours."

The world was so weird. Here I was being connected to friends of friends of friends, and it was completely normal. I had seen life go from a point in time where one would tell you not to speak to a stranger, to being introduced to a group of girls who barely knew anyone who actually knew me and yet everyone was fine with it. Walking inside I saw that the night had a closed-off kinda vibe to it. Passing by the maitre d' I saw a guy on stage who was clearly performing drunk. A suspicion confirmed as I stood there for the next few minutes listening to him stagger through his act. It was sad, this was something you would see every now and then, a drunk comedian was nothing new, but the reality of it always kinda killed me. I could never figure out if they were doing it to get the courage to get on stage, or if it was the courage to speak. After asking the staff about where to sign-up I struggled to understand the nature of this mishap, I mean, why label it an open mic? There was nothing more embarrassing than this moment. With no proof to show her as to my current abilities as a stand-up comedian I couldn't help but notice the fact of the situation that the man on stage was doing worse than anyone in the audience would have done in the same situation. As the friends of a friend showed up I was bummed to tell them of the reality of the evening. Like many groups before them they attempted to playful insist that I just perform right there, a talent I wish I possessed as an addition to my usual sidewalk manner. They were perfectly nice people and they did nothing to shovel guilt onto my already shameful walk, but I couldn't get it out of my head the entire time we were together.

Not being allowed to go on was the most embarrassing thing. Well not embarrassing, but annoying since I actually brought a crowd. I kinda got it though. They didn't know me, but it still looked bad on me. Especially since I had gotten them to change their plans for the night to come watch me. I apologized to the two of them and went off to the back of the room where I stood and watched the acts go on over the next two hours. I didn't even wanna hear it. It was hard to hear anyone go on that I knew was telling worse jokes than me. Perhaps I had made a cardinal mistake by not checking on whether or not it was an open-mic night or a features kinda night. Of course as my luck would have it, it was one of those features kinda nights. Plus, there was no set of reviews hovering above my head, not even a comic from the area who could say he had heard of me before. I wish they coulda let me go up and just agreed to pull me off I had started to bomb. I could agree to that. Though I reflect upon it now with a more fair understanding, at the moment I found few things similar to understanding when attempting to consider why the hell I couldn't have my shot. Then the more I watched the more I felt a first-timers sense of entitlement, as if I deserved to be on that stage because I had been on A stage before.

The stage was the only place I could practice. I never wanted to be that guy who practiced his jokes on his friends. It was like you could never stop selling yourself. I suppose that would be the nice part about being famous if you will, you wouldn't have to sell yourself or your work in the same way anymore. You wouldn't have to constantly reaffirm who you were to the outside world. In a lot of ways aren't we just what we say we are? And if so, who is to judge, and who is the audience? Judgement is usually meant to shame the offender. Shame as a tool to stifle humans has proven largely ineffective, only now has shame been attached to an uncoupling of your future possibilities from the operational realities of the world as it is.

"I'm sorry guys. My bad."

"It's cool man. That third guy wasn't even funny."

"I saw at least two guys I know you woulda done better-den'."

"Yeah. Thanks. If I didn't think that enough I'd likely never get myself on stage."

I went outside and waited while they watched the show as it would have passed even if I had gone up. Uncertain in my own skin for one of those rare occasions I kept from going to mingle with the other comedians and even tried not to...

"Hey, how did you learn to do that?"

"What do you mean?"

"Well how do you figure out the proportions?"

"Oh that's nothing, that shit's just technical."

"Well what's the hard part to you?"

"Deciding what I want to put my name next to. The moment I put this up people will be coming around posing next to it, I gotta make sure my work is tight."

With no chance of doing comedy for at least a week I had no reason to be staying in Boise. I had wasted time. A lot of time. Maybe I'm being harsh on myself, but it was wasted in the sense that I did nothing to get myself on stage. Annoying as it was I had to remember not to be so disappointed in myself for the lack of time spent on stage on the latter half of this trip, especially when I consider the distances from one mic to another.

DENVER, COLORADO
August 2016

"What you doing after the tour?"

A pproaching the Rockies my eyes widened at the sight of faded green peaks lined in a row ahead of me. Climbing the steeply pitched highways I heard my cars engine speak its age as another slow driver called for a quick downshift to speed past. Speed. Not really speed, if we were speeding I wouldn't be passing them, instead I'm just doing my best to keep a smooth sixty with double the RPM's that would normally be required at thirty. I remember my first time entering Denver. I was only 24, on the way to California on my first real road trip as an adult, or at least the first one crossing a time-zone. I would hate to call the ones I had before this unreal but you see it's a lot different when you're the one doing the driving compared to being driven as I had been on most of my trips to Florida.

Though it may seem like an unlikely place to associate with humor, Colorado as a whole gave me a good comedy vibe ever since the first time I saw *South Park* somewhere in middle school. It was poorly animated and done so purposely, with that animation being the only thing not evolving over the years. As far as Hollywood goes the creators of that show are the only ones who can truly do or say anything. They're modern day times most relevant utilizers of free speech with regards to addressing the most sensitive of issues. Admittedly sometimes done with zero taste, but they never hold back.

Seeing that I was only an hour or so from the city I sent a text to the number of the guy I had been connected to on *Couchsurfing*. He was a bartender in the city with a dog, a cat, and a two bedroom apartment.

"I'm coming up on the Fort Collins. Be in the city in about an hour. What time you off?"

A few miles later I received an answer, *"Hey bro, busy til about 7. Wanna meet me at this hookah spot by my place at 10?"*

"Cool."

"They have an open mic every Sunday if you're feeling up to it. I'll send you the address."

Out of the car stepped a half-Persian half-black man with a body covered in tattoos and a frame that looked like it was meant for hanging clothes. We quickly related as two guys who had traveled a lot up and down the coast with a fair amount of knowledge of the 95 corridor. He took the love of it far more seriously than I did. Representing his heightened dedication with a set of tattoos streaming down his arm, decorated by a set of stars representing cities going from bicep to wrist, starting in NYC and ending in Miami. When I got to his house we said our hellos in the parking lot before he ushered me towards his car where I fought through a series of fast food bags and empty energy drinks in order to find a space in his passenger seat.

"You smoke?"

"Seems I'm in Rome a lot lately."

"Awesome. Here, hold this."

Placing a softball sized apple in my hands he smirked at the look of confusion on my face as he left the apple in my hand and directed his fingers to the depth of his cupholders to find a stray lighter. Noticing the properly placed holes on either side I put the apple to my mouth and tried to imagine how this would work. It was odd doing this in a city where weed had been legal nearly a decade and there was no need to be discrete. I couldn't understand why we were still using such a primitive method in a state which allowed us to travel with rolling papers, bowls, bongs, and anything else we could want to use to smoke with. Nonetheless, here he was carving his way through this giant apple. It had to have been a honey-crisp, few other apples could have handled the necessary carving. Once we were done he noticed me still holding the apple as we approached the door to the lounge and asked,*"You're gonna eat that?"*

"Doing this tour on a budget. I'm not throwing away a $3 apple."

Eating the apple as we got out I closed the door and followed him to an entrance with black velvet ropes.

"Oh. I thought you said there was an open-mic."

"Yeah man. You can go up after that guy."

"I'm not gonna go on in-between music. WTF man?"

His friend pulled a script out from his book bag and asked me to take a look. A Cameroonian who was found out when I heard his French accent and took a wild guess by starting with the question, *"Parlay VOO Fransay?"*

"Wee, Vous Parlay?"

Pulling my hand up to indicate a pinch I uttered, *"un pwa." (If I did the literal spelling you would hate me more than the French right now.)* With that he laughed and pulled a notebook from his backpack. *"Take a look at dis."*

"What you got there?"

"Is a script I've been working awn."

"What's it about?" Listening to his summary of what it was and where it was going I tried to think of what to tell him and listened best I could above the music. We were interrupted by Meyhar informing me that he knew a place where they were doing comedy down the road tomorrow. Sadly I can't tell you anything in regards to the details as I promised I would not, but if it ever makes its way to the screen I'll be sure to let you all know. As I talked with him about his script he threw a few of his own comedic questions my way. *"Ever thought about trying to get on SNL?"*

"Not really. I don't know that I could give my jokes away to someone else."

"It's not hard if you're in a sketch mindset. You won't see a joke as a joke, you'll see it as a joke for the situation. Some stuff only works coming from the right person."

"Most art is like that. Either way, I just don't think I would want to be topically funny on command."

After speaking with him I went up and tried to tell a new story. It's wild how quickly time can get away from you when you're working with a new bit, especially when it'a story, because you always end up killing a minute and a half before you realize you've been speaking for thirty seconds. I did too much painting the picture for them to get why it was funny. Even so, I did well. Truth be told it was the most confident I had felt since getting back on my feet. I could finally walk around on the stage and move my hands without worry about letting go of my cutches. I was able to glide along and even walk over the microphone cord without any concern.

His girlfriend was nice. She was a Russian who had been living out here a while. Next I watched as Meyhar went up and made the same mistakes I had made when I first got in front of the mirror, mainly starting the story from the middle assuming people already know a lot about me. Once his performance was over we made our way to another spot in downtown called The Red Square where his girlfriend had more than a few tips for me. *"Don't say anything to the bartender. He'll take care of us if he thinks we're Russian."*

"What the fuck am I supposed to do if he starts talking to me?"

"Just don't say anything. Or just say Ya voz' mu yeshche and keep your head down."

"My head down? Am I not supposed to be here?"

"No it's fine! They're just old paranoid dudes."

"Right..."

I began wondering what was my country becoming? Could a place this broad and this populated remain united?

"You know anybody else in the city?"

"Yeah. A friend from college. Gonna go see them tomorrow."

"Not friendly enough to stay with?"

"I don't think her newborns would make for great housemates given my late night hours."

"Ahh. Good luck getting a word in on your visit tomorrow. My brother had a kid in April, I can't ever get his ass on the phone."

"He live around here?"

"Nah. Moved to Cali after college. Boys barely back this way."

The next morning when I woke up Meyhar was still asleep so I did my best to quietly pack up the things I needed for the day and headed out. On my way downstairs I came across the gym and found myself compelled to go inside as no one had yet to enter and turn on the lights. I looked in the mirror as I did some leg lifts and saw my muscles appear back to normal for the first time. Even my thigh had a definition that was for once back to bulky instead of a pitted piece of metal after a heavy impact. With the extra confidence I got through a few more sets and sat there panting before going to top off my water bottle. I felt like myself again, grateful each day that my injury had been temporary. Something sort of came back to me as I was getting my shit together that evening. Even as I put my shirt on in the mirror I was a bit happier than usual with how everything was fitting. I did as I told him I would and spent most of the day in Boulder. Mainly walking around the University. I found myself hearing about Boulder in one capacity or another much more over the last few years and I knew I had to see it. I only regret that the night I showed up there were no mics to speak of and light rains after six which made walking around less than ideal in this otherwise pristine setting.

Leaving Boulder I made sure to do one more pitstop at another one of our nations cultural landmarks and a particular point of interest for anyone performing anything on a stage. RedRocks was one of those places that had a cult level of recognition among music communities in the United States, especially with those groups most known for long running jam band sessions. A combination of phenomenal acoustics and views that are out of this fucking world, I mean it, it looks like Mars with a touch of green. Despite having felt better in the gym this morning the hike up the steps at Redrocks took everything in me to keep my knees from visibly shaking.

Pulling up at Emma's house just before sunset I parked my car on their patch of the culd-e-sac and kept my door shut as a giant German Shepard came rushing up to my door. No barking to speak of, but his curious nose met the top of my door and his quick breaths out quickly fogged up the bottom half of my window.

"Arlo! Get Down! Sorry Pat. He gets all excited anytime someone new comes around." - Emma

Looking down at the dog she rubbed his head and continued to talk to him more than me, *"He's not here to see you silly. He's here to see mommy." - Emma*

"Yo. You have a fuck load of bees out here." - Patrick

"Oh, yeah. Ignore them." - Emma

"Uh okay," I muttered as a few flanked my right side and then darted around my head, seeming to examine my aura with each swoop. Noticing my nerves Emma leaned in a bit more, *"Do you wanna move?"* In our continued conversation I found it so interesting how differently the idea could be considered. From one end, some friends would hear about me coming to their city and get very excited. Natalie had loved seeing me. Meyhar and his friends looked like they had the time of their lives and all in all I would say the crowd enjoyed me. It was times like this I asked myself why some people back home couldn't be happier for me. Why not just come along and enjoy the view of this crazy ride like my grandma.

"So you don't think this is a bad idea?" - Patrick

"Oh I think you're crazy. I hope you make it, but, all that running around and everything, that's not what I would want. I'm glad my husband has a simple job where he's home before sundown each day." Finishing her sentence with the happy smile of a lady bobbing a baby.

"Sorry we couldn't make the show. Kids."

I sat there and took in a drag of her cigarette as I stared up at the skyline thinking how I would never get some of those moments back. It just wasn't the same any more. You didn't get to hang out with people unless someone else was around, be it their dogs, their family, or their spouse. Those who can afford to give you some of their time often have to do so under the supervision of their family and parental obligations, with an understandable portion of their existence always off in a far away land traveling with the soul of their children. I saw that by the time they were done with their children I would be somewhere in the stages of raising my own, behind by at least a decade and living with my own reasons for not being able to make it over.

The one question I couldn't avoid from those who loved me was, *"What are you going to do when your trip is over? You might as well move somewhere like here. We're in the middle of the country. Could be a great place to get your comedy going."*

To this day I'm still not sure I made the right decision. The only truly right decision I made was making the phone call to my grandma when my mom mentioned that they might be putting her into surgery next week for some type of old people problem with her heart. The type of thing that happens to someone in their nineties. I suppose if I got in the car and had driven I could have been home late the next day, but by my projections at the time I still had five days or so left on my journey if I was gonna hit up Chicago. When we spoke on the phone she was her usual self in high spirits and urged me to continue with my trip as opposed to driving back to see her when she got out of surgery. Even ending the conversation with the hopeful promise of ,*"I'll see you in a few days sweetheart..."* Something to which I should have just said *"Love you"* and *"Goodbye"*, but instead I told my grandma something I still think about to this day. Something which I said because I was thinking about the pain she was in, not the pain I would be in. *"You know grandma, you don't owe it to any of us to stick around. I love you and I'm happy for all of the time I get with you and will get with you, but you don't owe anything to anyone. You've been a really great grandma. Just wanted you to know that."* Even so, she ended once more with a loving goodbye and an, *"I'll see you soon dear."* That would be the last time I would ever hear my grandmothers voice. All the time wanting to scream, *"Why is anyone performing open heart surgery on a 92 year old women? Why? What are we trying to accomplish? Does the physical burden match the potential future of the operation?"* A series of complaints and questions I would never get to throw her way as she would pass away on the operating table just one day shy of her 93rd birthday.

Laying there after talking with her I started going over my tapes in an attempt to get a grasp on the entirety of my material. The majority of my new material over the last two months was completely reliant not just on the mention but the actual presence of my crutches. Yet I no longer had my crutches to use as a crutch. Unless I told a way to retell the story I couldn't really use my new material the same way. I had become reliant on a prop of my situation. Just like my raccoon story. It was great, but it was way better with the photo.

Regardless of how positive I wanted to remain with the memories of my grandma and all of her encouragement it was here that the realities of my life were beginning to catch up to me. In one way I had escaped my reality by driving so far away from it, but in another way I had done nothing to change the reality waiting for me upon my return. There was no stage waiting. If I continued down this life for even longer, would I end up with no one waiting for me at the end of the day? My trip was almost over and in the end I did not know what I would be doing once it was all over. I had to ask myself what were the options from here. I felt just like I did after college, all of this paperwork to show and no idea what to do. Deep down I was somewhat discouraged to not have more to show for all of the time I spent on the road. I didn't wanna return home or even back to my cave of comedians as I could see everyone asking how I had missed the chance to finish a new act with 40 days of sitting down. Hell, by some standards I should have written a book. The ultimate problem was that I was managing too much. I was trying to develop my comedy routine while simultaneously building my following. All before or without knowing exactly who I was as a comedian and who I was planning to be in the future. Plus, to make a following actually want to follow you, you need to be delivering with quality material that makes them wanna follow you. Which only seems possible by someone going up more often than your average comedian.

Later that night I went to another open-mic downtown and decided to give something new a try by just going on stage and telling a story.

"You guys are nature people you might like this. You're weed people too. Let's talk about the meeting of those two things..."

From there I went on to tell them a story that I shall relay to you as I did to them. So I'm at work this one day and I get a text message asking me if I wanna take part in a bbq with my roommates. Now this new roommate barely knows me. So I didn't respond with *"Why are you bothering me at work?"* I instead was nice and said, *"Hey bro. Wish I could. Stuck here on the grind."* To which he replied, *"Oh, that's weird. Sounded like you were in your room."*

Now, I don't know if you've spent much time away from your house, but you don't want to be far from it when someone tells you it sounds like you're already there. So I sent him a message asking, *"Uh. is my door closed?"* To which he said *yes,* and led me to believe there was nothing to worry about. Since I was at work I went about my day and brushed the message off until I got home a few hours later. When I got there the house was empty. So I open the door to this stairwell to go up to my room and I first notice that all of my shoes are out of order. Which is not how I would leave them. Then I walk up and turn the corner to view my room and it looks someone came in and was looking for something very small. Like when they're tearing apart a room for a microchip. Except I don't have any fucking microchips. Nonetheless, my covers are off the bed, all of my papers are off of my desk, and things are just kinda fucked up. Weird thing was. Nothing is missing. I go and look where my computer and those types of things are, and though they might be turned over or moved, they're still there. Then I open up my night stand and find the only thing missing. Well, not missing, just mostly gone. There was a box in my nightstand that had your typical things. Condoms, vitamins, and a weed brownie. This weed brownie was now like a weed crumb. Which is when I determined my room must have been ransacked by a teenager. Didn't know what he was doing. Took the goods. And ran. So I did what any good man does. I cleaned my room. Put my shit back together, and went about my life. Time goes by. It's two days later. I'm downstairs. And I hear a shuffling upstairs again. Weird. I think, okay Patrick, let's go upstairs again and finally catch this mother fucker. So I swing open my door and looking down at me is the face of the most adorable confused looking raccoon you've ever seen. And he looks down at me with those big ass raccoon eyes and through those dark circles, darker than normal this time, I read a message that said, *"Bro...what the fuck was in those brownies?"*

At this point his head was stuck in the rails as he stared at me so I went into the kitchen to get some peanut butter for him. Okay that's a lie. It was almond butter, but I didn't wanna seem bougie. So I finally shuffle his little ass out the door and as he's leaving he goes, *"Can I at least get your connect?"*

Lincoln, Nebraska
August 2016

"It's as much corn as you think..."

I don't think I could have picked a worse time than crossing the Nebraskan border to start listening to the audiobook of *My Life*, the story of Keith Richards, a long time member of *The Rolling Stones*. His book starts with him getting pulled over in middle America in possession of drugs, and what was I doing? Driving through middle America, in possession of drugs. By no means my first time or the last, but I do dare to say it was my first time with the audible reminder of times before to reinforce my knowledge that what I was doing to be a poor decision. And for the first time all summer I didn't have some wrapped up leg to point to as a reason for why I had them. Crossing the state line I decided to stop and take a look back at the country behind me, with the flatness of the Midwest expanding ahead. I stood there enjoying the last bits of tall grass swaying in the wind and threw out any metaphorical grass from my pockets. Now completely healed I had no more reason to justify smoking myself into oblivion every time the memory of my leg bothered me.

With six-feet of cornstalks on either side blocking the setting sun from peering through, I began to feel like I had been watching the same movie reel on repeat for hours on end. One mile after another I floated through an endless stream of shadows resulting from stalks bright green and firmly pointed toward the sky, soaking up every last bit of evening sun the MidWest could offer. Though surrounded by blindspots I began texting a few friends as the day went on to see what options I had between there and Chicago. One had a girlfriend in Kansas, another a brother in law in Tulsa, neither of which was anywhere outside of a 6-hour inconvenience. The span of the country without any friends for me to crash with really opened my eyes to this country's lack of places for the traveler on the go to drop in and stay without a tent. At least none blatantly advertised. No real hostels to speak of either. Granted, not a lot for people to do to bring them all this way anyhow. Might as well take the train. Yet, as alone as I felt out here I can't imagine how alone someone who grows up here feels when they think of either coast as a 1,500 mile journey. I like to think I had a hard time wrapping my head around the idea of getting into showbiz, but it must have felt even more intense from these tiny towns.

Getting off the interstate I made my way to the obvious downtown with your typical brick laced streets and railroad style buildings on every side. I'm not gonna build up your hopes with regards to learning much about this place or it's comedy scene. I didn't do anything here, it was merely a stop off. I had never seen Lincoln and I was curious about what the city had to offer and what the university looked like. That draw became more reinforced as I got within a few miles of the city and saw the Nebraska Cornhusker's football stadium peaking over the horizon as the largest thing in any direction. Had I been there during the fall you better believe I would've scheduled myself to pass through on the weekend of a home game. More importantly, I would have tried to get myself on a local mic. Despite being told that colleges were a nightmare to perform at, my time in restaurants has shown me that this generation can still enjoy an inappropriate laugh.

Having spent nearly all summer on the road I started to see what type of loneliness this life could ultimately lead to as the years mounted up. Though I was fully aware that this could be the curse of any life with a tendency towards solitary pursuits. I was genuinely conflicted because I had found myself finally living the type of life I wanted to live only to find it was going to be completely counter to the type of life I wanted to have once I was successful. I wanted roots and yet somehow I had managed to pick a career that was counter to the idea of finding roots. Or ever getting the chance to create them. If I continued down this type of lifestyle how many empty days would I spend crossing state lines instead of being surrounded by those I love? The idea that some comics stay living like this for eternity is wild to me. Though I would imagine that's what people who knew me would think I wanted. Was I in some ways dooming myself to a life of solitude and loneliness and who says that's not what I would be getting at the end anyway? As far as I've seen it seems that to be the ultimate end because even surrounded by a family we're all alone within our own heads.

This was the only time I decided I wanted *to-be* something. Even knowing the amount of behind the scenes work which would come along over the years. It was oddly the part of the career which appealed to me the most. I enjoyed the solitude of working through that which was at hand. In some ways I wondered if it was just a thing which came to me as man entering my thirties, a time in which I was compelled with this urge to tinker. Even as I walked through the city I did so with an enhanced curiosity, some sort of early mid-aged reinvigoration of the soul. Whether it was environment or biology was still up for debate. The only thing over which I no longer had a debate was how important it was that I established my comedic identity in the next stage of my journey. I could do this for as long as I wanted, but until fans knew me as the guy they come to for a certain type of comedy I would still just be some guy floating around the open-mic circuit making people laugh here and there. Which was fine, but if I wanted this to be a career I needed to decide who I was going to be. This wasn't like life where I could be one person with my grandma, another with my girlfriend, and someone else to the person I meet on the bus. I had to put out one version of me onto the stage and hope that those who come enjoy it and encourage others to do the same, but the one thing I couldn't do was play the typical human game of wearing many masks at once.

As far as success as a comedian came there was no blueprint, only suggestions, only paths from which I could draw some advice. Those before me had become famous performing in such venues as *"Catch A Rising Star"*. Meanwhile my generation sat there with people finding them on YouTube, a place where it's way easier to click to the next rather than sit here and give someone their due. Trying to make it on the internet felt like jumping in the ocean hoping to be seen from space. I would have to navigate my own way through all of this by either algorithms or audiences. Nonetheless I would end up getting my first offer to do paid comedy from a LinkedIn message of all places. When it came in asking if I really did comedy it led to a few other messages and eventually, *"Could you do a few minutes at a show we are hosting during our fall festival this October?"*

"Absolutely, how much time you need?"

"15 minutes?" I looked at her response for a minute; fully aware that she was asking for three times more than what I KNEW I had.

"I can do that. Any rules or anything I need to know?"

"Keep it friendly for a small town crowd. That's about it."

This interaction caused a second spirt of inspiration in me that worked well with the idea of a deadline. I needed to live in a city like a training camp. The only thing that matters is the time you put into it. It needed to be an 8 times a week type of thing. Having five minutes was great, but I needed to have a real act if I was going to live up to the promise I Just made. At the end of the day I want to go beyond the open mics. I want to be invited on stages near and far. For this to happen I would need to get in more reps. I could see what had happened as a result of spending time more or less in the gym over the last decade, perhaps I would have to work the next decade to see what could come out of this. Though even that comparison couldn't be done perfectly, because the body will respond no matter what, the audience not always. Truth was I would need to put in so much more time. In the end I would need to be where I could perform the most amount of times in a week. I would have to somewhere to put in the work. The answer was simple, it was back to NYC. It was either move to NYC or find a way to not only start my own thing, but also find enough people to come in to canvas a worldwide audience. That's what NYC had that nowhere else did, flows of people that seemed to never end. Even people who went out and saw stand up a lot wouldn't see you more than twice a month. I may have jumped too early, but I now had a network of comedians and comedy houses around the US to bring back to NYC. If I was going to find the comedy in my life, if I wanted to find the funny, I would first need to see it. I needed to write it. I had only now started to understand myself. Perhaps that's because I had only recently begun to question myself. Wherever I went, I needed to sit still for a change. I couldn't promise the quality, but they would see the most refined version of what I had.

If I was going to continue doing this I needed to know what it was that set me out from the rest of them. I don't know why, but until now I had never considered what it was to have a voice and stick to it. Even if my identity were to shift from here I needed to at least write about the one I knew now while I was living it. I needed to write about what I understood. That's all I could really do. The comedy is usually in the tragedy. Speaking of tragedy, I'm still not quite sure how I lost track of my gas gauge while crossing over Iowa in complete darkness. At one point the construction going on overwhelmed me with orange lights and I didn't notice the one on my screen until it was closer to half of a *oh shit* level with more red above the arrow than below. Along with the construction the road was lined in both directions with 18 wheelers making their way through the midwest under the cover of night. I was lucky to even find a gas station when it was all said and done, too bad it was closed by the time I got there. Having only fumes left in my tank

I was forced to deal with reality and park my car near the pumps and wait til morning.

There, in the top right center of Illinois I sat, awaiting the arrival of a store clerk; hopefully, one who was the timely type. For my friends who supported me from afar, I always wondered what they would think if they got to look in on the little moments of my life like this one, could they handle the annoyance? Would they wonder why I bothered? Then again I wondered if the me before crutches would be handling this so calmly. After sending the necessary messages I ended up scrolling through my texts a bit more and ultimately landing on a friend of mine back in NYC. Somewhere in this I fell asleep in the front seat of my car with my legs buried beneath the pedals as a hoodie covered my eyes.

CHICAGO, ILLINOIS
August 2016

"Ever done improv?"

W aking up three hours later I saw dusk approaching as the lights of another vehicle finally pulled in. Once I noticed the storefront lights turned on and the pumps powered up I released the emergency break, allowing myself to drift down the gravel back to the pumps. Getting out of the car I saw the attendant look out a bit puzzled as to where I had come from so quickly. Surely his cameras would tell him later. After gassing up I started the engine and put the heat on full blast. It was one of those early summer mornings where the night had set a dew on everything and warmth would not return until long after the light of day had. And that wouldn't happen for the next two hours. Seeing as I didn't intend on sleeping at a gas station last night I also didn't intend on finding myself in rush-hour traffic at the early part of a Friday morning. No amount of intentionally bad planning would have done such a thing. Facing the same fate of those going to work in America's third largest city I sat on the interstate and crawled my way in, slowly creeping towards a sprawl of tall buildings and a wall of lakeside nothingness just beyond them.

Once referred to as *Paris on the Prairie*, Chicago is easily one of the most breathtaking cities our country has to offer. Its reputation for wind and terrible winters are as true as any, but its prime months are the best weather has to offer. With a lakeside setting the city also serves as one of the few metropolis's that actually increases in population over the summer weekends when most city goers would be escaping their cement dwellings in other regions of the country. Currently one of our largest cities in the U.S., it was an anomaly with 1.6 million people already living there in 1900. The first time I came to Chicago was when a group of long time friends decided to take a long weekend to the Windy City to celebrate a set of birthdays. Upon arriving I had been given the better part of the day to explore the city on my own and had readily taken the chance to discover some of the cities biggest sites, running by The Bean and some famous market before my friends arrived for happy hour. The architecture in Chicago is like none other this nation has to offer. Though some areas vary from one another with great degree, no area has so few similar things within its own blocks. A string of noticeably different builds lines each side of river wide enough to run two great big boats side by side. I would argue it is the most unique city in the hemisphere, architecturally speaking. The eclectic blend of pre-1870's dwellings, combined with the many commissioned works, it just makes this area hard to top. For the record, this level of oddity in design did not stop with buildings built post some fire. To confirm this I highly suggest looking into the story of the Giant Bean and how it was put there because some mayor was tired of looking at a parking lot. A must see when in the Windy City.

Driving through the south side of the city I saw one of the most obviously neglected parts of our country somewhere only comparable to that of New Orleans, on full sketchy display in the early morning sun. Though both carry their own set of issues it's unlikely that those issues from the top of the Mississippi have anything to do with the issues at the bottom. For one reason or another the upper-midwest has developed a bad reputation for getting the short end of the stick when it came to government funding. A mixed result of reprioritization by Washington and a reflection of the regional corruption which has long plagued the area and its politicians; with four of the last ten Illinois governors eventually serving time for corruption related charges. Not to mention the fact that they sold off the future earnings of their parking meters to Morgan Stanley and Abu Dhabi[7]. As if that wasn't enough, the city had been started with a rebuild taking place in the last century. The fire had made this place a blend of new and old all at once, arguably one of the most updated American cities from what it was when it first started. I mean, they kinda had to rebuild some of San Fran and L.A. due to earthquakes, but, you know what I mean.

I know it's not the utmost of importance, but, there seemed to be no roadside management anywhere I went. Grass was coming through the concrete everywhere; and this was in the one of the countries largest fucking cities with a history and notoriety that goes back generations. Not to mention no short of funds or industry to help supplement.

Improv is the only branch of comedy that truly scares me. One of the things which scares me about improv is that even when you're doing good that's not good enough, you've gotta go and change the topic. I think the idea of doing something on stage with someone else sees way

---

[7] Bothersome right?

harder than doing your thing alone. Just the idea of recovering your way out of your own fuck up seems easier. Though I'm not really sure what a fuck up in improv is, it's never really over until you've stopped, you can always keep going for the laugh. I think a crowd is more willing to watch an improv crew as long as they are entertaining, even if laughable moments are only scattered every once in a while. The same is not true with a one person stand-up act, that audience seems much more bent on you being particularly funny. Perhaps it's because there's someone more specifically to hate. Either way it'll remain one of my greater regrets that I didn't get a chance to see any improv while in the city most known for it.

If you had talked to me about improv before I started doing stand up I would have had a much different line of thought to give you. I can recall seeing improv first highlighted by Drew Carry via *Whose Line Is It Anyway* on whatever night of the week the network was choosing to air it. Though hilarious, the show made it look like it was some comedically advanced version of adult Pictionary. After seeing it I'm even more sure that an unfunny person cannot do improv. That might be one of the more odd differences between improv and stand up. I think an unfunny person could write enough funny material to fool you for a few minutes. Until further notice I might even be one of them. Yet I don't think an unfunny person could in any way fake their way through improv. I think improv requires a different type of genius on top of a necessary level of innate talent. In some ways they're the ultimate artists because they've mastered the art of adapting to the moment.

Through my wandering I came across the Palomar Hotel and noticed a sign outside which eluded to some type of wine happy hour from 5-7 that evening. I went in with an otherwise lack of options for places to hang out while it rained. While there I started talking to a couple who ended up being there taking advantage of the happy hour just the same as I was. They were actually locals and a few glasses of wine later I was being invited to stay with them. Well, not actually with them. The guy was a property manager and told me he had a few open rooms that he usually put up as weekend rentals. Feeling more in the mood to be alone than not I did my best to politely decline, but to no avail. Being too tired to fight their resistance to my persistence I gave them an *okay* and moved onto my next curiosities, *"So, where you performing tonight?"*

"Someplace near Lincoln Park. Where's your building?"

"It's literally walking distance. You got anything to do before the show?"

"Not really."

"Awesome. Follow me. I'll show you some views from my patio."

Entering a bronze lined elevator I looked around at the high ceilings and chandeliers trying to calculate whether they'd give up 3 levels or 4 to make up this sort of lobby. His apartment was the nicest place I had ever seen someone our age claiming to own. The views of downtown were incredible and the vaulted ceilings let the light expand to every corner of the room creating an almost unnecessary need for extra light. All with one noticeable difference from a NYC apartment, that being the luxury of a bathroom big enough to spread your arms in without hitting the walls. Though the feature of narrow foyers and tightly designed kitchens remained the same.

"How long you lived here?"

"They transferred me here a few months ago."

"Nice. You got about as much time here as I do."

"When were you here last?"

"Shit, eight, nine years ago maybe. Came here for a four day weekend and a friends birthday celebration. I don't know the lay out of the city very well, but I really enjoyed it. I remember the food being awesome."

"The snack joints here are where it's at. We'll go to this sandwich spot down the street later. You like pizza?"

"Who doesn't?"

"Perfect, I know a place. It's not like the places they show the tourists. And they won't look at you like a fuck-tard if you ask for a slice of thin crust."

"Not a fan of deep dish?"

"I don't go to a pizza shop to wait 30 minutes. Fuck deep dish."

"Fair point. Harsh, but fair."

An hour and two slices later I was relaxing on the porch of a bar hosting the closest open-mic we were able to find. There waiting I was hit with one of the first times that I could recall not feeling motivated to do a stand-up since I had started. I was just fucking tired. You know, the slept in my fucking car at a gas station then sat in several hours of traffic kind of tired.

By now I had been waiting long enough to not even care if I was going to be going up. I didn't understand what they were waiting for. Why it was so important to wait for the crowd which was never coming? Pearl Jam had a show and Kevin Hart was performing around the corner. No one was gonna be here. It was a beautiful summer night. There was a plethora of reasons for no one to show up. Still one delay after another came and went. *"Show's probably gonna start a little later…"* I would hear every twenty minutes or so. At this point I was only five minutes away from when I told the guy I would be leaving and here we were with another delay. By this point getting a performance under my belt in Chicago felt like something to check off a to-do list more than it did an urge. It was like a relationship the first time the sex felt stale.

Sitting there waiting I was reminded of one timeless fact; musicians are the luckiest performers. They can get people to vibe to the same song for hours in a way other performers cannot. You could never get a crowd to listen to the same comic hour on repeat. Meanwhile I'm positive that on more than a few occasions *Lynyrd Skynyrd* could have entertained a crowed with *Free Bird* for hours. Makes me jealous of people like *Dave Matthews, The Rolling Stones, KISS*; all of them. Any of them able to perform the same act over and over again; and though I can't speak to the pains of monotony as much as the singers performing the same song 30 years and running, there's gotta be some relief in knowing you never need to prepare a new set of words for the crowd to hear. That's the power of some of those anthem type songs. As a comedian I would not be able to travel around on my best jokes. Then again another school of thought is to always be giving the audience the best version you can give that night. Something of a Jordan way of performing with each time in the limelight meant to exemplify your greatness. Though I would argue a victory to be much more quantifiable in basketball.

It only took seeing one bar he knew before my triangle shaped dreams soon took a back seat. We got back to his spot somewhere after midnight. According to memory we were just stopping off before heading to some bar around the corner where we would spend the next two hours. The night was crazy. This guy knew every doorman at every place we went by. I found it hard to believe he was new to the city. Then there was always a bartender or some cocktail waitress who owed him a drink from the last time. As my luck would have it a majority of these drinks were funneled to me and quickly added up to create a more wobbly version of myself than I am used to. Going from one bar to another he eventually shuffled me and his girlfriend into an Uber. From there I couldn't tell you what part of town we went to next. Nor could I recollect just how many different liquors I had mixed. Then through a series of elevators and stairwells I eventually found myself on top of his building with a view of over 40 stories to take in the night sky. Glancing over the edge of the building his girlfriend commented on the light bouncing off of the lake. This led to a walk to water where we stood along a concrete wall looking down into a deep and frightening abyss. Jumping in the water I held my nose and hoped not to ingest too much of the city blended lake. While crossing the street back to his place I was hit with a sudden emptiness in my stomach followed by a quick rush of water up my esophagus. Until that moment in my life I had never understood what it meant to throw up in my own mouth. After that my understanding was forever and regrettably changed.

I saw a quote once that said, *"Every man is self-made, but only the successful ones have the guts to admit it."* Never before had that sentence made more sense. My hangover the next morning was self-made, and my guts definitely had a thing or two to say about it. There's no reason for a hangover to ever take place if you plan your life accordingly. You can drink water, you can sleep, you can even have a beer with your morning shower to give you an edge in the fight; just don't forget to trash the can and leave the shampoo.

Along with not choosing to be hungover I would also not choose to be hungover while having to do a ten-hour plus drive across the bottom part of the Mid-West. I rather sleep in and wait it out. Today wasn't one of those days when I had an option. The room around me woke up far earlier than I had planned to do so myself and once the rhythm of the day got going I couldn't really stop it. Sure, I could have driven around the city once more and meandered down a new alleyway for the heck of it or found some place to take a nap, but deep down I kinda just wanted to get home. Plus, it's Chicago, taking a nap in my car down some random alley sounded like a death sentence. I was too at fault for feeling the way I did and I wanted to be in the result of a different decision. Though we all know that in a lot of ways we are all always just in a moment of existence resulting from every decision we've made since, whether we think of it or not.

EXIT STAGE LEFT
September 2016

"When am I gonna get to see you perform again?"

I don't know if my body ever truly felt a sense of normalcy anywhere over the last few months. Car lag is just as much of a thing as jet lag. It's weird when you can't cross a timezone in an hour, then spend a week in another. All the while communicating within the hourly restrictions of your home base. On my way home I decided I needed to make one more stop before heading back to the city. Two hours later I made my way into a small town in Virginia and pulled onto Buttercup Drive and up next to mailbox 113 where a thinly curvaceous font spelled out my grandma's name in brilliant gold. My aunt had since arrived to take over the house and all that would come with dismantling the shells of life. Sitting there in her driveway I had to pause before going in as I suddenly began to cry without any thought given as to why. Though any deeper consideration could show it was the accumulation of guilt and sadness from not getting to see my grandma again. When I got inside my aunt expressed the obvious *"Hello's and happy to see you's"* as you would expect. Then she sat and did all she could to listen to anything I had to say before showing me a few things my grandma had left for me. My grandma hadn't been a person of money so the things she left were more of a sentimental value than monetary. I left a few hours later with a box of papers and a rocking chair to add to my collection of things to sit on.

Arriving back in New York City later that night I pulled up to my old Brooklyn apartment and used the same tired key code to get in as I had many times before. Propping the front gate open I pulled the rocking chair from my trunk and finally closed it for the first time in nearly 300 miles. Opening the door I was greeted by a set of dudes, some I knew, some I didn't, and a stack of mail all bundled up with a few rubber bands.

"You need help bringing anything else in?"

"Nah man I'm good."

"You saw that stack on the table? Bunch of stuff from Los Angeles."

"Full of good news I'm sure.."

"Nice Chair."

"Don't worry, it's not staying. I just can't close my trunk with it in

311

there."

"No worries. We can always use a smoking chair."

"No. No smoking. That's my grandmas chair."

Pulling up a chair next to me Jax leaned forward and grabbed the spiral notebook on the coffee table. Left to me was a rocking chair and a box filled with journals, one of which had been bound in a spiral notebook with a cover clearly made on a typewriter. *"Is this yours?"*

"Nah. Something my grandma wrote while she was living in Africa."

"Family full of writers huh?"

"Not really."

"What do you think it is you're doing on stage?"

"Performing...?"

"Performing material you WROTE."

"I don't know man. Maybe I'm not as funny as I thought I was."

"You're just a different type of funny. It's just bout figuring out how to use it."

"At the end of the day the odd truth is that I'm pretty sure I could write a book faster than I could finish an hour of comedy."

"Then write about your trip."

"I don't know. I feel a bit too close to it right now."

"You got anything else you could write about?"

"My trip down to Central America?"

Tossing it back on the table he got up and lit a cigarette, opening a window as he pulled on the slowly budding cherry at the end of his lips. *"Well there you go, write about that."*

"Maybe. I'm gonna take a few days and decompress first."

"Don't chill for too long bro. The game never stops."

"Yeah...I know."

"Speaking of the game. How'd you do man? How was the summer?"

"I did good. I guess? For my first year."

"When am I gonna get to see you perform again?"

At that particular word his friend jumped in from across the couch, *"What do you play?"*

"Nothing. I do stand-up."

"Yo Nick. Don't let him downplay his life. He just got back from touring the country!"

"That's badass. Where all'd ya go."

"You name it, I was there."

"Where is your favorite place to perform?"

"You know where people never say the pizza is like New York...?"

"No. Where?"

"In New York. There's just nowhere like it."

"True."

"Speaking of which. I don't know where I'll be performing yet, but it'll be sometime this week."

"Nice, lemme know!"

"Sure thing. Hey, I'm gonna run up to the roof real quick. I was about to head up there before I came in here anyways. I just came in to get this chair out of the car take a piss and drop off my things then I saw you guys."

"Want some company?"

"Honestly, no. I know I've been driving alone for a few months, but I could really use a few minutes to decompress."

Dragging a lamp up with me I put on some headphones as a means of drowning out the sounds of the neighborhood cats while I drifted off into thought. Starring off at the city lights I was able to relax without guilt for the first time in a while. More so than I ever had when looking out over some vista or wading through some tropical oasis not knowing what was next. Despite wanting to escape back to the jungle I would need to stay in the city for the next part of my journey. Though the road ahead of me held much uncertainty, there was certainty in the next part. It was all the same that I had been doing, just on a much bigger level. On the road to success there are a few simple layers. The first is trying, the second is continuing, and the last is being known for it. Open, Feature, Headline. Those were the levels to being a professional in this time. By the last stage the crowds are coming for you. How big those crowds are will then determine the monetary side of that success, but once they're coming for you, that part of the equation is cracked. Every artist eventually learns that if they're gonna make it past a certain point they've gotta have some type of active following. It all came back to the following. In the end the only thing that truly survives are those things with a following. Shakespeare had a following, Poe had a following, all religious works have a following, it's the following that keeps anything alive, never the creator. Though even followers have their limits to commitment. If this was where the most people were coming to, then it's where I needed to be as a performer.

The only thing I'm sure of is that at the end of the day comedy is a career of minutes. The amount of minutes you've got determines what you can do with it. Even once I got to the highest levels the struggle would never be over. I would always have to be making those minutes as tight as possible. I would always need more material. That's the thing with the arts. There is no end game. It would always be a game of more. And I had to find a way to either stay current or stay universal. I would always be chasing the next mic if I was going to stay in this game. I had to ultimately turn the question from, *"How much time you got?"* to *"So, where can I see ya?"* How long it would take for me to feel good about answering the first of those would depend on how long it would take me to get up to an hour of material under my belt. If it was a slow build, so be it. As of yet, I still wasn't a professional, but I could at least call myself part time. Then again, when are we anything full time in this life other than alive? Even then existing and paying attention are two very different forms of awake. Deciding to be all forms of awake before falling asleep I decided that I was going to commit to the arts no matter what for the next 10 years. I had to believe in the power of sticking with it. Just like a decade learning Spanish had done one thing, a decade on stage would do another. I would use this summer as a benchmark and continue to use other moments in the future as a means to measure where I thought I stood in the comedy game from time to time. Because as Churchill once said, *"No matter how brilliant the strategy, every now and then one must stop and look at the results."* With any luck the comedy of existence will continue long enough for me to turn some more of those results into material. Even if not, it's been a fun ride for someone who knows life is just about getting in more laughing than crying before we get the final light.

- MIC DROP

INSIDE THE GREEN ROOM

INSIDE THE GREEN ROOM

Coming along somewhere close enough to the end of the eighties to be considered a millennial, but not enough so that he can remember what the eighties were like, Patrick started his writing career as a go-to for the class delinquents not wanting to write their own papers. Bothersome as that may be to any teachers out there; a kids gotta make a buck. Since then he's scribbled his way through a little bit of everything from contracts to comedy. Growing up in the Shenandoah Valley, Patrick attended James Madison

Some stage, somewhere.

University, where he studied Political Science. After college his love of languages began to flourish and through a series of travels and jobs he became fluent in Spanish. Author of two books, (this one and *The Stateside Wander*) Patrick plans to complete his 5 part *Stateside* series in as soon a time as he possibly can.

Despite being seen as *well traveled* Patrick didn't actually step foot on a plane until he was almost twenty-years old. On those planes he enjoys reading (though most of his books are consumed on audiobook these days) and he claims to have loved documentaries since way before it was cool to talk about them. Check out the rest of his work at www.PatrickDiMarchi.com and keep up by following Patrick on Instagram @PatrickDiMarchi.

Travel Well, Travel Often
Patrick DiMarchi

OTHER WORKS

The Stateside Wanderer:
Two-Weeks of Hideaways and Hangouts
Along the Pan-American Highway

A story inspired by one character's tendency to roam in an increasingly connected world untethered from responsibility. This stream of conscious tale follows the day-by-day thoughts and happenings of an overly cautious traveler as he takes four small-town friends along a Central American road trip and into a realm of international hideaways known to travel with lesser luggage than most. Along the way the group encounters world leaders, 3rd world delays, and some of the hardest to find hostels in the Spanish speaking world. While spending two weeks crossing borders and trekking mountain top jungles visitors from the past and fantasies of lives left unfinished begin to resurface, bringing out an internal conflict long buried by childhood partners in crime. Living through the eyes of a seasoned nomad, *The Stateside Wanderer* brings out the humor, headaches, and memories of many first time backpackers as the group navigates through the nuances of life on the go, showcasing what it's like to experience the consequences of mischief, restlessness, and a heated past between friends. Open up and read along to meet 4, travelers going through 3 countries, touching 2 oceans, led by 1 translator.

DISCLAIMER:

As a note of fairness. If in ordering this you receive one of the older copies, indicated by a cover which shows a different title than that of the one listed above, please let me know and I will replace it with a new copy for free. To do so, find me on instagram, message me with a photo of the incorrect copy and your receipt and I"ll exchange your copy for an autographed copy of the newest edition.
THE STATESIDE WANDERER

<u>LOVERS AND HATERS</u>:
What are the critics saying of my other works?
Well, on average it's somewhere between these
two excited individuals…

Emma

★★★★★ Verified Purchase

Returning Reader

Reviewed in the United States on July 21, 2020

I'm writing this review as I read this wonderful
book for the second time. It's kind of like reading a
new, but familiar book since I read it the first time
by it's former tittle - as the "hello reader" first
pages talk about. I recommend this book not only
because the author has always had a mesmerizing
way of speaking (story telling is certainly a strong
point) but because it sends you on an adventure.
The descriptions put you right in the car, jungle,
volcano, beach etc with the fascinating characters.
I never had any desire to stay in a hostel, but I
definitely do now. Fair warning: the desire to travel
after you read this book will just about double, if
not triple in intensity. Read it. You won't regret it.

Amazon Customer

★☆☆☆☆ Verified Purchase

As intriguing as this sounded, it wasn't

Reviewed in the United States on November 30, 2021

If you want to read about someone who gets a
free trip to a tropical oasis and still manages to
whine and moan for almost 300 pages... then
this is the bad read or the month for you.

REVIEWS OF *THE STATESIDE WANDERER*

WHAT WERE YOUR THOUGHTS ON THIS BOOK?

This book has been published by an indie author. Reviews help us know how readers felt about their experience and ultimately help us grow as writers. They also help other readers decide what books are worth their time. Please do your part in helping both.

OK, SO HERE'S HOW YOU START: OPEN THE CAMERA ON YOUR PHONE.

OK GREAT. NOW SCAN THE CODE BELOW[8]...

From there it should take you to the Amazon sales page where you can leave a review[9]. If it doesn't, idk what to tell ya, this world is weird sometimes. Regardless, you should still tell your friends.

& as always, Thank You for your support.

---

[8] Instructions are not to be used or considered as coercion for higher ratings.

[9] Provided that you have an iPhone, otherwise I can't be certain.

Thank You For Your Time. Hope You Enjoyed.

Made in the USA
Middletown, DE
26 May 2023

31217971R00201